Lead Like People Matter

*What Emotional Intelligence and
Neuroscience Reveal About Leadership*

Helen Abdali Soosan Fagan, PhD

Lead Like People Matter
What Emotional Intelligence and Neuroscience Reveal About Leadership

Published by
Helen Fagan & Associates

Copyright © 2025 by Helen Fagan

All rights reserved. No part of this publication may be reproduced, stored in a retrieval system, or transmitted in any form or by any means, electronic, mechanical, recorded, photocopied, graphic, or otherwise, without written permission of the author.

ISBNs:

Print: 979-8-9992890-0-1
Ebook: 979-8-9992890-1-8

Library of Congress Control Number:

Subjects:
BUS071000   BUSINESS & ECONOMICS / Leadership
BUS097000   BUSINESS & ECONOMICS / Workplace Culture
SOC002010   SOCIAL SCIENCE / Anthropology / Cultural & Social

Because People Matter™ is a trademark of Helen Fagan & Associates.

Helen Fagan & Associates
Hickman, Nebraska

Printed in the United States

❦ Formatted with Vellum

For my parents, Hamzeh Ali Abdali Soosan and Khorshid Yazdanipour.

*You sacrificed everything for your children.
I hope this book advances your sacrifices in ways you never imagined.*

My family on vacation in Iran, ca. 1970

Foreword

One of the bedrock principles we have maintained in over forty years of providing training and development is that growth begins within. Before we can understand and work effectively with others, we have to understand ourselves, our own hot buttons, and our comfort and discomfort with those who are different from us. It is only from this solid foundation of self-awareness that we can begin to develop an understanding and appreciation of others.

Helen's book, *Lead Like People Matter,* takes this approach. Unlike many books about leadership development that provide competencies and models, this book takes another path. It helps those aspiring to lead to develop themselves as the tool and use their own vulnerability to connect with others.

Helen uses storytelling, one of the most powerful ways to teach and move others, because stories touch our hearts as well as our heads. Her own story is the vehicle she uses to help readers tap into themselves in order to be accessible to others and encourage those they lead to open up to each other. The bonds that are forged when we connect on the personal level are at the foundation of leading like people matter and the antidote to the division in our world today. Contact Theory supports this when it tells us that empathy for others grows not by knowledge about others, but by the reduction of anxiety that results when we form connections with those whose lives and perspectives differ from ours. This is the key to building an environment that values the people in the workplace, at home, and in the community.

This book is both conceptual and practical, providing research and critical information as well as concrete actions readers can take to develop themselves and others. It touches both heart and head as Helen uses vulnerability to explain why this development matters to each of us and then shows us how to do it with examples, questions, and processes to follow. To paraphrase the slogan of the women's liberation movement, that the personal is political, the theme for this book could be the personal is organizational. Helen gives us a guide for this continuous improvement process of confronting and sharing ourselves to invite others to do the same, so that we can all lead like people matter.

Lee Gardenswartz, PhD
Anita Rowe, PhD

Preface

Have you ever tried remodeling a home while still living in it? The chaos is unavoidable, dust in the air, routines disrupted, constant noise. Yet you keep moving forward because what exists no longer works.

That's where we are globally, and especially in the United States.

Now imagine taking on that remodel without the skills, knowledge, or even a blueprint. That's what many of us are experiencing today: the urgent need to rebuild systems of leadership, trust, and connection, without always knowing how, or where to begin.

The United States is still a relatively young nation. And like any aging structure, it has required periodic remodeling to live up to its foundational promises. Since its creation in 1776, we've seen these remodels surface every century or so:

- In **1863**, President Abraham Lincoln initiated a transformation with the Emancipation Proclamation, freeing enslaved Black men, women, and children.
- In **1964**, President Lyndon Johnson signed the Civil Rights Act, extending long-denied protections to Black Americans.

- And now, in **2025**, we face another reckoning. With rising polarization, challenges to civil rights, and increasing societal fatigue, we are once again called to decide: What kind of society do we want to be? Will we lead in a way that truly values human beings?

These moments of transformation have never come easily. In every era, people had to intentionally engage in the deep, difficult work of changing their mindsets and behaviors before driving broader societal change. They had to reject the norms that allowed others to be owned, excluded, or silenced, and imagine a society where all people are treated with dignity and equity.

Today, we stand at the threshold of another vital remodel. If we are ever to realize the ideals upon which this nation was founded, each of us must take responsibility for creating a more just, compassionate, and healthy society. We must transform our thinking and lead, not just from our roles or titles, but from our shared humanity.

That is why I wrote this book.

My hope is that it calls you into the work of becoming the kind of leader our world urgently needs. The remodeling has begun. The work is hard. It is necessary. Will you step in?

Introduction

This is not a typical leadership textbook, filled with theories, research, and data analysis, although it does contain some of that. It's not a self-help manual offering lofty advice, though I hope you find inspiration here. Nor is it a memoir, though I share my life story as a person on the journey of growth and transformation.

Instead, *Lead Like People Matter* is a blend of all three. It is a gateway to self-exploration, leadership practice, and meaningful conversation. It is a call to examine the ways we are wired for bias and belonging, for self-protection and growth, and to embrace the possibility of rewiring our brains' default settings.

Thanks to advancements in neuroscience and our growing understanding of emotional intelligence and intercultural competence, we now know this truth: change is possible. Even our default settings formed by culture, upbringing, trauma, or training can be rewired. As the saying goes, an old dog *can* learn new tricks.

This book is for anyone who wants to lead more meaningfully in their families, organizations, communities, or themselves. It's for leaders trying to navigate complexity, scholars hungry for new questions, and humans trying to live with more courage and grace.

What you'll find in these pages:

Stories drawn from my life as an immigrant, scholar, and leadership coach.

Insights from neuroscience, psychology, and leadership theory.

Reflections inspired by personal struggles that have deeply impacted me.

Tools to help you practice emotional intelligence, recognize bias, and lead across divides.

Case studies from research with leaders across industries who are committed to showing up with integrity, humility, and heart.

You'll also encounter wisdom from voices that have deeply shaped me—poets like Hafiz and Rumi, scholars like Anne Fadiman and Arthur Kleinman, and leadership thinkers like Kevin Cashman and Robert Quinn. While my professional roots lie in cultural competence and inclusive leadership in healthcare, this book expands beyond those roots to a deeper engagement with leader mindset development: examining its foundations, applying its principles, cultivating its practices, and advancing its transformative power across all sectors.

There is no shortcut to becoming the kind of leader who makes others feel seen, valued, and empowered. Just as athletes train and condition themselves daily to perform at their best under pressure, leaders must train and condition themselves by training their higher brain to respond with emotional intelligence, intercultural agility, humility, and courage when they are under pressure. Only through consistent and intentional practice can we ensure that when we are tested, we will lead well.

As a Persian who has lived on three continents, I honor my heritage by opening each chapter with wisdom from the poets of my childhood. My culture of storytelling and reflection runs through every chapter.

As you engage with this book, whether holding it in your hands, reading it on a screen, or listening to it on audio, I urge you to do the work of unpacking your own story. At the same time, cultivate a sensitivity to the stories of others. Learning to step outside of yourself and see the world through another's perspective is one of the most vital leadership skills we can develop. As the French American writer Anaïs Nin wisely said, "We don't see things as they are, we see things as we are."

My one request is that you come to these pages not just to consume, but to reflect, engage, and practice, both within yourself and in the world around you. There is much to discover. Before we move forward, I want to leave you with the words of Hafiz as an encouragement to press on: "I wish I could show you when you are lonely or in darkness the astonishing light of your own being."

Let's begin.
Helen

Family passport photo when we left Iran for England in 1976.

Chapter 1

Vulnerability

Destiny forced us to spend our lives this way;
We believe in fate and hold it to be true.

-S.M. Hafiz

We had just arrived in England. Heathrow airport was bustling with activity, and my brothers and I were restless and excited about the new life ahead of us. My father, whom everyone called Aghayeh Abdali (Mr. Abdali), was the only one of us who spoke English. As he tried to figure out where we needed to go next, we began playing with the rolling luggage cart. Suddenly, the cart got away from us, rolled across the sidewalk, and clunked into the side of a taxicab parked at the curb.

The cab driver flung open his door and began yelling—in English, of course. We didn't know what he was saying, and we didn't know what to say back. Agha (Sir), as we affectionately referred to our father, calmly responded to the driver in English, then called us over to sit down on a bench.

"You need to behave," he said gravely. "You must realize you may be the only Iranians people will ever meet. You need to behave in such a way that you represent your family and your country well."

With those words, I began my life outside my native Iran.

It was hot outside Detroit's Sinai Hospital ICU, but inside it was freezing. I sat at my dad's bedside thinking about my childhood, massaging lotion into his legs and arms, watching his static face for any sign of communication. The stroke he suffered after heart surgery had taken away his ability to move and speak. There was not much I could do but simply be there with him and help maintain his body's circulation.

I was desperate to communicate with him, but his only response to my loving words was to blink his eyes while tears rolled down his cheeks. After much trial and error, we finally realized he could no longer understand English, the language he had fought so hard to learn and for his children to learn. On this day, Agha responded only when we spoke Farsi to him. I fought with my emotions: anger and annoyance, desperation and sorrow, deep love, fear, and confusion. My feelings were the only real thing in a surreal environment filled with sterile machines and the stale smell of ailing bodies.

When Dad landed at the Detroit airport a few days earlier, he'd been having chest pains, so my brother took him directly to the hospital. The doctors decided to perform open heart surgery the next day. Our family flew in from around the country to be with him as he faced what would be the last of my father's many struggles.

My brain tried, without much success, to use logic to resolve what was happening. We had been through many terrors and tears as a family, and now we were supposed to be enjoying the conditional peace we had finally won. How would I live without my father? How could I let him go so soon? We had only recently been reunited after years of separation. The bitter struggles I had experienced because of early isolation from my parents and life in a country where I alternately was seen as a threat and felt threatened, made this moment even more desperate.

That afternoon, a nurse I hadn't seen before came into the hospital room with a young student or trainee. The nurse stood near my father's bed, scratching with a pen on his chart. Without introducing herself or explaining her objective, she began asking questions about what he was feeling. She became increasingly frustrated as I interpreted her questions into Farsi, then waited for Dad to answer as best he could by blinking his eyes. I knew he was frustrated, too, because I could see the tears forming again.

"*Dawg hasti, Aghajan?* Are you hot, dear Agha?" I asked. He blinked.

"He said no," I relayed to the nurse, my heart sinking with the realization that he must feel trapped within his body.

"*Helenam, meefahmi chi migam?* This is Helen. Do you understand what I'm asking you?" I translated. He blinked twice.

"Yes, he knows it's me." Did I detect a narrowing of his eyes in love? Tears rolled down his face every time he heard me speak. It broke my heart.

What would typically take seconds took minutes. The nurse walked away without saying a word. As they passed through the doorway, the nurse leaned over and said to the trainee, "I wish they would learn to speak English. It would make our jobs so much easier."

Anger and horror rose in my chest. My head began to spin at the nurse's words. She didn't think my father could speak English. Perhaps she thought he was unintelligent, which was so far from the truth. She didn't realize how hard we had worked to learn English and make a life here. She didn't understand what we had been through to get to this place, and how heartbreaking it had been for my father to realize his children would never go back to the country he loved. In my mind, she had insinuated so many things with her words. She had plunged a knife deep into my already broken heart. The depth of my hurt and the heat of my anger compelled me to let go of my father's arm, rise from my seat, and follow the nurse through the door and down the hall, fueled by a fever of disdain. I approached her in the hallway from behind, spinning her around with my words.

"You have no idea who my dad is," I spat, "or what his position was in Iran. How dare you judge him in his condition! He's done and seen more than your puny brain can fathom. He has more intelligence, courage, and dignity in his little finger than you will ever have in your whole brain!"

I don't remember all that I said. I now describe that diatribe as "verbal vomiting." I'm not proud of the way I behaved. This is not the way I want to represent my family and my country of birth. But, in that moment, I became a slave to my emotions.

The nurse apologized for her insensitivity, and I could see she was indeed remorseful, nervous, even afraid of what I might do. But I didn't care. When my dad lost his ability to speak to me and put his arms around me, a big piece of me began to die, and the niceties of social interaction escaped me. I didn't understand my feelings, let alone have any chance of understanding what had made her say such a thing.

My rage went beyond the nurse. I wondered how we, as a nation, could say the United States has excellent healthcare when we have healthcare providers who are this ignorant. This was not the first time I had experienced this type of pain. The nurse's insensitivity dredged up all the sorrow, shame, and pain I had felt so many other times in the years before my father's death, first as an immigrant from what many considered the hostile nation of Iran, then as a minority citizen of the US.

Flash forward a decade. I walked rapidly down the hall of Bryan Hospital in Lincoln, Nebraska, a fairly large hospital system with a Level II trauma center, where I led the diversity and cultural competence initiatives. I was on my way to a lunch meeting with one of the hospital chaplains, a trusted colleague and friend. He was preparing to meet with several of the hospital's decision-makers regarding what would ultimately become a breakthrough case in culturally adept medical care at our hospital. I walked through the door of the cafeteria, took a seat, and settled in to hear the details.

A truck had struck a twelve-year-old boy while he was riding a bike in his small-town neighborhood. Our helicopter team had airlifted him fifty miles to our trauma center, the closest to his home. At the hospital, the team sprang into action, doing what they could to save his life, but told his parents the prognosis was grim. The young boy's heart had stopped several times, and his brain was showing no activity. Eventually, doctors determined he had suffered brain death due to the lack of oxygen to his brain and the severity of his injuries.

As part of standard protocol, hospital staff approached the family about organ donation. Several hours and many tears later, the family informed the chaplain they were ready to proceed and would agree to organ donation on one condition: a family member must be present in the operating room while the organs and tissue were retrieved.

"Help me understand what makes this important to you," the chaplain asked.

In the faith traditions of their Native American tribe, the family believed the spirit of their son rested in his heart. They wanted a family member to be present to witness that the heart had fully stopped beating, allowing the spirit to be freed. Otherwise, they feared the boys' spirit would remain trapped, continuing to live in another person's body.

The chaplain listened to the family, empathized with their concerns, and reassured them that he understood the sacredness of their request. His next challenge was approaching hospital decision-makers to determine whether granting the request was legally and logistically feasible.

"I'm not sure how to do this, Helen," he admitted. "I don't know what to say. Can you help me think it through?" His concern was understandable since the hospital had never done this before.

I pondered the issue for a few minutes, considering what I knew would be objections from multiple perspectives: legal, safety, and procedural.

"Remind hospital leaders of the decision we made as an organization," I said slowly. "Tell them we've made a commitment to respect the cultural needs of our patients. I've been out in the community sharing that commitment—that's why my role exists."

I had been hired, among other things, to be an advocate for patients with culture-related needs and to assist hospital personnel who lacked experience navigating cultures beyond their own experiences. Many had never realized the role culture played in who they are as individuals and the influence of the healthcare culture on their understanding of health and illness, let alone how the hospital's own institutional culture affected patient care decisions.

The hospital staff, and many of the leaders, had engaged in multiple hours of learning intercultural competence, which included cultural self-awareness, health equity, and medical anthropology. I was a member of the ethics committee, which had already decided that cultural needs should be met whenever possible, as long as it did not violate federal or state laws.

I reminded the chaplain of some past examples: We had deactivated overhead sprinklers multiple times to allow patients to use incense during prayers, and we had regularly accommodated requests for female medical staff for Muslim women.

"This is no different," I explained. "This is another opportunity to demonstrate our commitment as an organization. Tell our decision-makers that this is a valid cultural need, and, if we are to stay true to our core values, and our commitment, we must follow through."

After an intense and emotionally charged dialogue over the next several hours, decision-makers confirmed that no legal barriers prevented us from honoring the family's request. The hospital agreed to allow a family member to observe the organ retrieval in the operating room. Later, the Nebraska Organ Retrieval System informed us that this was the first time in the twenty-five-year history of organ donation in Nebraska that a Native American family had agreed to donate their loved one's organs and tissue.

When reflecting on this outcome, my thoughts often drift back to my father's time in the hospital, wishing I could have impacted that situation to have had a different result.

In hindsight, the solution to the Native American family's request may seem obvious. But in the moment, it was anything but clear what "doing the right thing for the right reasons" would entail. For this organ and tissue donation to happen, two important factors had to align:

1. The physicians and the chaplain needed to approach the request with a certain mindset of openness and cultural humility, something the nurse in my father's care appeared to lack.
2. Hospital administrators had to embrace the request and take it seriously, despite its uniqueness.

It is not lost on me just how important the mindset of everyone involved was in this critical case. Patient experiences and sometimes their very lives depend on the mindset and perspectives of the decision-makers. The complexity of navigating a challenging hospital situation like this often depends on the diverse experiences, mindsets, and expertise of medical personnel and administrators, each with highly specialized roles, distinct training, and unique motivations.

Culturally complex medical situations tend to have the best outcomes when decision-makers and care providers approach them with a certain level of intercultural humility. But where does that come from? Are people born with it, or is it developed over time? And if it is developed, at what point, and what motivates people to put in the effort to develop it?

In this case, people at our hospital had been willing to grow in their cultural knowledge and skill with both colleagues and patients long before this young boy became our patient. It wasn't surprising. We had been working as an organization for four years toward this kind of cultural competence. I had led Bryan Hospital's council through a considerable amount of work to ensure we were delivering culturally competent care. On the ethics committee, my role was to help the team see the case through the eyes of someone whose cultural experiences had shaped their understanding of health, illness, death, dying, birthing, or disease from a completely different angle. If we are to be successful in navigating these cases to achieve positive health outcomes, we must be willing to accept that the patients' and their families' perspectives may differ from ours, and that is okay.

As I left the cafeteria after my conversation with the chaplain, I allowed myself to feel a small sense of satisfaction that our hospital was doing well in this area. But I also felt something was missing. Some of our staff had not embraced this accommodation request as much as I thought they would. Why were some people willing to embrace cultural requests while others resisted? What made the difference for people like our chaplain?

These questions haunted me so much, especially as I began teaching at Bryan College of Health Sciences, that they became the foundation of my doctoral research, and ultimately the guiding thread of my life's work and what has led me to write this book.

I didn't know it at the time, but the two moments—the nurse's callousness toward my father, and the hospital's groundbreaking decision for the Native American boy's family—were the painful crucible moments that led me to a career I believe my father would be proud of. I now have a deeper understanding of the challenges faced by healthcare professionals like the nurse who cared for my dad, and why I reacted so strongly. I also have a deeper understanding of how we can create breakthroughs, such as the one in the twelve-year-old boy's case, not just in healthcare but across a wide range of fields and contexts.

People feel incredibly vulnerable when they are out of their comfort zone, especially when they are sick, injured, or at the mercy of decision-makers who lack understanding, humility, and an openness to learning from others. This pattern goes far beyond healthcare. In every field, the greater the difference between people, the higher the likelihood of tension, especially when emotional intelligence is lacking. The ability to navigate these differences with awareness and skill is crucial for fostering collaboration and generating innovative solutions. But that will never happen if we see ourselves as better than others.

Through my work with professionals across a wide range of

industries, I've learned that successfully navigating our human differences requires more than knowledge; it demands emotional intelligence, psychological capital, and an understanding of how humans are wired (neuroscience). However, challenges arise not only on an individual level but also from larger systems that thrive when they can pit groups against one another. If structures are designed to pit us against each other, then bridging our differences becomes even more difficult, ***and absolutely critical.***

As the world becomes increasingly interconnected, those who will succeed are not just the ones with expertise, but those who excel in connecting with others from all walks of life. Navigating relationships in a globalized society requires approaches that foster meaningful and constructive interactions, rather than reactive, instinct-driven reactions that often come from our emotionally hijacked brains. Reflecting on my experience in the hospital that day, I realize how much better outcomes can be when we approach these interactions with empathy and intentionality, rather than allowing uncertainty and discomfort to dictate our actions.

In their book, *Leadership in a Diverse and Multicultural Environment*, authors Mary Connerly and Paul Pederson reinforce the idea that boundaries between diverse people are being shattered. "National boundaries no longer define the world of organizations (Connerly and Pederson 2005, 2). The free movement of labor continues to intensify as organizations diversify geographically." Large and small countries interact with customers and employees from multiple nations. This includes companies in many different industries, such as GM, Budweiser, Disney, and Medtronic, as well as Apple, IBM, Google, and HSBC.

"Global flow of goods, services, and finance have continued to expand significantly since 2012," According to a 2022 report by the McKinsey Global Institute shared on their website. These flows reached unprecedented levels, with goods trade hitting a record high in 2021. "The report highlights that the growth in global flows is now being driven by intangibles, services, and talent, with data flows growing at nearly fifty percent annually between 2010 and 2019."

In a separate paper published on their site, "The McKinsey Global Institute's Connectedness Index ranks countries based on their participation in global flows. Developed economies remain more connected than emerging ones, with Germany, Hong Kong, and the United States topping the list." However, some emerging economies have rapidly climbed the ranks; for instance, India gained sixteen places between 1995 and 2012, reflecting growth in services flows. Flows linked to knowledge and know-how are driving global integration. "Flows of services, international students, and intellectual property grew about twice as fast as goods flows in 2010–19."

These trends underscore the increasing importance of digital technologies and knowledge-intensive industries in the global economy. As global flows continue to evolve, countries and businesses that effectively harness these trends are likely to experience enhanced economic growth and integration.

Meeting the demands of this global integration is relatively easy in some ways—many citizens of the world have long desired this coming together of people and information. However, one significant hurdle that can prevent us from fully embracing a global community is our inability to overcome personal biases so we can interact in positive ways with those who are different from ourselves. Neuroscience reveals that humans are wired to prefer similarity, a phenomenon often referred to as ingroup bias. In his book, *Social: Why Our Brains Are Wired to Connect*, Matthew Lieberman, MD, wrote, "our brains have a natural tendency to favor those who are similar to us because it activates areas associated with trust and safety" (Lieberman 2013, 45). This evolutionary mechanism, while helpful in forming close-knit groups, can hinder our ability to connect across differences.

To move beyond these innate preferences, we need to develop the psychological capacity and emotional intelligence to address the unconscious programming that often leads to misunderstandings with others. As emotional intelligence pioneers Lee Gardenswartz, Jorge Cherbosque, and Anita Rowe explain, "emotional intelligence is the ability to understand and deal with feelings, both your own and those of others, in a healthy and constructive way. Your ability to be effective in this diverse world, on and off the job, depends on it" Gardenswartz, Cherbosque, and Rowe, 2010, 2). Developing this capacity requires introspection and a willingness to confront our vulnerabilities.

When we don't know what we don't know about people who are different from us, our brains instinctively revert to positions of suspicion and caution. This reaction often stems from drawing on our limited personal experiences and the collective beliefs of our own cultural programming. The fear of encountering pain or repeating past hurts shapes our responses to the unfamiliar. As social neuroscientists John T. Cacioppo and William Patrick, who researched loneliness, discovered, "our social pain system—wired to protect us from rejection or harm—can amplify feelings of distrust toward those perceived as different" (Cacioppo and Patrick 2008, 123).

Overcoming this hurdle demands courage: the courage to acknowledge our pain, confront our biases, and learn to ask questions rather than make assumptions. It requires unraveling how past experiences hold us hostage (often unconsciously) and prevent us from becoming leaders who can effectively bridge differences. By fostering curiosity and empathy, we can transcend our evolutionary instincts and build meaningful connections across boundaries.

Can it be done? Daily news is still rife with attacks and killings motivated by misunderstandings related to race, gender, and class. Elderly people are misunderstood, neglected, and abused. Government officials must navigate delicate negotiations between feuding countries. Pastors often find themselves moderating disagreements between ethnic groups that want to worship in different ways. Teachers must referee conflicts between students whose values differ. Families face clashes related to gender, sexual orientation, even politics, and religion.

Each and every one of us must find a way to deal with differences at whatever level they appear in our daily lives. We all must face our own hesitation and inability to overcome and heal our personal memories of pain and find a better way. Then, after we learn how to do this, it is our responsibility—and privilege—to teach others.

The first step is understanding what makes us who we are.

I was born in Masjed Soleyman, Iran, on July 31, 1964, the second of four children. Until I was sixteen, it was just my two brothers and me. My baby sister was born in Iran much later, while my brothers and I were living away from our family in the United States.

When I was a child, we lived in a modern ranch-style house on Kharg Island in the Persian Gulf. Our home was filled with beautiful Persian rugs and artifacts from around the world that my dad collected from his travels. We had everything we needed in our lavish home, including a gardener and a maid to help my mother. My mother was sophisticated, fashion-minded, and well-dressed like Jacqueline Kennedy and Sophia Loren. Our vast gardens were filled with flowers and banyan trees. My brothers and I liked swinging from the vines of the trees, and I enjoyed watching my dad tend to his beloved flowers.

I grew up loved, respected, and deeply cared for. My parents, siblings, and I enjoyed strong ties with our large extended family. We often visited my grandparents' humble home in Masjed Soleyman, where they raised chickens and goats and maintained a small number of fruit trees.

Summer was my favorite time of year. When we gathered with my aunts, uncles, and cousins, we ate, danced, and listened to lots of stories, and often heard family elders reciting the sonnets of Omar Khayyam and Hafiz. I knew my cousins well enough that it seemed as if they were my brothers and sisters. Most evenings, while the adults talked of global issues, we played until the sun went down. We slept peacefully under the stars on the rooftop, knowing all these people would love and support us no matter what life brought our way.

My family and many others in our circle lived a life of prosperity among the breathtaking natural, cultural, and architectural landmarks in our temperate Middle Eastern region. Our family was deeply respected because of my father and his position with the National

Iranian Oil Company. Although he felt pride in our history, customs, and culture, my father also admired Western culture, education, architecture, and healthcare.

Kharg Island was a major oil exporting location in the northwestern corner of the Persian Gulf. My father had advanced through the ranks and was head of everyone who came to work in the development of oil exploration and exportation. He brought people from all over the world to work for the oil company. Through his exposure to diverse people, places, and cultures, he recognized the value of knowing multiple languages and making a conscious effort to learn about the world. He was the kind of leader who led with the underlying belief that people matter. We moved to several different cities to accommodate my father's position with the oil company, but most of my memories are of Kharg Island.

Because English was and still is the standard international language for business and science, my dad taught himself English and spoke fluently with those he hired from other nations. I would listen to him speak English with his colleagues and friends from around the globe, and I became determined to speak the language someday myself. My family laughed at me as I pretended to speak English like my dad.

When my dad came home from the oil company at night, he was no longer an important global leader. He was just my dad. He sat with me for make-believe tea parties and told me stories about a loving and hardworking family of mice to calm my fears of the creatures who ran in the fields near our home. He picked me up, danced around the room with me in his arms, and sang nonsensical songs, calling me his *holoo koochooloo*—his little peach. We often watched American television together as a family. I was in love with the *Six Million Dollar Man* and swore I would someday meet Lee Majors and impress him with my English-speaking ability. Gosh, I had a crush on him!

As Dad learned more about the world, he developed a strong desire to provide the same knowledge and advantages for his children. He wanted us to be exposed to the world and to receive an excellent education. My parents had dreamed of sending us to college in England and were convinced that we would be more successful if we learned English at a young age. For that reason, my father told us we would soon move to England to attend primary school. Although this was what many cosmopolitan, affluent Iranian families were doing, our extended families were against our move, especially since my brothers and I were so young. But no one could talk my parents out of it.

In 1976, when I was twelve and my brothers Allen and Mehrdad were eleven and thirteen, my parents put their plan into motion. For the next few years, my mother, brothers, and I would live and study in England during the school year, then return to Iran in the summers. Even my mother would attend school to finish what she hadn't been able to complete before getting married. My father would continue working in Iran to pay for our schooling. As we each completed college, we would move back to Iran to live and work among our nation's leaders.

Oblivious to the fact that my parents' dream would die with the upheaval in Iran during 1978 and 1979, we left for England. It was exciting at first, but reality set in when I realized my dad—my knight in shining armor, storyteller, and friend—would not be with us for long, and that I would have to say goodbye to my family and friends in Iran.

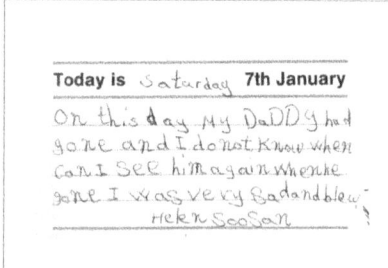

The entry from my childhood journal the day my father left us in England. I was just learning to read and write English.

Suddenly, I was in a new land, learning a new language, adjusting to a new culture without my dad, who had given me strength and made me confident in myself. During the first summer, my brothers and I lived each with a different British family during the week to force us to learn the language quickly. Those in-home stays, along with daily private English tutoring, helped us become proficient enough for the start of school in the fall. That was a tough summer on so many levels, though I still have fond memories of picking fruit from the fruit trees on the way to English lessons and being amused by the oddities of the English language. I heard about "butterflies in someone's stomach" and wondered how they got there. I was an avid reader, and my English tutor told me about *Heidi,* then gave me the book. She sensed I'd find solace in Heidi's journey. She was right.

When school began, for the first time in my life, I was not accepted without question. The British children made fun of the way I talked and the color of my skin. They even made fun of the way I smelled because of the food I ate at home. It was a rude awakening for this daddy's little princess, who, to that point, had grown up with everything she needed and had always been treated with love and respect.

I wasn't sure how to respond to the insults, so I looked at the situation philosophically. I let it make me stronger. I vowed to speak English so well someday that no one would be able to tell it was my second language. If you know me today, you know I have accomplished this goal. In 1977, my mom's youngest brother, Mehrzad, moved to England to attend college. He saved the day for us! He made being in England fun. He could drive, so he took my brothers and me everywhere. Mehrzad, who is kind and deeply generous, temporarily filled the void left by Dad's absence. He took our minds off the things other children said about us, and we pushed our feelings deep inside. To this day, I have a special bond with Uncle Mehrzad.

It was never my parents' intention that their children would not return to Iran. We didn't need another country to help us prosper. We had a great life; they simply wanted to find a place for us to get the world's best education and to expand our worldview. We immigrated legally and thought it would be temporary. I remember thinking it was strange how in one place we were loved and revered, while in another place we were degraded and stripped of dignity, as if we were an inconvenience rather than human beings.

Migration has been an integral part of human history across all regions of the world. For thousands of years, people have moved to find better access to resources such as food, water, and grazing land for their animals. The restriction of movement between nations, as we understand it today, is a relatively modern concept in the long timeline of human existence.

In some cases, people don't move, but boundaries do, instantly turning residents into immigrants or vice versa. The United States, for example, engulfed a part of Mexico that today comprises the states of Texas, Arizona, and California.

Some people are forced into migration to escape war and violence. Others choose to migrate to new areas for better access to jobs, healthcare, and education, just as my family did when we left Iran.

The summer of 1978, when I was fourteen years old, was the last time I was in Iran during my youth. We went home to see family and friends. I enjoyed showing off my genuine English ability (no more pretending) and seeing my cousins again. They were impressed with what I had learned.

There was something different about my birthplace that summer, though. When we landed in Tehran, I saw tanks and armed men in the streets. Dad and the male members of my extended family were constantly talking about the Shah, the Ayatollah, the SAVAK (Iranian Secret Service), and the United States. My family members, while not political, were educated and have always engaged in intellectual and philosophical debates about humanity, life, and global issues. The summer was a mixture of joy and intense concern.

When we returned to England, the British government informed us they would not renew our visas when they expired at the end of 1979. We would have to return to the unrest in Iran and abandon my parents' plan to educate us in the West, or we would have to find another country that allowed international students. My parents had already sacrificed so much, and they didn't want to give up on their dream. My dad had friends all over the world and believed he could find another place for us to receive an excellent education, so he began to search.

Several of Dad's friends and his cardiologist had moved to America. They provided information about places where we could attend school in the United States. Two of my mom's brothers were already in graduate school at American colleges. Regardless of their positive experiences there, my uncles begged my father not to bring any of us to America, especially me. They didn't believe the American lifestyle would be good for young children. My parents, again going against the wishes of others, decided to simply transfer our original English-speaking education plan to the United States. I remember my dad telling my uncles that whatever opportunities his sons had for education, his daughter would too. It was a good idea, but it was not to be—at least not in the form we had hoped. The US Embassy in London would not issue my mother a visa that would allow her to stay with us. My parents were issued only visitor's visas, with enough time allotted to get us settled in a boarding school, after which they would have to return to Iran.

And thus began a new chapter of my life that would test me to the core.

The United States of America has had a conflicted relationship with newcomers for more than four centuries. From the time of our nation's early settlers and the launching of the slave trade in the 1600s (which lasted until 1808), to Irish and German settlement (1820-1870), and immigration of the Chinese during the Gold Rush (1848-1955), then the influx of Eastern Europeans (1880-1920), and the desperate immigration of the Jewish population during WWII (1939-1945), most of us can trace our roots back to a ship or plane that brought our ancestors here.

Countless Mexican Americans are citizens of this country, not because their ancestors immigrated but because the national boundary lines moved. In the southern US, this began when Texas gained its independence from Mexico in 1836 and became part of the Union in 1845, and it ended with the close of the Mexican-American War. In 1848, with the Treaty of Guadalupe, the state of Hidalgo in Mexico ceded to the US about 525,000 square miles of territory that now lies in California, Utah, Arizona, New Mexico, Nevada, and parts of Colorado and Wyoming.

Between 1860 and 1920, the immigrant share of the total US population fluctuated between 13% and a peak of 14.8% in 1890, mainly due to high levels of European immigration. Restrictive immigration legislation in 1921 and 1924, coupled with the Great Depression and World War II, led to a sharp drop in new arrivals. As a result, the foreign-born portion of Americans steadily declined between the 1930s and 1970s, reaching a record low of about 5% in 1970. After 1970, the number of US immigrants more than doubled, growing to 13.3% of the population in 2014 (Batalova 2025).

According to the Institute of International Education (IIE), in the 2014-2015 academic year, more than 974,900 international students were attending American colleges and universities, contributing $30.5 billion to the US economy, representing more than 373,000 jobs (Witherell 2015).

Most people who enter the United States from other countries have a vision of America as an incredible place of unlimited opportunity and promise. My father was no different. He expected that our time here would be filled with adventure, possibility, and the chance to meet people who would inspire us. He revered everything about the United States: its education, healthcare, engineering, architecture, and technological advancements. He believed those who found their way to the US would have the opportunity to be educated and achieve their dreams. He loved the idea that women living in the US had just as much opportunity to do anything they set their minds to as men. He loved the ideals upon which the United States was founded.

"*E Pluribus Unum*," Latin for "out of many, one," was more than a motto to my father. Like many, he saw it as a declaration of unity, purpose, and collective identity. These words, etched into the foundations of American symbolism, echo from the base of the Statue of

Liberty to the chambers of the United States Capitol, reminding us of the enduring ideal that a diverse people can be bound together in a shared pursuit of freedom and democracy.

Originally coined during the formation of a new republic from thirteen distinct colonies, this phrase affirms the strength of plurality: of many voices, backgrounds, cultures, and dreams converging into a single national spirit. It reflects a foundational belief that unity is not found in uniformity, but in embracing and harmonizing our differences. Inscribed on official seals, monuments, and institutions, *E Pluribus Unum* is a call to every generation in this country to honor the strength that human diversity brings, and to shape a future where every person, regardless of origin, contributes to the shared story of "we the people."

Yet, despite my father's unwavering faith in these ideals, our experience in America would prove to be painfully different from that vision. The vision that inspired my parents to leave their children at a boarding school in central Florida.

At the tender age of fifteen, I landed in New York City on a Pan Am airliner with my mother, father, and brothers. We began driving south. It would be hours before we would reach Florida Central Academy in the town of Sorrento. At first, I was excited. The summer before, I had watched the movie *Grease*, and I thought that's what our new life in the US would be like. I expected to have fun and meet exciting new friends—and, of course, learn everything my father wanted me to learn, as well as perfect my English speaking and writing.

As we traveled toward Florida, it began to sink in that my mother would not be with us, and I would only see my brothers sporadically each day, because we would live in separate dorms. I grew sadder with every mile of city and country that passed by the windows of the car. I was afraid of being alone, and even more scared when I thought about living and studying with other boarding school students from all over the world.

In my first days within the confines of the academy, I could only think of myself as fear and anger consumed me. Before my parents left, I remember having a major meltdown. *Why would they leave me? Would they ever really come back for me? What was there for me in this strange place? Nothing!* It didn't help that I was a teenager, naturally full of questions about myself and worried about everything from the strange changes in my body to my unknown future.

Today, after many years of thinking, analyzing, and discussing with my parents, I now understand that those days in Florida were some of the most difficult of their lives as well, as they contemplated their forced return to Iran. I admire the courage it took to leave their fourteen-, fifteen-, and sixteen-year-old children thousands of miles away. Even then, they intended us to return to Iran someday and make Iran a better place.

In a matter of days, culture shock settled over me. So many things were different from England and Iran. My roommates shaved their underarms and legs. They wore makeup, had boyfriends, smoked cigarettes, and drank. None of this was "normal" or familiar to me, and when I didn't do these things, they made fun of me. It felt much like the ridicule I had endured in England. For the first time, I felt a memory of pain associated with being different. Because of the painful experiences I had endured in England, I made unfavorable assumptions about Florida, the United States, and the people living around me.

I begged my dorm mom, Louise Anderson, to let me move in with two older Iranian girls, Farah and Sophia, and she allowed this. We were all new arrivals in the United States. I taught them to speak English, and they protected me. They became the family I was missing —and so did my dorm mom. Before my parents left for Iran, they had asked Mrs. Anderson to promise to watch over me, give me a piece of fresh fruit every day, and teach me how to do my laundry.

I found two places I felt comfortable at the academy: the library and the stables. I'd had horseback riding lessons in England, and I knew how to take care of the magnificent animals. I spent many hours brushing down my favorite, Socks. I would sit on the fence and talk to him, telling him how sad I was or describing the events of the day. I felt a connection with him because he was gentle, and I needed any possible connection I could find with something gentle. The horses and books helped me slow down and calm myself. They were the only things that felt familiar. Nothing else looked, felt, smelled, or tasted like anything I had known before.

Questions

1. Crucible moments are moments that leave a lasting impact on a person, shifting their identity in some way. Can you think of a moment in your life that fundamentally challenged or reshaped your identity? How did it change you?
2. Because of our brain's wiring, we all have biases. Our job is to uncover them and then learn not to allow them to drive our critical decisions, both on and off the job. Reflect on your biases. Whom would you not want your children to bring home and introduce as their future spouse? How could this impact your relationship with your child? How does this impact your decisions at work?
3. Have you ever felt like an outsider, or realized that your "normal" was different from someone else's? How did you navigate that experience?
4. How do your biases influence the choices you make—where you live, who you befriend, and how you vote?
5. Have you ever assumed something about someone based on their background, only to be proven wrong? What did you learn from that experience?

Chapter 2

What We Don't Know

That heart which stands aloof from pain and woe
No seal or signature of Love can show.
                    -S.M. Hafiz

NOTE: *While this chapter addresses challenges specific to healthcare, the insights and practices can be applied to any organization or industry to experience how cultural humility can improve outcomes.*

An Afghani family brought their elderly mother to the Bryan Hospital emergency room after she had been experiencing abdominal pain for quite some time. The woman did not comprehend any English. She had come to Lincoln, Nebraska, from Afghanistan as a refugee to settle with her daughter's family. She had been forced to leave her homeland because of the war on terror that commenced after New York's World Trade Center was attacked on September 11, 2001. The woman's daughter and son-in-law, who were with her, spoke very little English. They were taking classes, but it was proving very difficult for the daughter to learn the complicated new language.

Neither of the women could read or write—even in their native language, which made learning English more difficult for them.

The woman was admitted to the hospital, and a few days later was diagnosed with end-stage cancer. Over the next few days, it became apparent to healthcare workers that circumstances would make this a more challenging case than usual. Because the woman was Muslim, modesty during physical examinations was required, and the family requested a female physician. Further complicating the case was the fact that the daughter and son-in-law were unwilling to discuss end-of-life issues with the patient. They would not openly talk with her about her impending death.

To properly care for this woman, hospital staff had to step outside of their personal comfort zones and discover creative solutions to provide culturally and linguistically appropriate care. It was imperative that the woman's medical care include culturally competent interpreter staff, with translated written materials that the son-in-law could read and explain to his wife. Clinical and support staff who knew how to ask about and negotiate cultural issues had to conduct culturally sensitive discussions with the family regarding treatment consent, advance directive forms, even appropriate food choices.

When the elderly woman died, the family requested time to wash and anoint her body with special oils. No one had asked to do this before. The hospital staff wasn't sure how to respond or manage the request; they weren't used to allowing family members to handle the body of the deceased. When a patient dies in an American hospital, the rules say the body can't be released to anyone but funeral home officials. The staff had worked hard to accommodate all the family's needs when the patient was alive, but there was no context for accommodating this last request within the rules and practices of this hospital so far away from the country of the woman's birth. I received a phone call late one weekend night asking me to help.

I explained to the department manager that, according to Muslim tradition, the family of the deceased must anoint the body with camphor oil, then wrap it in cloth at the burial site and put it into a wooden box. The manager and her staff had never heard of this tradition. Even the hospital chaplains were at a loss. To bridge the cultural gap, I sought to explain the family's request by drawing a parallel to death traditions familiar to most of the hospital staff—those rooted in Christian practices in the United States. In the US, when a person passes away, their body is often embalmed with specialized fluids and carefully prepared by a funeral home to resemble how they looked in life. This process provides comfort to grieving loved ones and helps them say their final goodbyes in a way that honors the deceased.

In much the same way, for many Muslims around the world, anointing the body with oil and wrapping it in cloth is a sacred and deeply significant practice. It is not simply a ritual but an act of devotion and reverence, ensuring that their loved one is honored according to their faith's customs. By likening the use of camphor oil to the embalming process, I offered the hospital staff a familiar reference point that helped them understand not just the *what* but also the *why* behind the family's request. With this newfound perspective, their apprehension transformed into understanding, replacing fear of the unknown with a sense of clarity and connection.

Once the staff grasped the cultural and emotional significance of this practice, their attitude shifted from confusion to compassion. Rather than feeling burdened or inconvenienced by an unfamiliar tradition, they began asking thoughtful, solution-focused questions:

"How can we obtain the oils they need?"

"Is there a way to connect them with community members who can support them in carrying out this sacred tradition?"

At its core, this situation was not about resistance to cultural differences, but about two groups—hospital staff and the grieving family—struggling with the same underlying frustration: the inability to provide the best possible care in a moment of profound vulnerability. The staff, though aware of the cultural differences, had been grappling with the helplessness of not knowing how to assist. The family, on the other hand, carried the deep fear that they might not be able to honor their mother's final rites in accordance with their faith.

By serving as a cultural interpreter, I was able to facilitate not only understanding but also genuine empathy. In doing so, I witnessed a transformation where uncertainty gave way to a collective desire to help, and where cross-cultural connection replaced hesitation with humanity. The beauty for me was being able to be a bridge in a difficult situation. I want to offer these lessons to others who desire to be bridges.

Conflicts in healthcare settings can be among the most challenging to navigate, especially when differing cultural perspectives collide. I encountered this firsthand during my father's final days, when a seemingly simple interaction with a nurse revealed the deeper complexities of cultural expectations and institutional norms. When individuals enter a hospital or clinic with an injury or illness, they are not just physically vulnerable; they are also emotionally distressed, experiencing heightened anxiety, pain, and fear. For caregivers, treating patients is part of their daily routine, but for patients and their families, it is often an emotionally charged and unfamiliar experience.

Neuroscience research, including findings from Daniel Kahneman's *Thinking, Fast and Slow*, helps explain why these interactions can become fraught with tension. Under stress, the brain's prefrontal cortex—responsible for logical reasoning and rational decision-making—becomes impaired, while the amygdala, the brain's emotional processing center, becomes more dominant. This shift makes it more difficult for both patients and caregivers to engage in calm, rational thought, often leading to heightened frustration and conflict.

Caregivers, operating within the structured world of healthcare, often follow an implicit set of cultural norms that are deeply embedded in their professional training, as well as their personal values shaped by family, region, and nationality. When patients or their families engage in behaviors that fall outside of these established norms, it can create friction, sometimes escalating an already difficult situation. However, understanding that both parties are navigating these interactions while under cognitive and emotional strain can foster greater empathy. By recognizing how stress impacts decision-making and communication, healthcare professionals can become more intentional about creating space for understanding, rather than reacting defensively or dismissively.

Ultimately, acknowledging the role of cognitive bias and stress-induced reactions in healthcare conflicts allows us to move beyond immediate frustration and toward meaningful, culturally competent care.

To further complicate matters, patients often enter the hospital or clinic with unspoken expectations about how they will be treated. They rarely verbalize these expectations because patients assume that healthcare providers intuitively understand their needs. *I'm a human being, and you are a human being; you should know what I need.* This assumption overlooks a fundamental reality: every individual, whether a healthcare professional, patient, or family member, operates with their own set of beliefs, experiences, and assumptions. Healthcare professionals, armed with years of education and clinical expertise, sometimes inadvertently allow their medical knowledge to overshadow a patient's expectations, lived experience, or expertise. Even the most culturally aware and adaptable healthcare professional can, at times, forget a crucial truth. Recognizing this dynamic at the moment it matters most is essential not only for achieving excellent patient outcomes but also for cultivating meaningful and compassionate interactions between those seeking care and those providing it. Our most recent research confirms that developing this level of awareness—and being able to apply it precisely when needed—is entirely possible. But it doesn't happen by chance, and certainly not without intentional and consistent effort. It cannot be achieved through a single one-hour training session or an occasional overseas experience. Instead, it demands continuous learning, self-reflection, and a deep commitment to understanding the needs of patients as if they were our family. It is a practice that must be nurtured over time through real engagement, active listening, and the willingness to challenge one's assumptions.

Communication is a key to overcoming these conflicts and misunderstandings. In the book *Intercultural Communication*, authors Larry Samovar and Richard Porter define intercultural communication as any time "the parties to a communication act bring with them different experiential backgrounds that reflect a long-standing deposit of individual or group experience, knowledge, and values." The word "long-standing" is a clue as to why intercultural communication is so difficult. Every person's background is deeply embedded with certain habits of communication.

Samovar and Porter explain that communication in the healthcare environment is complicated because layers of culture intersect, and these cultural layers differ for each person involved, including medical providers, patients, family members, pastors, and social workers. The layers of culture include:

- Overall culture of healthcare
- Unique culture of each area of healthcare (e.g., nurse culture, physician culture, non-clinical culture)
- Ethnic/national traditions and the deep-rooted values associated with a patient's country of origin, race, religion, or family
- Expectations shaped from each individual's experiences, both positive and negative.

If we add the volatility and trauma of life-and-death situations, we have a complex combination of conditions ripe for painful misunderstanding. Emotion is the fuel that feeds this fire. Dr. R.W. Breslin, in his book *Understanding Culture's Influence on Behavior*, said that human beings have their strongest emotional reactions when their culture's values are either violated or ignored.

Most of us in Western cultures are socialized to avoid pain, so it's not surprising that no one wants to talk about the issues causing emotional, culture-related pain in medical settings. In my opinion, this is one element that has led to disparities in healthcare.

Statistically, disparity in healthcare continues. While we know that race and ethnicity play a role, so does "educational attainment due to a difference in exposure to environmental risks and access to healthcare and socioeconomic opportunities and resources" (Commonwealth Fund 2024). Recent studies highlight that racial and ethnic disparities in health and healthcare remain a persistent challenge in the United States. For instance, the Commonwealth Fund's 2024 State Health Disparities Report reveals that Black and American Indian/Alaska Native (AIAN) populations experience higher rates of chronic health conditions and lower life expectancies compared to their white counterparts. We see evidence of similar disparities in the legal system. Such disparities are noted in numerous sources, including *The New Jim Crow* by Michelle Alexander and *Just Mercy* by Bryan Stevenson, which cite multiple cases. We also see this in the faith sector, where, in the words of Reverend Martin Luther King, Jr., "It is appalling that the most segregated hour of Christian America is 11:00 on Sunday morning."

Addressing disparities in every sector of society requires a dual approach: individual transformation and systemic change. One cannot exist without the other. Systemic change is only possible when numerous individuals in a system have a paradigm shift in their mindset enabling them to see the world from multiple perspectives and challenge the system's accepted norms and practices. Meaningful progress in any system, be it healthcare, housing, the legal system, or communities and nations, depends on the collective willingness to drive the change by cultivating mindsets that value a society designed to work for the collective good of all.

Individual growth alone is not enough to shift entrenched systems. Real change requires a shared commitment. We must move beyond isolated efforts and embrace a collective responsibility to drive systemic transformation. Encouragingly, most healthcare professionals I have encountered are willing to not just do this work but are deeply motivated by their desire to help patients who are often navigating fear, anxiety, and a profound need to be seen and understood.

For all these reasons, healthcare serves as a powerful testing ground for cultivating a mindset that prioritizes a society built for the collective good. It is a space where human vulnerability and professional responsibility intersect, offering invaluable lessons not just in patient care but in understanding and addressing the broader disparities that persist across society.

Culture-based questions in medicine, such as those raised by the needs of the Afghani woman and her family, are becoming more commonplace. Patients are more likely today to find themselves being cared for by medical staff who are influenced by a culture different from their own. This has underscored disparities in healthcare to an increasing degree. As awareness has increased, the complex challenges of accommodating culture within the healthcare environment have been examined more frequently in modern studies and books.

In *The Spirit Catches You and You Fall Down*, the story of young Lia Lee, a Hmong Chinese toddler who had epilepsy, researcher Anne Fadiman examines the clash between cultures that affected Lia's treatment. For more than a decade, Fadiman studied the beliefs and traditions of social workers and hospital staff at a hospital, and the many ways those contrasted with the vastly different beliefs and culture of Lia's Hmong family.

Fadiman's book is filled with accounts of events and struggles that demonstrate the misunderstanding, miscommunication, and distrust between Lia's professional caregivers and her family. Decisions made both by Lia's parents and her doctors may or may not have led to numerous crises of care on the one hand, and the unexpected traumas in the child's life on the other. Her professional caregivers believed the power of Western medicine would help her most, but Lia's family preferred the power of their cultural traditions. It had worked for them in Laos—why wouldn't it work in the United States? They believed the illness itself was simply *qaug dab peg* (the spirit catches you and you fall down), the wandering of her soul.

Patients aren't the only ones who experience disparity in the medical field; healthcare providers sometimes face their own crises. While this book doesn't delve into those issues, other authors have explored them. One such work is *Black Man in a White Coat: A Doctor's Reflections on Race and Medicine* by Damon Tweedy, MD. In this powerful memoir, Dr. Tweedy examines not only the challenges that Black doctors encounter in the medical profession but also the disproportionate health burdens that affect Black patients. His story is particularly compelling because it is both professional and deeply personal. As a Black physician, he has spent years studying the health inequities that disproportionately impact Black communities, only to find himself diagnosed with a chronic illness that afflicts Black patients at significantly higher rates. Through his journey, Dr. Tweedy seeks to humanize the statistics, transforming impersonal data into lived experience. While he does not claim to have all the answers, he believes that by sharing his own experiences, he can contribute to the larger conversation and ultimately to improved health for all Black individuals.

Both books and the stories of the people in them imply that solutions for overcoming health disparity are rooted in something personal, not just the science of medicine or the practices of medical institutions. A patient's situation, emotions, and ability to cope are dependent on that unique individual's many layers of expectations, which are indelibly linked to the many layers of culture that influence and define them, as well as the layers of culture that have influenced them in the past. The way patients behave in a medical setting can be influenced by their family history, work environment and coworkers, religious beliefs, peers, geographical setting, good or bad past experiences with medical staff and medical settings, as well as factors such as age and gender. The same can be said of the medical personnel who treat those patients.

It can be incredibly difficult for those in the majority—whether by race, nationality, or culture—to truly grasp the harm caused by disparities in healthcare, let alone feel a personal stake in solving them. If you are an American, born and raised, accustomed to seeking medical care in your own country from professionals who share your language, background, and customs, you may never have experienced the fear and disconnection that others feel. Medical disparity might be invisible to you, simply because it has never touched your life.

Now, imagine that everything you've ever known is suddenly ripped away.

Imagine a future in which the United States and Canada are at odds. Canada becomes the aggressor in the conflict, and Canadians begin to hate the US and its citizens. Over a couple of decades, the problem escalates, and physical conflicts between Canadians and United States citizens near the border become violent. Your family lives in the southern part of Montana, where there are wide open spaces and little worry about the violence. Most members of your family watch news of the conflict with interest, but they think of it as someone else's problem, and they don't pay close attention.

The idea of war on home soil seems unthinkable. Until it happens. Practically overnight, Canada, with the help of anti-American allies, launches a full-scale invasion, taking control of Washington, DC, and major metropolitan centers across the country. The government collapses. The land you've always called home is no longer yours.

But the worst is yet to come. Canada, now under a new totalitarian regime, has begun an ethnic cleansing campaign. German Americans, labeled as undesirable, are targeted for elimination. You watch in horror as your community is torn apart. People vanish overnight. Anyone who resists is executed on the spot. Your entire family, except for your spouse and elderly mother, is murdered. The country you once felt safe in is now the most dangerous place in the world for you. There is no time to grieve. No time to think. Survival is the only priority.

Your spouse convinces you that your only chance is to flee—to run thousands of miles south, across the border into Mexico. With nothing but the bare necessities packed in a bag, you begin a desperate journey from Montana, traversing an unfamiliar, hostile landscape, fearing at every turn that you, too, will be caught and killed.

When you finally arrive at the border, exhausted and terrified, Mexico grants you asylum. You are among the lucky ones. Just a few days later, Mexico shuts its borders before an expected flood of refugees overwhelms its fragile infrastructure. You and your surviving family are sent to a city willing to accept refugees, under one condition: you must quickly learn the language and integrate into the community to support yourselves.

With no other choice, you throw yourself into learning Spanish. But language doesn't come fast enough to meet the demands of survival. You are still struggling with basic words when tragedy strikes again. Your mother falls gravely ill and is in unbearable pain. Panicked, you rush her to the hospital, praying for help.

Now, Put Yourself in This Moment

How do you want her to be treated? What kind of care would you expect for her? Imagine the hospital staff speaking only rapid Spanish, their words a blur of sounds you don't yet understand. You try desperately to explain your mother's condition, but the doctor shakes his head impatiently. A nurse sighs in frustration. Someone makes a joke in Spanish that you can't quite translate, but you know it's about you. And then, the unthinkable happens. Your mother dies, far from the home she knew.

You try to explain that you need to honor your family's burial traditions, but no one understands. There is no funeral home willing to embalm her. You can't find a place that offers cremation. The customs you took for granted in the United States simply do not exist here. Your grief is compounded by helplessness. You have no idea how to lay your mother to rest in a way that feels right, that gives you closure.

Would you hope that someone showed you compassion? That a doctor or nurse took an extra moment to listen, to understand? That someone helped you navigate a system that was never built for you?

This is the reality for many refugees and immigrants seeking medical care in an unfamiliar country. Their fear, their grief, and their isolation are not abstract concepts. They are lived experiences. If this were your story, would you want someone to care enough to help?

As a country, the United States is still on an uphill climb when it comes to successfully managing and overcoming healthcare disparity, but it is improving. Overall, there seems to be greater knowledge of religious and cultural differences, and information about non-majority cultures is more readily available. The presence of knowledge doesn't mean behavior will change, but it is a start.

Let's step back into history for a moment to take a brief look at the roots of healthcare disparity. The stories you are about to read seem horrifying to us in the twenty-first century, but they explain a great deal about the unconscious tendencies of human beings to protect ourselves, as well as our blind spots, and our inclination to act on our fears. It sometimes took decades of study, analysis, protest, and political action to right some of these wrongs. The fallout from events like these has left us with lingering disparities that we often find difficult to explain. On a fundamental level, these accounts of real events demonstrate why it's sometimes so difficult to overcome the differences between us.

The first account is of Henrietta Lacks, a young black mother of five children in Maryland. In 1950, Henrietta was diagnosed with an aggressive form of cervical cancer. During her operation, doctors took two cervical tissue samples from her body and, without her knowledge, used them in research.

Author Rebecca Skloot told Henrietta's story in her 2010 book, *The Immortal Life of Henrietta Lacks*. Skloot explains that Henrietta's tissue was given to Dr. George Otto Gey, a researcher at Johns Hopkins Hospital in Baltimore. He discovered that Henrietta's cells reproduced at a much higher rate than normal cells and could be intentionally divided many times without dying, a very unusual condition that made the cells ideal for conducting experiments.

After Henrietta's death, Dr. Gey launched a commercial line of cells from the samples without notifying the Lacks family. At the time, it wasn't illegal to sell or use discarded tissues taken from a person's body during a medical procedure. In the following decades, Henrietta's resilient cells continued to be divided and used for experiments by medical researchers, labs, and doctors around the world, leading to several important biomedical breakthroughs and the creation of a multimillion-dollar industry. Jonas Salk used her cells in the development of the polio vaccine, and, according to my research (Wikipedia, n.d.), scientists have used Henrietta's cells to study cancer, AIDS, gene mapping, radiation, and the effects of toxic substances, as well as to test human sensitivity to certain manufactured products. Researchers have grown an estimated twenty tons of Henrietta's cells and filed nearly 11,000 related patents.

Henrietta's family was unaware of any of this until a large number of the cells became contaminated. Members of the medical community contacted the family and asked for blood samples they hoped would replace the contaminated cells.

Henrietta's story has become a landmark case in both medical ethics and cultural bias in the treatment of non-majority patients. In her book, Skloot uses the case of Henrietta's cells to help readers understand the human side of scientific experimentation and why many patients distrust the American healthcare system. Unethical experimentation on human patients has become unacceptable in the twenty-first century, yet distrust remains for many entering the healthcare system.

The question of human experimentation without a patient's knowledge is the most prominent aspect of Henrietta Lacks' story. But it's impossible to hear the story today without wondering whether Henrietta's race or socioeconomic status influenced the doctor's decision not to inform her family about the phenomenal properties of her cells, especially after the cells became widely used in prominent medical breakthroughs. At many points along the way, many different doctors or researchers could have decided to share this information with her family. Why did no one choose to reach out to the family? We have no way to know this, but we have many other examples of race-related healthcare disparities to indicate the answer often has to do with differences in power and privilege, and sometimes money.

Another famous example of healthcare disparity has its origins at the Tuskegee Institute in Tuskegee, Alabama. In 1932, the Tuskegee Institute began a study in partnership with the US Public Health Service to understand and trace the natural history of syphilis in order to get funding for treatment programs for the Black population. At that time, 35% of Blacks in their reproductive years suffered from the disease. Participants in the "Tuskegee Study of Untreated Syphilis in the Negro Male" originally included 600 poor black sharecroppers in Macon County, Alabama: 399 with syphilis and 201 without the disease. There is no evidence that the researchers ever obtained informed consent from the patients. Instead, researchers told participants they were being treated for "bad blood," a term widely understood by the Black population to include several health issues, including syphilis (US Public Health Service Syphilis Study at Tuskegee 2015.)

The men participating in the study received free medical exams, free meals, and burial insurance. After losing funding for treatment, someone decided to continue the study, but those who were infected were never told they had the disease and never received treatment. At the beginning of the study, doctors performed spinal taps to determine who had the disease. Some have conjectured that researchers continued the study without syphilis treatment simply because they wanted to learn about the progression of the disease in the body until death.

The study was initially intended to last only six months, but it continued for forty years. Thousands of study participants died of syphilis. Penicillin became widely accepted as a course of treatment in 1947, but those in the study who had the disease were never given penicillin. In 1972, Peter Buxtun, a social worker and epidemiologist working for the US Public Health Service, discovered the truth about the program. Buxtun was born and raised in Prague, Czechoslovakia. He was stunned to learn that an experiment similar to the Nazis' human experimentation in concentration camps was going on in the

United States. He leaked his findings to a reporter after several attempts to get the Public Health Service to stop the experiment.

As a result of Buxtun's leak to the press, Senator Edward Kennedy conducted congressional subcommittee hearings in early 1973. The subcommittee found that the men had agreed to participate, but they had been misled. None of the participants were given all the information necessary to constitute informed consent, and none were ever given the option to quit the study. The panel advised stopping the study immediately. In the summer of 1973, a class-action lawsuit was filed on behalf of the study participants and their families. As part of a $10 million out-of-court settlement, the US government provided lifetime medical benefits and burial services to all living participants and their families. The last participant died in January 2004, and the last widow receiving benefits died in 2009.

The history of the Tuskegee study is well-known among black Americans. Due to the account of human experimentation, many Black patients say they wait as long as they can before seeking medical care. They still distrust the system. Many Blacks will seek care only from Black health practitioners.

As with the case of Henrietta Lacks, we must ask how the decisions that led to this horrible situation were made. For our purposes, it's not a matter of blame; it's a matter of wanting to understand what happened within the hearts and minds of the individuals who made the decisions. The study of this type of motivation and behavior is what we call social science research.

Were the people who designed the Tuskegee program and continued the study even after funding was pulled aware of the ultimate consequences for participants: pain, suffering, and ultimately death? If so, why was that okay with them? If they were not aware of the gravity of these consequences, what was blocking their understanding? Does it have anything to do with race or the fact that the sharecroppers were poor? Would a study such as this ever have been put into place for well-to-do white males with syphilis in the 1950s? Did those who initially made the decisions realize they were risking legal consequences? Or was there something within their personalities or personal experiences that allowed them to justify their actions, remain blind to that possibility, and continue conducting the examinations?

It's easy to imagine medical practitioners in those days, hungry for knowledge, desperately looking for human subjects to help them understand diseases and find cures. Perhaps, by default, they gravitated toward citizens on the lowest rung of society. Perhaps they justified their actions with the thought that they might ultimately save many millions of lives. Were those the same kinds of thoughts the doctors had about Henrietta Lacks' immortal tissue?

Throughout history, people have been willing to compromise compassion and ethics for what they have believed to be good causes. It's unfathomable today to think that people could not have seen what was wrong with the Tuskegee study. Then again, why did people believe not long ago that it was okay to use experimental drugs on homeless people as long as we paid them?

Now let's take this examination of the people involved in the Tuskegee program one step further. After the program was dismantled and the lawsuit resolved, one wonders what those early decision-makers were thinking. Did they suddenly understand the seriousness of their actions? Did they feel remorse, or were they still blind to the pain of the study participants and the unjustness of the program? Again, we aren't looking to blame. We are simply trying to understand what led to the decisions, so we can determine what we can do to prevent such terrible things from happening in the future. Is it possible for those who are blind to the pain they have caused to understand what has gone wrong within themselves? Is it possible for them to change?

Is it possible for any of us to change?

Questions

1. How has your cultural background, experiences, and identity shaped your assumptions about healthcare, fairness, and access to services? How might your perspective differ if you were part of a marginalized or displaced community seeking care in an unfamiliar system?
2. Reflect on a time when you felt powerless or unheard in a healthcare, workplace, or institutional setting. How did that experience make you feel? How might that compare to the experiences of refugees, immigrants, or historically marginalized individuals navigating the healthcare system?
3. Knowing our brain is wired for bias to protect us, how can you actively work to recognize and challenge biases in your personal and professional interactions?
4. If you are in a leadership position in healthcare, what specific steps are you willing to take to ensure that culturally diverse individuals receive equitable treatment, respect, and care? How can leaders create policies that go beyond compliance to foster genuine inclusion?
5. If you are in a leadership position in education, government, finance, or another industry, what can you glean from the exploration into the healthcare dilemma to apply to your industry?
6. After reading about the real-life disparities in healthcare, what actions can you take to contribute to positive change in your community? How can you use your voice, privilege, or position to advocate for a more just and equitable society, not just in healthcare, but in housing, the legal system, and other areas?

Chapter 3

Costs of Belonging

*Fear is the cheapest room in the house.
I would like to see you
in better living conditions.*
-S. M. Hafiz

My father had a scar—large, unmistakable—stretching from beneath his chin down part of his neck and shoulder. I never knew the full story, just that he'd been burned by hot water in an accident long before I was born. But as a little girl, that scar was a source of wonder, not fear. I studied it openly, with the curiosity only a child can carry, free of shame, free of caution. I didn't worry about hurting his feelings. I knew that he knew I loved him.

One day, I told him, without hesitation or filter, that his scar looked like an egg-and-tomato omelet. It was a dish beloved by southern Iranians, familiar and warm. He laughed. Not the kind of laugh to dismiss me, but the kind that held a deep sense of recognition. And in that moment, he didn't brush it off. He leaned in. He saw the moment for what it was: a chance to teach me something far more important than how to cook an omelet.

"You can't tell anything about people from the way they look," he said gently, his eyes calm and knowing. He told me how people would stare, speculate, and make up stories in their heads about his scar; stories that were almost always wrong. What others saw as something strange or tragic, he had come to see as something that shaped his strength.

His scar carried both a curse and a gift: the curse of constant judgment, but also the gift of deep adaptability. Life had taught him early how to face discomfort—how to rise above the hurt, the whispers, the sideways glances—and instead meet people with grace. He learned not just to live with the scar, but to live with purpose.

My father was never bitter. Never angry. Never a victim in spirit, no matter what people might have assumed. He was full of quiet resilience. He found joy in his work. He loved and protected his family fiercely. He didn't let the pain of his past define him; he used it as fuel. His emotional strength didn't come from ignoring hardship but from choosing not to let it harden him.

He taught me, not through lectures, but through how he lived, that real strength is not loud—it's steady. That empathy isn't weakness—it's power. And that when life marks you, in ways visible or hidden, you can still lead with kindness, courage, and hope.

His scar became a symbol to me, not of damage, but of depth. Of survival. Of resilience. And of a father's quiet, unwavering love that taught his daughter how to stand strong in a world that too often looks only skin-deep.

On November 4, 1979, a group of Iranian students attacked the US Embassy in Tehran and took more than sixty hostages. The news was filled with conjecture about the reasons why this had happened. Some believed it was because then-President Jimmy Carter had allowed Iran's ousted king, Mohammad Reza Shah Pahlavi, to come to the United States for cancer treatment. Others believed it was far more than that—a dramatic way for the revolutionaries to declare a break with Iran's past and build momentum for a new Iran free from Western influence.

Perhaps it truly began decades earlier, rooted in Iran's desire to nationalize its oil industry, or maybe it stemmed from the CIA's intervention and overthrow of the government in the 1950s to protect Western interests in Iranian oil. Analyzing and speculating about the actions and motivations behind the Iranian Crisis, as it came to be known, is beyond the purpose of this book. The crisis marked a turning point. It paved the way for the establishment of the new Islamic Republic of Iran and for the Ayatollah Khomeini as its supreme leader. It was also the beginning of a long and broken relationship between Iran and the United States.

It also marked a mass exodus of Iranians to different parts of the world. By the mid-2010s, it's estimated that two-thirds of Iranians were in their thirties or younger, while one-third were over the age of seventy. Iranians between thirty and seventy years of age had left the country in the late 1970s and 1980s or were killed during the Iran-Iraq War of the 1980s. The majority of emigrating Iranians settled in the US, primarily in southern California, where large communities took root.

During the Iran hostage crisis of 1979, many people in the United States became wary of Iranians. For some, it was the first time they had heard of Iran. Most knew little to nothing about the country and its people, other than the horrible stories they were seeing on the news, and many Americans became angry and fearful of Iran. In the absence of a meaningful personal connection with the people of any group, a person's brain has nothing to challenge the information it receives from media and other sources. The brain accepts the new information (in this case, obtained mostly via news) as the way "everyone is."

I believe the workings of the human brain played an important role in the way Americans felt about Iran and Iranian immigrants after the 1970s crisis. As human beings, we are born with a need to self-protect. This becomes incredibly evident during times of perceived danger.

Neuroscientists and social psychologists call the part of the brain that automatically engages at such times the fight-or-flight center (the amygdala). Thanks to advances in neuroscience, we also know that human beings tend to connect with people like themselves and are naturally mistrustful of people different from themselves—unless they have worked hard to develop new neuropathways that allow their brains to balance emotion with logic and engage with curiosity, instead of resorting to fight or flight.

In times of crisis (like the Iranian hostage crisis), the empathy center of the brain tends to shut down, and mental vision becomes narrow. The ability to think critically, a function of the neocortex, becomes impaired. This is because, in moments of perceived danger, the brain shifts into survival mode, making quick, life-or-death decisions. The instinct to fight or seek control becomes more intense. These responses were essential for our prehistoric ancestors as they fled from wild animals.

While most of us no longer have to outrun predatory animals, the fight-or-flight response still serves us today, like when we react to an oncoming car or rush to stop our toddler from jumping into a pool. At those times, we need this primitive part of our brain to do exactly what it is designed to do. At other times, such as when there is a lack of adequate information, which is not a real threat to us, we need to recognize how to manage our primitive emotions—to regulate the impulses of our brain, especially when they are shaped more by perceived fear than by facts and human connection.

And some prey on our innate fight-or-flight response by stoking these perceived fears. America has become, and continues to become, more politically polarized. While this is a complex issue without a simple fix, we can become less polarized if we choose to step away from our devices and engage in genuine, face-to-face conversations with people across political lines. Some benefit from the political polarization of 330 million Americans. Quite honestly, it pays well, and they profit most when they can keep us divided, angry, and mistrusting of one another. The revolution we want and need is not in someone else but in our hearts and minds.

When the American hostages were taken in November 1979, I was in my dorm room at Florida Central Academy and had no idea what was going on. None of us did. You have to remember that there was no cell phone, or internet, or social media. Slowly, the news began to pour in. One of our classmates told us that there had been an attack on the US Embassy in Iran. At first, we didn't know hostages had been taken. The story unfolded slowly. Many Americans watched special reports after the nightly news. These nightly updates on the Iranian Crisis gave birth to what is now the television news show *Nightline*.

As teenagers, we were unsure what to think about this horrible event in our home country. At first, my brothers and I didn't think about what it meant for our families. The incident had taken place in Tehran, hundreds of miles from our home on Kharg Island, or from Masjed Soleyman and Ahwaz, where most of our relatives lived. But as other Iranian students talked, we began to worry about our loved ones across the sea. Our families started calling, and we shared updates, passing bits of information from person to person throughout the school. Some of the students were from Tehran. We heard that someone's family member had been detained, or another person's family was trying to leave the country. Deep fear settled into my belly as I became more and more afraid for my family, and my fear worsened when the war with Iraq began. We were fearful of what might happen in both Iran and Florida. What would this mean for our future?

This added a new dimension to the personal ridicule and humiliation I'd been experiencing since 1976. Before the hostage crisis, I was mocked mostly because I was generally different from the insecure British and American teenagers who felt threatened by all the unknowns associated with me. They also didn't like that I wasn't willing to change to suit them. After the crisis, this fear of unknowns gained new definition and focus. The events in Iran deepened the suspicion of some people and turned some people's disdain into hatred. Some of the newer Iranian students, including me, my brothers, and friends who had just arrived at the academy a few months earlier, felt this hatred and fear coming our way even from fellow students.

As the hostage crisis continued, the expressions of fear toward me and my fellow Iranians at the academy became more public. There were verbal assaults almost daily. People protested, yelling in the streets and carrying signs that said, "Camel Jockeys go home," or "Deport all Iranians." I remember the first time a person called me a Camel Jockey. She laughed and then said, "I'm just kidding, you know that, right?" Another person's father called me a Sand Nigger and followed it with, "But you are the prettiest Sand Nigger I know." These are small things that, in and of themselves, are not a big deal, but a hundred small verbal offenses toward one person build up and often damage their long-term mental health.

When my brothers and I talked with our parents, they told us everything was fine. They didn't want us to worry. Many years later, I found out they were *not fine*. They had been evacuated in the middle of the night to Abadan, then later to Tehran, because Iraq had attacked Kharg Island.

One day, shortly after the hostages were taken in Iran, school officials gathered all Iranian students, put us on a bus, and told us the US government required us to go to the Orlando International Airport. I still don't know what specific information immigration officials at the airport were looking for. They examined our official papers and asked questions about why we had come to the US and how our families were employed in Iran. I think some students were detained and perhaps sent back to Iran. The rest of us were driven back to school on the bus and told we could stay there as long as we continued our education.

The Ku Klux Klan (KKK) made it known that we weren't welcome. I knew nothing about the KKK until that time, although I heard we were in the heart of KKK country. My first clue was. When my dorm mom, Mrs. Anderson, refused to allow me to go to a barbecue with a boy whose father was a leader in the KKK.

"You'll become the barbecue," she joked, with enough of a serious note that I relented.

After the hostages were taken in Iran, the KKK looked for ways to make their opinion of us known. During a hayrack ride for students at our school, we heard gunshots, and the adults instantly took us back to the dorm. The rumor was that the KKK was shooting our way because they knew there were Iranians at the school. If it was them, I must assume they were only trying to scare us. I don't think I was aware enough of what was happening to be as terrified as I maybe should have been. I remember thinking, "They don't even know me. How can they hate me?"

Some of the non-Iranian students, teachers, and local citizens would talk about the hostage situation in ways that made us feel unwelcome and afraid. One day, I went shopping with a group of Iranian students at Altamonte Springs Mall in Orlando. A store employee began chatting with us. She seemed nice, and it felt good to have a normal conversation with a friendly member of the community. When she asked where we were from, one of my friends said, "Iran." Instantly, we were politely but firmly thrown out of the store and told never to come back. We were in shock and disbelief.

This experience wasn't an isolated incident. At that time, stores were selling dartboards and T-shirts with "Death to the Ayatollah" on them. People were singing "Bomb, Bomb, Bomb—Bomb, Bomb Iran" to the Beach Boys' tune, "Barbara Ann." We heard and read jokes about Iranians being Ragheads. On more than one occasion, I was told, "Go home! You don't belong here."

What could I do? I couldn't change where I had been born. I couldn't change who my parents were. Didn't they understand that the political situation in Iran had nothing to do with my teenage world at the academy? I felt embarrassed to be Iranian, but a part of me wanted them to know about the beautiful parts of life in Iran: the hot summer nights in the village on the hill, the expansive home on Kharg Island, and the loving embrace of my cousins and grandparents. Not every Iranian hated Americans. Not every Iranian was a terrorist. When I lived in Iran, my life was remarkably similar to theirs.

In my mind, there was only one thing I could do: not admit to being Iranian. It was a matter of physical safety and emotional survival. When people asked me where I was from, I began asking, "Where do I look like I'm from?" People would guess all kinds of places. Mostly Mexico, sometimes Greece. My typical response was, "You are so smart!" or "How did you guess?" This was a measure of protection I used for many years after the hostage crisis had cooled. To this day, if I meet someone new and they have openly voiced disdain for people from the Middle East, I will not mention my place of birth. It saddens me, and I wish it weren't so.

Mrs. Anderson was faithful to her promise to my mother and father. She left a piece of fresh fruit on my pillow every day. Instead of teaching me how to do my laundry, which she believed would add to my stress, she took my laundry home with her and returned it clean. She saw my sorrow and sadness in the days, weeks, and months after my parents left and wanted me to know she cared.

The United States seemed very strange and confusing to me in many ways. Mrs. Anderson took me to my first American football game. "Why are they so puffed up?" I asked her. I had thought they were going to play soccer, because in Iran we call soccer "football." I spent my first Thanksgiving and Christmas breaks in the Andersons' home, because Mrs. Anderson wanted me to see how typical American families celebrated the holidays.

Through her words and actions, I could tell that Mrs. Anderson was truly concerned about what happened to me. The day the authorities gathered us up and loaded us onto the bus, she was as upset as we were. She grabbed her son Andy, who was five years older than me and happened to be visiting his mom that afternoon, and said, "He'll marry you if he has to, to keep you here!"

I don't know what life would have been like at that time without Mrs. Anderson watching over me. Even though I missed my parents and was afraid of what might happen, everything was a little better because her empathy, care, and consistent support made me feel a bit more grounded in this strange land.

I settled into a routine, and the months began passing more easily. I graduated from high school just eight days after my sixteenth birthday. I had been accepted to several US colleges, but I didn't want to leave the security and comfort I had found. I decided to stay in Sorrento and attend the community college, so that I would be close to the Andersons. When it became difficult for my parents to send money out of Iran, I moved in with the Andersons. I worked hard at school. Some days, I felt like I was walking a tightrope, balancing homesickness, fear of the unknown, and the heavy weight of responsibility. But having a safe place to land at the end of each day made all the difference.

Then, when I was almost finished with my associate's degree, my mother and eighteen-month-old sister, Helena (whose name I got to choose to be like mine), were finally able to move to the United States. The moment I heard the news, my heart raced with a mixture of disbelief, joy, and overwhelming relief. After years of uncertainty, a part of my family was coming back together.

Helena was born in August of 1980, nearly a year after my parents had dropped us off at the boarding school. I had never met her in person. I had tried to piece together what my baby sister might be like from the occasional photos and stories from phone calls. I had imagined her face so many times, and now I would be able to play with her and get to hold her. My mom and Helena got visas because my younger brother had finished high school but was still a minor. The thought of reuniting with my mother felt like taking a breath I didn't realize I had been holding for years. So much had changed. I had changed. She had changed. My Mom's deep devotion to her children and their safety took a toll on her that affected every facet of all our lives from the day we were reunited. I had no idea how my life was about to change. Once again.

The process of migration is difficult. When an organization is moving employees (expatriates) to another country, the company works hard to help them acculturate (adapt) to the new country. Even with support, displaced workers often experience months of sadness, loneliness, and trouble adjusting.

Immigrants don't usually receive such support from an organization, so the distressing feelings are exacerbated. Refugees, who are forced to flee their homeland to find safety and security, experience emotional turmoil at an even more intense level—what some might call exasperation on steroids! My brothers and I were a little bit of both. While we started as international students, our experience became similar to that of typical teenagers, immigrants, and refugees all rolled into one. What we went through emotionally was even more intense because we were so young and had no family with us. At a time when most teenagers are beginning to explore their identity and search for belonging among their peers, we were trying to make sense of who we were amid a hostage crisis, separation from our parents, and a war in Iran. Not to mention that our funds were cut off, and our ability to pursue our education became more difficult.

The adaptation process of moving from one country to another happens slowly and requires a great deal of support for the process to be successful. It's difficult to understand if you haven't experienced this. A big hole is created when you leave your home country. You feel disoriented in the new culture and uncertain how to handle even the small daily tasks, which vary from country to country. An immigrant can experience a rollercoaster of emotions: the highs and excitement of experiencing new things and of having made a decision and following through, then the lows of homesickness and frustration with new ways you are expected to behave. This emotional cycle is normal, and acknowledging it can help ease the burden of the transition.

Offering support to those navigating cultural transitions and educating bystanders about how to be compassionate and encouraging can make all the difference. Without such support, so much can go wrong. But when adaptation (not forced assimilation) goes well, it stands as a powerful testament to the strength of the human spirit. It often results from intentional support, acceptance, and encouragement by both those adjusting to a new way of life and those welcoming them into it.

A refugee experiences mostly lows, including sorrow and fear, but there are a few highs, too: the relief of having escaped danger and the excitement of encountering a new place. Both immigrants and refugees can have delayed reactions to all the changes, and the first few months in a new country are filled with overwhelming sensory input that can make everything feel disorienting.

If you're not an immigrant and want to understand what it feels like, try this: Imagine you have moved to a new city in a region you're not familiar with. You can't go back because war has broken out in your hometown. Imagine your family is still there. Now, you're expected to learn a new language, work, and go to school, all at the same time. And on top of all that, you don't even know if you'll be allowed to stay. Can you feel it? The fear. The exhaustion. The grief. The quiet ache of being untethered. The frustration of being misunderstood. Maybe even a flicker of excitement that brings you shame, and a determination to survive and thrive despite it all.

Now, imagine that in the middle of all this chaos, people get frustrated with you because you aren't speaking the language correctly. Some make fun of you, while others just plain ridicule you and tell you to go back to where you came from. How would you cope? And how would you feel if the new city is constantly changing its policies whether you and others from your former city will be allowed to stay?

Psychologists and researchers have spent decades studying what happens to the human spirit in moments like these. We know this process of cultural adaptation is deeply challenging, emotionally, mentally, and physically. For children, the need to feel safe and secure is most urgent. The older the person, the longer it takes to learn a new language and to adapt to the changes.

There's more than one way to adapt, and the how makes all the difference. Sometimes adaptation is forced; that is called assimilation, and it is often the most damaging. At other times, adaptation is a choice; that is called acculturation, and it is far healthier because it involves a personal decision to fold oneself into a new way of living and being. Assimilation demands, "Who you were is not good enough to be here." Acculturation offers the freedom to choose. The person chooses by reflecting, "This is a new place, and I want to figure out how to live in a way that honors who I was and who I am becoming in this new land, and for my children and their children to celebrate their roots as they spread their wings."

I know the difference well, because I've lived both. Early in my journey, I felt pushed to assimilate by hiding who I was and exhibiting the least amount of my Iranian identity in order to be accepted. However, as I grew, I found my way toward acculturation, and the shift was life-changing.

Assimilation says, "I can't pronounce your name. Can I call you Tom, Sally, or John?

Acculturation says, "I see people struggling to say my name. I wonder how I can find a way to help them say it without it losing its meaning?"

Assimilation says, "You don't know our language? You must be too lazy or too stupid to learn it.

Acculturation says, "Learning a new language is hard, but I'll keep trying, no matter how long it takes me."

Assimilation wants instant transformation—a microwave-like society's expectations of newcomers. We want humans to be like the AI learning that is now part of our lives. Acculturation allows for growth over time. A slow-cooked society, more like a crock-pot, where there is patience, support, and space to breathe. And at the heart of it all, assimilation often leads to resentment, disconnection, and resistance. This has the exact opposite effect we want when we are forcing people to change at the pace of AI. Acculturation leads to dignity, confidence, and lasting acceptance and belonging.

Most of us, when entering a new world, would choose to acculturate, adapting at our own pace while preserving our sense of self. But far too often, newcomers are expected to assimilate on someone else's terms. Understanding the difference is where empathy begins. Supporting the difference is where change happens.

I loved my mom and was excited to have her nearby again. But my time in the United States had changed me not just on the surface, but in ways that shaped how I saw the world and myself. It was a necessary change. To survive in my isolation within the American world, I had to accept living the "American" way, at least to some degree. In my formative teenage years, I took on American characteristics by choice and created the life of an American girl. I learned how to do this with Mrs. Anderson's help, as well as by watching and imitating other teenagers around me.

I sometimes wonder if I would have changed as much if the hostage crisis in Iran hadn't happened at such a formative time in my life. As a sensitive teenager, it was so important to be accepted. Belonging wasn't just a want; it was a deep longing. I was willing to do what was necessary to avoid feeling different and avoid some people's contempt. That's why I would allow people to guess where I was from instead of telling them I was Iranian.

When I moved in with my mom and sister in St. Petersburg, Florida, I realized that my mom and I had both changed drastically. Mom wanted what we had in England, but her time in Iran had transformed her into a strong Iranian-Muslim woman: modest, quiet, and focused on education for her children at all costs. By contrast, I had become an active, independent seventeen-year-old who danced between two cultures but had started to find her rhythm in American life. I attended the University of South Florida in the fall of 1982, as Mom had expected me to do, but we began to argue about many things.

When cultures collide, it is painful for all the people involved. When the collision is between mother and daughter, the pain cuts deeper and lingers longer.

One of the biggest problems was that our work ethic was now different. I valued my education, but I had learned how to have fun. My mother, who had become even more conservative, felt that any distraction from education had to be removed. She wanted me to spend sixteen hours a day studying, eight hours sleeping, and nothing else. She was an introvert who was happy being at home by herself. I was an extrovert who needed to be with people. I learned by talking and doing, as opposed to my mom, who learned by reading and writing. We weren't just from different generations; we were now from different worlds. I think she believed, because of the way I had changed, that I was unwilling to comply with any of the rules she set.

My mom was horrified that I had a boyfriend. It was nothing serious, but to her, he was a threat to my education. She began to check up on me, in my mind violating my right to privacy. I didn't believe associating with Americans detracted from my education. On the contrary, I believed it enriched my education. I loved being around people from all parts of the world and learning from them. I thought socializing was an education in itself. I enjoyed talking with the Andersons on the phone, for example, getting updates about the people who had become my surrogate family.

I know my mom was simply reinforcing what she felt was best for me, but I felt she was forcing me into a mold I no longer fit. Each time I stepped into our home, I felt smaller and more confined, as if the girl I had become wasn't welcome there. When I came home from school, I felt like a caged animal, miles away from everything familiar to me. Today, with children of my own, I look back on this time with greater understanding. My mom was desperate to protect me. I was desperate to live my own life.

So, I escaped.

I ran away and lived with my friends and former roommates from Florida Central Academy, Farah and Sophia. They lived in Clearwater, about forty miles from the university, but I didn't care how far away it was from school or my mother. My independence was worth the hardships. I hitchhiked to college from the girls' apartment three days a week and worked at a nearby McDonald's restaurant. Money was tight, freedom was hard-earned, and some days we lived off the scraps the restaurant was about to throw away, but I felt free.

In one important way, I did not stray from my parents' wishes. They had already paid for my schooling, so I refused to quit. My mother and sister had waited in line with me for hours during registration at the University of South Florida. Back in the early 1980s, college registration wasn't a quick online process—it was an all-day, in-person event that required standing in long lines, moving from table to table, and filling out forms by hand. The image of my mother and sister sitting patiently on the floor of the registration hall, waiting as I made my way through the maze of paperwork and bureaucracy, *is permanently burned in my memory.* It wasn't just the time it took—it was their quiet support and their presence in that moment that made it unforgettable. Although I didn't want to live with them, I couldn't bear the thought of quitting when my parents had sacrificed so much for my education.

When the semester was finished, I had a choice: Stay where I was, move in with my mother again, or move back to the Andersons, three hours away. I chose the Andersons. I wanted to be free to make my own decisions and go to college without feeling as though I was always being watched. I know my mom felt betrayed, and I am sorry now to have caused her that pain.

To earn money for tuition, I began working at another McDonald's, with Mrs. Anderson's daughter, Laura. Laura is my American sister, and she and her husband, Wayne, are some of our closest family members to this day. When we walked into the new-employee orientation, the first thing I saw was the behind of a young man who was bent over, preparing a video for our session. I liked what I saw and whispered to Laura, "That's the butt I'm going to marry." It was a joke, but it wasn't long before I began dating Scott Fagan.

I buckled down at work and saved money for school. I had nine months to save for the fall semester. Then, one day, I received a letter demanding my appearance at an immigration hearing. My mother had given the US immigration office my name and address at the Andersons and had told immigration officers that I was working illegally. The betrayal hit me like a wave, cold, forceful, and suffocating. I was furious and heartbroken at the time. Today, I know my mother's belief that I was ruining my life had been so strong that she decided the best way to protect me was to force me back to Iran.

"What can they do?" Scott asked as we talked about it on the phone.

"They can deport me," I said matter-of-factly.

"I won't let them do it," he said.

"What are you going to do, marry me?" I asked, laughing. And to my surprise, he said that is exactly what he would do. I reminded him he was only seventeen and still in high school. And he would be leaving to fulfill orders for the US Navy a month after graduation.

"We are too young," I said, serious now, "and I don't want you to marry me because you feel sorry for me." I'd heard this before when Mrs. Anderson said Andy would marry me. I thought this was the same kind of thing—an expression of love and concern, but not a serious proposal. Scott insisted he did not feel sorry for me. He professed his love and said he couldn't bear the thought of me going back to Iran.

The next day, I received a beautifully written letter from Scott asking me to marry him. He said he didn't care how young we were and believed we could make it if we tried. I loved him, too, so I said yes. Our plan was to get married the following December when he completed boot camp and telecommunications school. I would go back to school wherever we landed after that.

Finally, I felt at peace with my life.

I was the future wife of a US sailor, and I knew where I belonged: With him. The Andersons were not happy with my decision, but they were moving to Dallas anyway and knew I would have to find another place to live if I wanted to stay in Florida. They gave me a car and some money, and I moved in with a fellow McDonald's employee—a single mother of two children.

Scott took me to the immigration hearing in June. As my fiancé, he was allowed to go into the hearing with me. The judge was not sympathetic. Despite our engagement, which he may have seen as an attempt to circumvent the law, he told me that if I didn't leave voluntarily by September, I would be deported and not allowed to come back anytime soon, if ever. Scott and I were shocked. Both of us were silent on the drive home, each of us lost in our thoughts.

The next day, Scott showed up at my door. He had talked with his parents. They would sign for him, since he was under the legally marriageable age, which meant we could get married before he left for boot camp on July 21st. I couldn't believe it. I felt so loved and cared for. I couldn't wait to be Mrs. Scott Fagan. I knew it would not be a popular decision with some of the people in my life, but I was at peace. I began to feel excited, as any young bride should.

We set the wedding date for July 8, 1983, only three weeks away. My friends Farah and Sophia thought I was crazy to marry an American without my parents' permission. My friends at work thought I was pregnant. I wasn't. In fact, we waited several years to have children to prove it. Louise Anderson expressed her worry. She convinced a friend to come to McDonald's and try to talk me out of it. She didn't want me to give up on my parents' dream for my life, and really believed I was marrying Scott to get a green card. Much later, I found out Scott's parents also believed our marriage was simply a way for me to get a green card, but they wanted to support their son in his effort to help me, and they knew we could get a divorce afterwards and be done with it.

Farah told my older brother about the wedding, and he told my parents. It is not an exaggeration to say they were devastated. This was not the future they had wanted for me for so long. At the time, young and in love, I didn't understand. But I do now. I probably would feel the same in their shoes. At that time, though, as a bride-to-be full of excitement and confidence in my future, I couldn't understand their displeasure.

Honestly, I didn't feel that I was being forced to marry Scott to stay in the United States. I knew my father had the connections to keep me in the country. But I believed then, and have always believed, that God intended for Scott and me to be together.

Even though we were different in many ways, including the ways we were raised, we were instinctually drawn to each other, as opposites often are. What we shared wasn't perfect, but it was real. On a deeper level, we felt a strong emotional connection to one another and a sense of commitment. We understood each other, were deeply in love, and believed this was the right thing to do.

Our decision would mean some major changes in Scott's life. As the husband of a non-US citizen, especially an Iranian citizen, he couldn't be in telecommunications because it required a security clearance. So, he switched careers and became a Navy engineman (diesel mechanic). In my mind, this decision proved he really loved me. With a new chapter rising to meet me, the trauma of my early years began to loosen its grip. The anguish I felt during my first years at the academy started to fade, the Iranian crisis suddenly seemed light years away, and I felt much of my pain being overshadowed by happiness.

Questions

1. What is your gut reaction when you hear about protesters in another country? Do you feel empathy, judgment, confusion, or curiosity? Why do you think you respond this way? What personal experiences, media influences, or cultural messages might be shaping your reaction?
2. We have all endured challenging times. In what ways have those experiences shaped who you are today? How have you allowed those challenging times to make you stronger? Better? Wiser? More resilient? More purposeful? How are you using those experiences to help others grow, heal, or feel seen?
3. Think about a time when you had a strong disagreement with a family member. Did you ever consider why they may hold the belief that you disagreed with? What values or life experiences might have led them to that perspective? Where may that belief have come from, and what in your life has caused you to believe differently?
4. Have you ever been in a situation where you felt like an outsider? What helped you feel more included? What would have helped? How did that experience change the way you relate to others who are different from you?
5. When was the last time you changed your mind about something important? What influenced the shift, and what did it teach about your ability and willingness to be open and adaptable?

Chapter 4
Shifting Perspectives

*Love sometimes wants to do us a great favor:
hold us upside down and shake all the nonsense out.*
-S. M. Hafiz

As our wedding day approached, I was happier than I had ever remembered feeling. We were so poor, we had to make do with what we had, but everything was going wonderfully under the circumstances. Love was our only luxury, but it was more than enough. I would wear the dress I had worn to Scott's high school prom. We would be married at his parents' church, and the Reverend Vanus Smith would preside over the ceremony.

Everything happened in a blur, as if time itself had conspired to push us toward the altar. Scott bought a suit from the Salvation Army and then purchased two silver wedding bands at the flea market. We went together to get our blood tests and apply for the marriage license. We sent no invitations; we would have only about ten people with us at the wedding.

The afternoon before the wedding, I was at home shaving my legs.

The phone rang and I left the shower, one leg shaved and one unshaven, to answer it. A coworker at McDonald's was calling to tell me that a man was there asking for me. The man said he was my father and claimed he wouldn't leave until he talked with me. In that instant, the world seemed to shift beneath me, like a story I'd put away was reopened without warning. I was anxious and excited—I hadn't known my dad was in the US. I remember smiling the minute I heard his voice on the phone. I still hear his voice, and it calms me instantly. My younger brother and our youngest son both have his same voice.

"I heard you were getting married, and I want to talk to you," he said. His voice carried a weight I hadn't felt in years, part memory, part mourning. All of a sudden, a little dread mixed with the excitement, but I told him I would meet him. I quickly finished shaving, dressed, and drove to McDonald's. When I walked in, I saw not only my dad, but also my older brother, my little sister, and my friend, Farah. While Farah and my brother took my little sister to the playground, Dad and I sat in one of the booths at the back of the restaurant and talked for a long time.

He told me I didn't have to get married, because he would contact the judge and talk to him. He would take care of everything. I told him I really loved Scott and truly wanted to be his wife. I could see he was sad, and I understood. It was not his dream that I would get married at eighteen. He wanted me to go to school and reminded me that I had promised him I would become a doctor and help save people's lives.

"You will be poor," my dad said, stating the obvious. "It was not my goal to bring my kids to America, only to have them live without money and not go to school. You know we have sacrificed everything to bring you and your brothers here because we wanted an excellent education for you."

"I know, Dad," I said, acting as grown-up as I could for an eighteen-year-old who was about to marry a seventeen-year-old. "I respect that. I have not forgotten my promise, and I will do my best to make sure your sacrifices were not in vain. But I have found my path —a path where love is not a detour, but the way forward. If only you could see that I can finally touch the happiness you have wanted for me. This is my home now, Agha. Please understand."

In the end, he did understand, or he said he did, for my sake. Was it because he knew he had no choice? Maybe. Parents do that sometimes because they don't want to irreparably destroy the bond between themselves and their children. I believe it was the same reason Scott's parents had agreed to our marriage. Letting go is a quiet heartbreak, spoken in silence and sealed with hope. We must let go of our children. And it's never easy, no matter what country we are in.

In the book *Thinking Fast and Slow*, Daniel Kahneman does a great job of helping the reader understand the two systems of the brain: the fast system (unconscious, automatic, associative, intuitive, judgmental), which he calls the System 1 brain, and the slow system (conscious, deliberate, logical, rational, inclusive) which he calls the System 2 brain. He draws back the curtain on how our minds truly function, offering us a map to our inner terrain.

In unpacking Kahneman's research, we see that thoughts, beliefs, and attitudes can move from the slow, deliberate System 2 brain to the quick and reactive System 1 brain through repetition (both conscious and unconscious). This neuroplasticity—our brain's ability to rewire itself—is a quiet miracle that invites us into the possibility of change.

Understanding this distinction gives us hope that humanity is capable of engaging the conscious brain to think deliberately and move beyond biases and stereotypes, which are the unconscious shortcuts through which our minds attempt to sort good from evil. Bias is not always borne of malice; it is often *the* residue of what we've learned without knowing we've learned it. No one understands how to embed information into our unconscious programming better than marketers who are trying to sell us "stuff". The "stuff" begins with an idea. Through repetition, emotion, and strategic storytelling, they bypass our critical thinking and lodge ideas directly into System 1.

That's why autopilot—moving through life without conscious engagement—is one of the greatest enemies of System 2 development. *Social media has become the strongest source of unconscious programming.* The algorithms are set up so that the more you watch or like a certain type of information in your feed, the more it will give you that. Thus, while we think everyone is getting access to the same information, in fact, we are being presented with the exact opposite sides of a story repetitively to the point that we become outraged when a friend or family member shares information that opposes what we believe to be true.

Sometimes, I use a dollar bill to help students, clients, or teams understand this concept. I present a dollar bill as I stand in the middle of the group. I ask one side what they see. Then I ask the other side what they see. They are all looking at the same dollar bill, but from different vantage points. Some are looking at the front, while others are looking at the back. This is what happens when we are being unconsciously fed information. We then argue about what we are seeing, to the point that we are outraged and no longer willing to sit with each other and accept that there may be some level of truth to what the other person is sharing, and perhaps we could explore and learn from each other.

And there are those who profit from this process. It even has a name: The Economics of Outrage. If you've had no opportunity to build strong, deliberate pathways in the conscious brain, you may be willing to listen, understand someone who is different, even accept them in the moment. Yet once they leave your presence, your unconscious brain takes the wheel again, steering you back through the familiar, well-worn grooves that fear differences and create judgment of those differences. And in times of tension, exhaustion, stress, or perceived threat, that unconscious, default System 1 brain takes over. In trying to protect us and conserve energy in the process, it drives us to do and say things that we, at best, regret and, at worst, create laws that harm those who are different, all while convincing ourselves we are doing what is right.

The System 2 brain is the last part of the human brain to develop physically. It doesn't even begin development until birth. It helps us make meaning of the experiences our five senses have. A child cries when hungry and gets fed. The System 2 brain makes connections between the moment of hunger, crying, and being fed. The System 2 brain continues to develop and build such connections over our lifetime. The latest technology has enabled us to see the neuropathways (hairlike connections) connecting as a person is learning something. For example, when my mother called immigration to have me deported, and I felt betrayed, my System 2 brain created a neuropathway between my mother's action and my sense of betrayal. Think of these as two separate neuropathways. When I became a parent and was in therapy for my trauma, I began to make a new connection. My mother behaved out of love. I could forgive her. I could forgive myself. I could move forward without inflicting trauma on my own children because of the trauma I knew and was comfortable with.

The System 2 brain is a muscle, and like any muscle, it must continually be exercised to keep it strong and agile. We know muscles weaken when left idle. The System 2 brain's form of atrophy is to quickly go offline and rely on the System 1 brain to give meaning to new experiences. If I hadn't addressed my trauma, when my son did something that reminded me of the betrayal I felt, I would have behaved out of fear and lashed out in ways that would have damaged him. In the book *The Body Keeps the Score*, Dr. van der Kolk talks about the amygdala (a central part of System 1) as being the brain's smoke detector. When trauma has occurred and is left unprocessed, it signals us by keeping us in a hypersensitized and irritable state, with our stress hormones firing when unwarranted. The trauma is relived internally (a function of System 1 brain), often without a conscious connection (a function of System 2 brain) between the trauma that occurred and the thoughts and actions of today.

One of the most compelling arguments for general education or liberal arts classes in higher education is that they activate the System 2 brain and exercise it on an ongoing basis for four or five years, teaching learners to think critically, synthesize information, and confront complexity. It is not just education; it is muscle training for the brain—the kind of brain that can hold contradictions and empathy at the same time. When learners engage in general education courses such as philosophy, literature, history, art, or music, they are strengthening their capacity to access the System 2 brain intentionally. I've seen this unfold in my classrooms, in the clients I've coached, and in my research.

A dean of students at a health sciences college told me that nurses who complete a bachelor's degree with a wide range of liberal arts courses often outperform their peers in nursing skills courses. The reason, she explained, is that the liberal arts courses build the student's ability to synthesize everything they are learning in their technical classes (anatomy and physiology, pharmacology, chemistry, medical terminology) and apply it to real-world patient care, using critical thinking, ethical judgment, and decision-making. They aren't just memorizing data; they're building bridges between knowledge and humanity.

Similarly, a chief of police I was coaching shared that, in his experience, officers who have taken liberal arts courses during their undergraduate education tend to make better decisions and demonstrate greater problem-solving skills. This is not to diminish the value of technical education, far from it. But these examples highlight the reality that higher-order thinking requires the System 2 brain to be online. And that means we must create learning opportunities that challenge the brain to stretch and grow beyond formal education.

We build physical strength by tearing existing muscle fibers to create space for new muscle tissue to grow. The brain is no different. To create new ways of thinking, we must disrupt the old. Transformation isn't neat and easy. It requires friction, discomfort, and at times, pain. And if we haven't developed the System 2 muscle, it will be the first to disengage when we experience differences. Because we are wired for comfort with similarity, we often will perceive differences as a threat in the initial engagement. This leads to the intense activation of fight-or-flight (System 1) and the inability to access our logical, balanced, thoughtful system (System 2). In that emotionally hijacked state, our willingness to understand the perspective of another person is blocked, and judgment steps in to "save us" from the perceived threat.

But here's the hope: once someone intentionally forges new pathways in the neocortex, it becomes possible to interrupt the fight-or-flight response, and to step on the balcony of our own thoughts, examine them, and choose a different response under the perceived pressure.

I'm not a medical scientist, so I can only wonder at the thousands of micro-changes in the brain that make this possible. I find myself captivated by the questions this raises—questions that led me to research and explore the intersection of neuroscience, human development, intercultural mindset, and expanding leadership effectiveness. If it's true that establishing new pathways in the neocortex helps people become more accepting of others, what do we need to do to guide their development? One thought that crossed my mind was this:

> Authentic, ongoing, positive interactions with those who are different from us, coupled with honest self-reflection, may be the neural catalyst we've been searching for.

These moments of connection create synapses in the neocortex that allow empathy and understanding to become an instinctive part of our approach to differences. This might explain why Scott was able to see past the differences between us, even during a time when people like me were feared and vilified. It might explain why my father, who had spent his life preparing his children for leadership in Iran, could suddenly pivot and support my marriage, knowing full well it would forever alter my ties to our homeland.

Consider people you know who are profoundly different from one another yet share a bond of respect or even love. It's likely they have developed a strong capacity for empathy that transcends surface-level differences. Empathy is not the absence of fear, but the decision to stay present with it. I believe that when someone sits with their doubts and biases long enough to recognize those same fears in others, empathy grows. I've seen it over and over again in my work educating and coaching leaders; the more a person develops the art of introspection and empathy, the more capable they are of embracing those who are different from them.

In my experience, hardship can be a powerful teacher of empathy when given the space to guide the development of System 2. Take Scott, for example. His early struggles and his ability to think deeply gave him a depth of maturity and compassion that others twice his age often lacked. Despite enduring overwhelming difficulties, some refugees and immigrants I've worked with develop immense empathy and use their struggles to build resilience and bounce back stronger. Others, though their suffering is similar, seem only to accumulate bitterness and resentment.

The truth is, hardship alone doesn't produce empathy, emotional growth, and maturation, which I call emotional intelligence. It's not uncommon for those who have been hated to become cynical and hardened by hate. In criminal psychology, it's believed that serial murderers lack the neurological development needed for empathy. So, what makes the difference? What causes one person to lean toward compassion, while another is consumed by bitterness?

Perhaps, as you read this, you're thinking of someone in your life who struggles to accept others. The reasons for this are numerous and complex, encompassing biological, political, psychological, and spiritual factors. To connect authentically with your own experiences, and from there, build a bridge to the experiences of others is the slow, deliberate process of developing our System 2 brains, ultimately leading to a higher level of empathy and understanding than we currently possess. And that messy, uncomfortable, and deeply human process is what creates mindsets and levels of conscious existence as a human race that will enable us not only to see through our own eyes but also the eyes of others. A mindset that doesn't just react, but pauses, leans in with curiosity, and reflects. And from that curiosity and reflection, we grow to be human in ways that haven't existed before.

I would have loved my dad no matter what, but I loved and respected him all the more because he heard me that day at McDonald's, treated me as an adult, and allowed me to make my own decision. In that moment, he didn't just hear my words; he saw my heart. He saw me not as a daughter to guide, but as a woman finding her way in a new land and new role. Until then, I had felt that very few people really heard me. My conversations with most people in my life had always centered around *their* views of me and *their* hopes for me. I had been cast in a story written by others, but no one had yet asked what I wanted, who I was becoming, or what meaning I saw in my own life. I felt freedom in this feeling and in the joy and wonder of our wedding day.

My dad went everywhere in a suit. He was already dressed to walk me down the aisle, and that is what he did, despite his feelings. That quiet dignity, that willingness to show up, even when his heart was being torn, was the greatest act of love he could give me. Our wedding was simple. I carried a silk bouquet from a friend's wedding a few weeks earlier. We served a homemade Duncan Hines cake, which my sweet mother-in-law baked, at our very small reception. The whole wedding cost less than $75. There were no extravagant decorations, no designer gown, no professional photos, just two young hearts, a borrowed bouquet, and a stubborn belief in love. We have a handful of photographs from that day and a one-night "honeymoon" thanks to Scott's stepdad, Robert Bliss, who worked at Walt Disney World and gave us two tickets to Epcot Center for the day. No one thought we would last six months as a married couple, let alone a lifetime.

Anytime I slow down long enough to remember that day, I am filled with a sense of the peace, strength, and confidence I felt with every step I took down that red-carpeted aisle of the church. My father walking me down the aisle was more than tradition; it was a passing of trust, an unspoken blessing. Scott honored me and showed true love by changing his professional career in the US Navy to create space for our life together. In a world where women are too often asked to bend and shrink, the two most important men in my life made space for me to expand. This outpouring of respect and compassion humbled me. It made me determined to live up to the promises I had made.

A few months after our wedding, we visited my parents, sister, and brothers in Tampa, Florida. My dad took Scott aside and sat him down with his accounting books. He showed Scott all the money he had spent on his children and shared with him the sacrifices, dreams, and hopes he had for my future. He laid bare the weight of fatherhood, not just the numbers, but the longing behind them. He made Scott promise to do whatever it took to help me advance my education and love me unconditionally above everyone else. Scott promised him that. And he has kept his word.

My father walking me down the aisle.

In July 1991, my father and my little sister, then just eleven years old, came to visit us in Virginia Beach, Virginia. We were living there because Scott was stationed aboard the USS Boulder. Dad would stay with us for about a month before heading to Detroit, where my younger brother was completing his surgical residency, and then finally returning to California, where my mother, older brother, and younger sister were living. It had been six years since I'd last seen my dad. He had returned to Iran in 1985 and had been unable to obtain another visa to re-enter the US until earlier that year.

Nearly two decades had passed since my father and I had shared anything longer than a fleeting visit, since the days when I was small enough to fit in his arms and believe he could protect me from anything. There would be no make-believe tea parties. He could no longer pick me up and dance with me in his arms. This was real life now. And I had so much to tell him to bring him up to speed on the bountiful life I had carved out of his early sacrifices, even if that life didn't quite match the future he had envisioned for me. A part of me clung to the hope that he still thought of me as his *holoo koochooloo*, his little peach.

Scott and I, along with our sons, Jonathan, then five, and Alan, a little over a year old, went to pick up my dad and sister from the airport. As we waited amid the swirl of travelers, the overhead hum of arrivals and departures seemed to slow time. My mind drifted into the past, awash in tender images of spring daffodil blossoms, visiting our grandparents in Masjed Soleyman, the salt air and scent of our home on Kharg Island, and our life in England. I cherished those childhood memories, not just of a place, but of a people, our family, and the country that shaped my first understanding of love and belonging. I still wanted to make Agha proud. I wondered if any of that old affection would ever return to us.

Then, uninvited, a different image entered my mind: tanks rumbling through the streets of Iran that last summer long ago. And with it came the sharper understanding, an adult perspective on what that must have meant to my father. Fear. Disappointment. The helplessness of watching a dream unravel. How had he and my mom endured such uncertainty? Did they have regrets, realizing it could be difficult for their children to return to Iran, suspecting the country would never be the same again? What gives parents the courage to live apart for the sake of their children's futures? What silent grief accompanied each goodbye? How had they overcome the many detours in their plans? I had always carried the sting of being from a place many Americans viewed as hostile and suspicious. Had my father felt that pain too?

Standing there, at the Norfolk airport, watching planes touch down and lift off, I asked myself for the umpteenth time: had I made the right decision to marry Scott and stay in the US? And then I answered myself. Again, not for the first time. Of course, I had. But time has a way of layering even the clearest of decisions with new questions. Now, after so many years apart, I wondered if my father would agree.

The truth was it hadn't been easy. I had my own hardships to share with my dear, precious Agha. After our wedding, I had stepped into yet another culture—the unspoken rituals and rhythms of the US military culture. Becoming a Navy wife was not just a role; it was a quiet transformation. A Navy wife is often lonely and removed from family, tasked with adapting over and over to unfamiliar surroundings. In many ways, it was familiar to me. What I hadn't grasped then was that my new life would echo an old ache: separation.

My life became lonely once again. This time, I was left to raise our sons while Scott was at sea, serving our country, so that we could build a future. I didn't resent him; he had already sacrificed so much for me. But the loneliness was real. It carried me back to darker memories: of being in England without my father, and later, at the boarding school in Florida, where I was isolated from my parents and the sense of safety and love I'd known.

There were other sorrows, too—the kind that visit most young couples. I had suffered two miscarriages. I had bounced from job to job, forced to restart every time the Navy moved us. Finances were *always* tight. We grieved together the sudden loss of Scott's twenty-two-year-old brother, Jerry, who was killed in a car accident. We carried the weight of my immigration status. We faced crisis after crisis. And even between Scott and me, bound together as we were, our cultural differences sometimes made us feel like strangers to one another. We disagreed on parenting, money, household roles, and the influence of extended family in our decisions.

In the middle of all that turbulence, I found a lifeline. I volunteered to be an ombudsman for Scott's ship. That role kept me tethered not only to him and the Navy but also to a purpose beyond myself. I was helping other young wives navigate the loneliness, the upheaval, the emotional whiplash of military life. What I didn't realize was that this would become my first true education in bridging and holding space for others' pain. I was twenty-seven and felt twice that age.

When I look back now, I see it clearly. So much of my pain came from separation. I had been apart from my family for years, then apart from Scott for long stretches at sea. I didn't know then that a heart can break from absence, not just loss. All the moving, the adapting, the bouncing back took a toll. My lifelong motto has always been, "That which does not kill me makes me stronger." And so, with every move, every goodbye, I forced myself to be strong. I pushed through. I stayed positive.

But strength, when wielded like armor, eventually becomes its own cage. Little did I know the cost of bearing that armor, the cost of denying the ache, the cost of pretending I didn't need to grieve. It would be decades before my body would force me to slow down and finally feel everything I had tried to outrun.

During Dad's visit with us in Virginia Beach, Scott deployed once again, leaving me and the boys with Dad and my sister for most of that month. At my dad's request, I kept the boys home from daycare to be watched over by their grandfather and have fun with their aunt, a decision that felt both natural and surreal. I went to work each day in the human resources department of First Hospital Corporation (FHC), which owned sixteen psychiatric and drug/alcohol rehab hospitals across the country. One evening, I showed Dad my resume and described my role at work. He nodded with quiet recognition. Much of what I was doing, he said, reminded him of his early career at the oil company. It was a moment of connection that startled me with its tenderness; our worlds, once distant, were overlapping at last.

Each evening after the kids went to bed, we had uninterrupted hours to catch up and rediscover each other. Our conversations ranged from parenting to global economics, from the pain of war to big dreams for the future and closed the distance I'd worried had grown between us. Our bond of love hadn't faded. We were still closer than most fathers and daughters who had been separated for years. It was simply magnificent watching my dad play with our boys just as he had once played with me. I watched from the outside now, as if peering through a window at a scene from my childhood, watching him sing, laugh, tell stories, and kiss little foreheads with a familiar gentleness. The memories came rushing back: sun-dappled moments from another life, another continent. Agha adored our precious boys as he adored me. My heart was full in ways it hadn't been for what seemed like a lifetime.

It became a time of unexpected healing, a chapter I wanted to freeze in place so it would never end. He saw how happy I was in this life, even with all its struggles. We shared more than memories; we shared our hearts. In those hours and days together, he spoke of dreams fulfilled and dreams deferred. And now that I was a parent myself, I could finally see his decisions through a parent's eyes. His fears made sense. His choices, which had once seemed confusing, now seemed noble. He also found space to share my hopes, dreams, disappointments, and fears.

One day, we walked side by side on the beach, the wind tugging at our clothes. The boys ran along the shore, their laughter woven into the rhythmic crash of the waves. Dad turned to me and said, "I want you to make this your homeland."

At last.

I could be at peace with that part of my journey. I could believe, truly believe, that Agha no longer grieved my decision to get married so young. I could stop wondering whether I had disappointed him. But then, unexpectedly, a quiet unease crept in. Instead of relieving the conflict inside me, his acceptance magnified it. He had crossed an emotional ocean to meet me where I stood—but something in me still floated between shores.

Dad wasn't feeling well during his visit. He needed to take naps after I got home from work each day. I could see that he was in pain, but he insisted on having the boys stay home with him and my sister, and on rising each evening to cook Iranian food, rich, fragrant meals that tasted like childhood. He cooked not just to nourish us, but to offer love in the way he always had. We even managed a short trip to Washington, DC, while Scott was away. We strolled through monuments and museums, the boys and my sister wide-eyed with wonder. At the same time, Dad quietly took care of official business, renewing our passports at the Iranian Interests Section in the Pakistani Embassy, as Iran had not had an embassy in the US since 1979.

I entertained the boys and my sister while he disappeared into the building. When he returned, his expression was heavy. He told me about a woman he had seen in the embassy, trying to arrange the return of her husband's body to Iran. Dad was upset by her struggle. "I kept thinking, if something happens to me, just bury me here," he told me. "I want to be near my family." His words broke my heart and struck me like thunder. He loved Iran, but he loved us more. Somehow, that revelation filled me with both comfort and sorrow.

When had it happened? When did his inner vow change from "my kids will return to Iran," to "they belong in the United States"?

"You won't have to worry about where you will be buried for a long time," I told him. But I was wrong.

Doctors would later say he was likely having mini strokes during the time he was with us. I didn't know it then, but I felt it deep in my bones—the fragile preciousness of every moment we shared.

True to form, Dad had brought his suit. So, I asked him to sit for a family portrait. As we waited for the photographer, I studied my family—the ones who held my heart. Scott, with his American confidence and unshakable calm. Agha, dignified and Iranian through and through, even as he spoke of burial on American soil. My sister, shaped by San Diego and suburbia, was more American than Iranian. My sons, born here, with Persian, Native American, and Western European blood coursing through their veins.

But what was I?

I had chosen America. I had embraced its promise. But my blood didn't come from here. And I had once been hated for that. I had chosen to remain here, but I loved what I remembered of my childhood in Iran. I loved the cadence of the language, the smell of saffron, the poetry in our daily conversations. And I could not, would not, deny my heritage. So, what did that make me? American? Iranian? Something in between? Something altogether new?

My Agha playing with his grandsons in a Washington, D.C. hotel room, 1992.

Jose Antonio Vargas, journalist, filmmaker, and immigration rights activist, is the CEO of Define American, a "non-profit media and culture organization that seeks to elevate the national conversation around immigration and citizenship in America." Define American is about more than policy. It's about people. It's about humanizing immigration and transforming the way immigrants are perceived. I believe, at the core, it's about helping immigrants feel seen, safe, and at home, as the "friends, neighbors, classmates, colleagues and community members they already are." As human beings. As contributors. As individuals deserving of dignity and, for many, a reasonable pathway to citizenship.

Interestingly, the word "illegal" is not only dehumanizing, but also inaccurate. As the organization's website points out, "Being in the US without proper documents is a civil offense, not a criminal one." Supreme Court Justice Anthony Kennedy affirmed, "As a general rule, it is not a crime for a removable alien to remain in the United States."

The Define American website is filled with powerful stories of undocumented immigrants in the US "coming out" and sharing what it means to them to live in the United States and how they contribute to it. Their stories aren't just personal; they're profoundly American and parallel those you hear while visiting Staten Island. Ultimately, this movement is about immigration reform. Still, I believe it's about something even more urgent: learning to care for one another as fellow residents of the same soil, to see our differences not as threats, but as threads in the fabric of a richer, more expansive, and pluralistic society. In the context of a hopeful vision for America's future, isn't that, after all, what it truly means to be American?

Since before the American Revolution, people (immigrants) have arrived in the United States, sometimes slowly, sometimes in surges. As technology advanced and travel became more accessible, people around the world gained unprecedented exposure to nations and communities beyond their own.

Then came the internet, and with it a seismic shift in how we engage with one another. In an instant, people of all races, ethnicities, and nationalities became connected. Years ago, I didn't have to hear whether others agreed or disagreed with me. Today, I see their opinions on social media every waking minute. I can board a plane and be in China before the day is over. I can run a small business from my living room and have a customer in Italy, whom I've never met, but speak to daily online. In a single neighborhood, people live side by side with vastly different religions, values, traditions, and worldviews. In all of these ways, the opportunity to meet and interact with people who are different from us has exploded, and there's no denying that much good has come from it.

But our increased exposure to one another has also brought pain. If the transportation technology had not existed to allow my parents to bring me to the United States, I never would have experienced the agony of being labeled a "Sand Nigger" or the humiliation of hearing shots fired over my head, possibly courtesy of the Ku Klux Klan.

Yes, many beautiful things are happening between people today. But despite all our advancements, humanity still struggles with the same age-old barriers: language, perception, values, beliefs, social norms, and life goals. The pain of being different and being marginalized or mistreated for that difference has burdened countless lives, both immigrant and native-born.

These tensions seep into every corner of our lives: into homes, workplaces, classrooms, congregations of all faiths, neighborhoods, and boardrooms. Just think of the friendships, partnerships, and breakthroughs we miss out on every single day simply because we fail to deeply understand and accept our humanity, and those who, by fate or chance, enter our world carrying identities we fear and dehumanize.

The divisions run deep. Women fear men. The elderly fear teenagers. The elite fear the poor, and the poor resent the privileged. Many cisgender fear and judge the queer and transgender community. We see evidence of our discomfort and fear in the ongoing clashes between police and Black communities—a symptom not only of flawed systems, but of long-standing, unhealed wounds in our national consciousness. These aren't isolated incidents; they are patterns embedded in generations of policy, practice, and perception. The disparities persist, not only in policing but in access to healthcare, quality education, and safe, stable housing. The COVID-19 pandemic laid these inequalities bare, disproportionately impacting communities of color, revealing once again how race often determines the care we receive, the schools our children attend, and the zip codes we are allowed—or denied—the chance to call home.

In today's political climate, where debates over history, identity, and belonging have become increasingly polarized, we are witnessing a surge in laws and rhetoric that seek to suppress discussions of race, gender, and privilege in classrooms and workplaces. Rather than leaning into complexity, many are retreating into denial. Rather than confronting hard truths, some are choosing to silence them. But erasure is not healing. And censorship does not lead to understanding. In fact, these efforts often deepen division and distrust, making it harder for us to do the very work that healing requires: to acknowledge, to listen, to empathize, and to act.

Paradoxically, as our world gets smaller and more interconnected, many of us have responded by retreating inward, erecting walls of protection rather than building bridges of connection. While it's natural to seek rest and grounding in times of rapid change and uncertainty, true rest happens in community, not in isolation. Yet instead of connection, we often surrender to the noise. Thousands of polarizing messages amplified by algorithms designed to fuel outrage for profit pull us deeper into our echo chambers. Rather than summoning the courage to dismantle them, we absorb the anger, internalize it, and let it spill over like hot lava onto those we label as "other."

No matter the source of cultural clash—be it ethnicity, nationality, race, religion, gender, ability, or age—there is a cost. The damage is personal, professional, and systemic. And the questions remain: How do we help those who don't understand the impact of their words and actions? Who don't see a need to expand their perspective? Who don't know what needs to change? People have been working in this space for decades, and still, so much fear persists.

We cannot keep going this way. When acknowledgement and appreciation for human differences are seen as obstacles to human advancement, the consequences are profound. Relationships erode, communities fracture, organizations collapse, and nations go to war.

We work hard to eliminate those who hold different beliefs, values, and approaches. We demonize those "others" instead of seeking understanding to grow as a humanity in love with understanding and the collective good. We must develop the desire, the will, and the courage to engage with the same level of compassion, grace, and support we offer a child learning to walk for the first time.

With all the access to information and exposure to differences, shouldn't we be getting better at this? Perhaps. But maybe knowledge and experience alone aren't enough. A person can be educated and still be unwilling to see that their way is not the only way.

This work takes personal effort and responsibility. Every human being must practice the muscles of bridging differences. Every teacher, pastor, coach, and leader sets the tone for those around them. But the work begins within each of us, with the willingness to accept that people are different and the true desire to connect across those differences. In my lifetime, I've seen this exhibited with grace and conviction by two spiritual leaders and by an entire nation. Desmond Tutu and the Dalai Lama modeled this work in their deep relationship, a connection rooted in humility, laughter, and an unshakable belief in the dignity of all people. And the country of Rwanda has offered the world a profound lesson in what it means to heal after devastation in the wake of the 1994 genocide.

What binds these examples together is not perfection in execution, but perseverance in the process. Both the individuals and the nation faced unspeakable pain. Tutu and the Dalai Lama each carried the weight of oppression, exile, and injustice. Rwanda, scarred by the horrors of neighbor turning against neighbor, chose not to be defined by its darkest chapter. Instead, it embraced truth-telling, forgiveness, and the difficult process of rebuilding community. In all cases, the bridge-building began with a willingness to see the humanity in the other, to soften hardened hearts, and to choose connection over vengeance. They remind us that even amid unimaginable wounds, healing is possible. But only when people and nations choose to do the inner work first.

Even when we are attacked and feel justified in defending

ourselves, we must recognize that retaliating often deepens the wound. Instead, we must summon the strength to pause—to hold space between our emotions and our reactions. When we approach confrontation with curiosity instead of combat, we create the possibility for learning, growth, and connection. It isn't easy. It's uncomfortable. It is messy. This is the kind of work that calls us into our higher-order brain—the part capable of empathy, reflection, and transformation.

My research affirms what I have seen in practice: human beings rarely change their approach to engaging with the "other" unless that change is *intentional and deeply personal*. And it rarely happens in isolation. It requires community. It requires support. It requires people who have already walked the path, individuals with high levels of emotional intelligence and psychological capital (hope, resilience, efficacy, and optimism), who can serve as guides and companions for others still finding their way.

What's the end game? My deepest hope is that a hundred years from now, humanity will look back on this time as a turning point, a pivotal shift in human consciousness, when people began to learn how to connect authentically across differences. When the capacity to engage with empathy, across culture and identity, became as fundamental as literacy. I believe we will see that this shift created synergy in our organizations, healing in our communities, and maybe even peace across borders. If we can figure this out together, our cross-cultural agility might just be the glue that binds the diverse parts of our world and propels us forward. The next step is not only asking what it will take to make that shift but daring to become part of the answer.

The Norfolk, Virginia, airport was the last time I saw Agha standing up. As he walked to the plane to leave us, he paused, turned around, and looked at me with the quiet tenderness only a father can give. He raised his hand, waved, and blew me one last precious kiss, a kiss I will never forget.

When he arrived in Detroit, he suffered a heart attack and later a stroke. Six months later, my dad, my hero, Hamzeh Ali Abdali-Soosan, died on February 19, 1992. The stroke caused him to exist in a locked-in state for six months, fully aware but unable to move or speak. It was the most helpless season of his life—and of ours.

We were devastated, lost, and shattered. Our hearts, already broken from so many partings, broke all over again. After many conversations, my siblings, Mom, and I made the painful decision to bury Agha in California, far from Iran, the land of his birth and the soil of his dreams, but close to my mother, brother, and sister, and the grandchildren and great-grandchildren who would carry his legacy forward.

During those long months in the hospital, the painful truth about cultural rigidity and systemic blind spots came into full view. My father, a dignified, professional, progressive man, lay motionless in a hospital bed, dependent on caregivers who could not understand him, his culture, or his pain. He believed, as so many did, that the United States had the best healthcare system in the world. But as I stood beside him, translating what I could and buffering when I couldn't, I began to question how we could claim excellence in care when intolerance lingered in the very rooms meant for healing.

One careless moment exposed the fracture. A nurse, unaware I could hear her, turned to her aide and said words that redirected the trajectory of my personal and professional life. Her words sliced through the air, and something inside me shifted. That comment in that sterile room where my father lay dying ignited the questions that would define the rest of my life. How can we expect good outcomes in care when bias goes unchecked? How can we train people to heal bodies while neglecting the wounds of ignorance and fear?

That moment became my call to action.

In the years that followed, the healthcare environment became both my laboratory and my mission field. I immersed myself in study, research, and dialogue. I watched how fear of difference plays out in high-stakes environments. And I began applying what I learned not just to healthcare, but to education, corporate leadership, and community development. I helped students uncover and overcome their fears of one another. I guided organizations toward unity and collaboration. I supported communities learning to embrace newcomers and shifting demographics with grace.

But the most unexpected discovery came not from the nurse's words, but from my response.

I realized, much later, that I, too, had been intolerant that day. I hadn't built a bridge; I had drawn a line. I had stayed wrapped in my pain, unable and unwilling to see hers. Perhaps she was overwhelmed, exhausted, or untrained. I didn't ask. I didn't try to understand. I only protected. I shut down. My System 2 brain, the part capable of reflection and empathy, went offline.

It would be a decade before I learned that on that day, something more than cultural understanding on the part of the nurse was needed. That empathy must flow in both directions. That healing is not a one-sided effort. And that if I wanted to be part of the solution, I had to examine not only the systems around me but the assumptions within me.

That day changed everything.

Questions

1. Think of a time when you witnessed or experienced a microaggression. A microaggression is a comment or action that subtly, perhaps even unconsciously or unintentionally, expresses prejudice toward a marginalized group. It might come in the form of a joke, a comment, or a dismissive gesture. What was said—or left unsaid—that stayed with you?
2. Can you imagine what it feels like to be on the receiving end of many such moments over time? What might it do to someone's sense of belonging, worth, or confidence to endure these daily, seemingly small acts?
3. How have others in your life encouraged you to build a bridge across differences? What did they model for you? How did their actions challenge or change your perspective?
4. When have you missed an opportunity to build a bridge? Looking back, what held you back? Fear? Discomfort? Uncertainty? What might you do differently now?
5. What steps are you willing to take, starting today, to develop your capacity for empathy, connection, and cultural humility, even in moments when your instinct is to retreat or protect?

Chapter 5

Getting Comfortable with Change

> *At the first I knew not*
> *that city's worth*
> *And turned in my folly*
> *A wanderer on earth.*
> - Rumi

On March 16, 1992, we walked into the federal courthouse in Norfolk, Virginia. While I was filled with a multitude of emotions, I was ready to pledge my life and loyalty as a citizen of the United States. I felt every mile of my journey against my ribs. A representative of the Daughters of the American Revolution handed me a tiny American flag. Its crimson and snow-white stripes, its bright stars against deep navy, reminded me of all the contrasts that make this country hum: wealth and want, elders and children, native and newcomer, and every shade of skin and love.

I was thrilled and had no hesitation at all. This was exactly where I was meant to be. Back then, we weren't allowed to take cameras into the courtroom, so I don't have photos of the moment I became a US citizen. I do have a rich bank of memories to mark that day. Scott and our sons stood at my side along with Cathy Callahan, my boss and the vice president for human resources at First Hospital Corporation, and Commander George Marvin, captain of the ship where I had served as ombudsman and Scott's commanding officer. They came to support us and to bear witness to the seismic change in our lives. Later that afternoon, when I arrived at work, my coworkers presented me with a cake decorated with a green card with a red slash through it.

Citizenship meant survival and dignity for our family. Since 1985, when I first began the journey to becoming a citizen, we'd spent hundreds of dollars and countless hours fighting to keep me here, wrestling with forms so picky that a missing dot could send the application back to the bottom of the pile. No government office has ever treated me so roughly as the former Immigration and Naturalization Service (INS), but on that day, the struggle finally ended. I thought of it as a finish line—freedom from the grips of the INS office.

Tears streaked my cheeks throughout the ceremony. I glanced at the back of the room where Scott cradled our boys, who were nearly two and six, and felt a fierce relief. They won't remember this moment, I thought, but more importantly, they will never have to battle through what their dad and I had endured. My gratitude for Scott's steadfast love almost split my chest. His commitment to endure the years of struggle began the moment he heard I was going to be deported. And he was there by my side through it all. While I was filled with joy, I was also still mourning the loss of my father. It had only been four weeks since he passed away. I missed him deeply. His voice had always soothed me to the very core of my being. I longed to call him, to let him hear the triumph in my voice.

At the close of the ceremony, I received a certificate of naturalization. One sheet of paper, yet it unlocked an exciting and longed-for new level of freedom. I eventually learned that the piece of paper has little relevance in how people perceive or treat you. Some will still treat a legal citizen with a foreign name as though they just snuck across the border. But that piece of paper reshaped the way I thought of myself, and the freedom I felt in every cell of my being. The true value of citizenship is that it gives you rights. You can legally vote. In some states, you must be a citizen to buy a home. I could now get a US passport and travel without fear. I could remain in the United States indefinitely.

When you come from a different country, it can take a long time to feel like an American, even after becoming a citizen. While you are working to become a citizen, you experience great fear and trepidation. The certificate meant that the long, anxious season of "becoming" finally gave way to a calm, confident sense of belonging. For Scott and me, this was especially momentous because this settling-in coincided with his transition from ship duty to shore duty, and we had some exciting choices ahead of us.

I became a citizen because I wanted a voice. Voting, serving, lifting others—that is my nature. Now I no longer had to glance over my shoulder for immigration officers. I could look straight ahead, find my place, and get to work for the people who share this sprawling, complicated, beautiful country with me.

Our family with Scott in his Navy uniform. I am proud to be part of this country.

The day I became a US citizen was a calm, sunlit eye in the middle of a much larger storm. For a moment, the world stood still. But almost as soon as we stepped out of the Norfolk courtroom, life swept us back into a whirlwind of responsibilities, complications, and relentless pressure.

In 1993, my mother and sister returned to Iran to observe the traditional Muslim ceremony and feast marking the first anniversary of my father's death. We had applied for their green cards months before they left. Because their applications were still being processed when it was time for their trip to Iran, they had to request special permission to leave the country. But then, life did what life does; complications arose in Iran, and they missed the deadline to return. Their reentry permits expired.

That one twist in timing cost us five years of limbo. My little sister was thirteen when she left, became a young woman in those missing years, growing from a child into a young adult outside the borders of the country that had been her home since she was three years old. For me, it felt like living with a knot in my chest every single day. My mother often called and asked for help, and I struggled to figure out what to do. And there I was: technically a free, official citizen, yet still caught in the emotional tangle of an immigration process that continued to tear holes in the fabric of our lives.

During those years, grief visited again. My dad's parents passed away. Their deaths unleashed another storm of emotion and impossible logistics. How do you mourn from across the globe? How do you show up for your family, your culture, your ancestors, when oceans and paperwork and money stand in the way? Sending flowers felt hollow. Taking time off to travel would mean leaving my young children behind, and we couldn't afford the flights anyway.

And still, the phone would ring. My relatives would ask, "Why can't you come to the funeral?" I couldn't tell them the real reasons. Not without shame. Not without heartbreak. I couldn't say, "I don't have the money," or "my boys are too small for me to leave." So, I cooked. I poured my grief into saffron rice, stews rich with turmeric, and the warm scent of tea rising from the stove. I fed the people around me—my husband, my friends, my coworkers—because I needed to feel the closeness of community. Mourning looked different here, but I was doing the best I could.

My family in Iran didn't understand. "Why can't you come to the wedding?" they'd ask, when joy returned to their lives. But even then, I was torn. Longing to be there, to celebrate, to belong, and feeling trapped by the same financial barriers and logistical roadblocks that had kept me away in times of sorrow. The weight of those questions never left me.

In May 1992, just months after my citizenship ceremony, more change arrived. Scott was done with sea duty. It should have been an exciting time for us. Scott had had his fill of ships and wanted to be as far away from the ocean as possible. The Navy only offered two options: Salt Lake City, Utah, or Lincoln, Nebraska. He was at sea when he was offered these two duty stations, so we talked about it by phone.

"You choose," Scott told me. "You've followed me everywhere the Navy sent us. It's your turn."

I had no idea where Lincoln was. "I've heard of a President Abraham Lincoln and I really liked what he had done for this country," I said. "Where is Lincoln, Nebraska?"

"Open the map to the first page. See the state in the middle where the crease is?" Scott said. "That's Lincoln." We decided to check Lincoln out.

Before we left Virginia, during one of our final conversations, my boss Cathy Callahan leaned across her desk with a gaze that held both tenderness and quiet insistence.

"Helen," she said, "you're a smart woman. You could get a job, or you could go back to school. You made a promise to your father. Maybe now is the time to honor it. Do something about what happened to your family when he was ill."

Cathy wasn't just offering advice; she was handing me a lifeline. She knew what it meant to chase a dream while raising children and working full-time. She had done it herself. Until that moment, I'd never believed I was smart enough. I had always felt a step behind, burdened by the weight of adapting to a new language, a foreign culture, and unfamiliar classrooms. But Cathy's words cracked something open in me. Her faith lit a flicker of belief where doubt had lived for years.

We made a house-hunting trip that August. Driving through the overpass that brings you into Lincoln's downtown, Memorial Stadium rose on the horizon like a monument carved into the skyline, a magnificent and impressive sight that still gives me goosebumps when we drive by it. We walked the University of Nebraska-Lincoln campus together with our sons, and something in me stirred. Cathy's words and the promise I'd made to my father to return to school one day felt real and attainable. For the first time in a long time, hope rose like a sunrise.

We moved to Lincoln, Nebraska, on November 1, 1992. It was my thirtieth move before the age of thirty, but something felt different this time. While we didn't know it at the time, this was to be more than just another place we'd land for a few years. Due to an injury to Scott's spine, Lincoln became our forever community. We planted our roots deep in Nebraska soil. And for the first time, we began to sense belonging and Lincoln felt like home.

When I first applied to the University of Nebraska-Lincoln (UNL), they turned me down. I was incensed. My GPA in my last semester of classes wasn't impressive, and my guess is the admissions committee didn't have to look hard to find reasons to say no. My academic record reflected a single, brutal semester at the University of South Florida filled with incredible hardships. I didn't have a place to live and was hitchhiking from a friend's apartment in Clearwater to the campus in Tampa. Every day was a struggle to survive, let alone study.

I couldn't accept the rejection from UNL. I could hear Cathy's words, "you're a smart woman." Those words gave me the confidence to appeal their decision. So, I picked up the phone and called the admissions office and scheduled an appointment. I told the admissions officer my story and explained that my circumstances had improved significantly in the last ten years. "If you let me in, you won't regret it," I said. It took some convincing, but they eventually relented and allowed me to enroll.

Three years later, I walked into that same office, this time holding a diploma in my hand. I had earned a bachelor's degree in management and economics with distinction while being a mom, wife, and working part-time. I smiled, held up my degree, and said with full-hearted satisfaction, "I TOLD you!"

I graduated in May 1996, but the journey wasn't just about academics. Somewhere along the way, I found myself again. I even had the incredible opportunity to study abroad at Oxford University for a summer semester, where I took courses in British political economy and international economics. It felt surreal, this Iranian American woman studying global economic systems on cobbled streets under ancient stone towers.

To make going back to school work, I pieced together a patchwork of scholarships, part-time jobs, and internships. Scott and I were still living below the poverty line on his military income and what little I could earn. We relied on WIC benefits to feed our boys and enrolled them in the reduced-lunch program when they started elementary school. But somehow, through late nights, early mornings, and sheer grit, we made it.

While at UNL, I became president of the student chapter of the Society for Human Resource Management. That role connected me to people across Lincoln. One of them was Doug McDaniel, the director of human resources at Bryan Hospital. When he spoke about the hospital's mission and culture, something inside me clicked. I had worked in healthcare in Virginia and Texas. I knew I wanted to return to the field with the education and determination to make a bigger impact.

After graduation, I excitedly applied at Bryan, but the hospital didn't have any openings at the time. I wasn't worried. They weren't going anywhere. I found a position working in human resources and accounting for a local company named Square D. There, I got my hands on everything from union operations to writing my first affirmative action plan. When a position finally opened at Bryan, I was ready. In April 1999, I was hired as an employment coordinator, responsible for recruiting staff across hospital departments.

By August of that same year, Doug McDaniel pulled me aside. He told me he wanted to create a new role focused on diversity and cultural competence, a position inspired by his experiences with Leadership Lincoln. He had committed to advancing opportunities for diverse talents as the demographics of our community were rapidly changing. And now he was ready to put action behind that promise.

A few months later, I was named the first coordinator of diversity and cultural competence programs at Bryan Health. There was no manual, no roadmap, just a job title and an open field. So, I did what I knew best: I started asking questions. I conducted an organizational analysis. I sat down with community leaders, especially those working with growing populations in the Asian, Hispanic, Black, and Middle Eastern communities. I asked what they thought of Bryan. I listened. I took notes. I wanted to know if people saw Bryan as a welcoming place to work and/or to receive care. What were the unspoken barriers? How did the broader community view our hospital?

Inside Bryan, I held conversations with employees from all backgrounds and across all levels, from entry-level aides to upper management. I wanted to hear directly from them: What made this a great place to work? What made it hard? As I facilitated employee orientations, I kept the questions going. Are you glad to be here? Do you feel seen?

The more I listened, the clearer the picture became. Diversity at Bryan wasn't just about hiring a certain number of people from a certain race or demographic. It stretched into patient care, communication, and culture. It wasn't just an HR issue; it was a clinical one, too. That shift was unexpected, even to leadership. But we leaned into it, and our vision for diversity work began to evolve.

Outside the hospital walls, I became involved in Lincoln's New Americans Task Force, a coalition of community agencies working to support refugees and immigrants. I saw firsthand how much Bryan needed to understand the unique healthcare needs of individuals coming from other countries, and how much opportunity we had to become not only the community's hospital but also a workplace for people rebuilding their lives.

I look back at that period, just a few short years after being rejected by the university I eventually graduated from, and I marvel at the distance I traveled. I was no longer that frightened teenage girl alone in a Florida boarding school. I was a professional. I was making a difference. And in quieter moments, I let myself believe something bold: that maybe, just maybe, I was part of something bigger. Maybe I could help shape a world that saw people like me not just as outsiders, but as essential voices for realizing the dreams of humanity in this country.

For years, since the incident with the nurse during my father's final months, I had carried a quiet but burning prayer in my heart: Somehow, someday, may I use my pain and education to help change healthcare in my community. When Bryan Health offered me a position, one that promised a chance to influence the system from within, it felt like an answer to that prayer. I threw myself into the work with everything I had.

Every night, after tucking our boys into bed and cleaning up the last of the dishes, I'd open my briefcase and dive into a growing mountain of research. I read landmark government reports, combed through work from the George Washington University Center for Cultural Competence, and devoured case studies from health systems across the country. My free time was no longer free—it was filled with highlighters, dog-eared articles, and scribbled margins.

The more I read, the clearer it became: Bryan's efforts would not be successful unless rooted in a three-pronged approach. One that addressed our employees, our patients, and our broader community. And it absolutely needed to be tied to the organization's strategic goals. Anything less would be performative.

Once I finished my initial organizational and community analysis, I presented my findings to our senior leadership team. I suggested that their ideas needed to be expanded beyond assigning someone to celebrate diverse holidays and hold job fairs to reach diverse populations. If that's what they wanted, I wasn't the person for the job. But if they wanted real change, if they wanted to build an organization that truly understood and served its increasingly diverse population, I was all in. It wouldn't be easy. We'd have to ask hard questions of ourselves and hold each other accountable for our decisions to ensure alignment with our commitment. But I was ready.

And then I got to work.

I began analyzing hospital processes and policies as though through a microscope, attempting to learn why things worked the way they did. In general, I looked for opportunities and limitations that affected the growth of our diverse employee population. I asked many difficult questions. What are the barriers that keep the majority of our ethnic or racial minorities working in housekeeping and dining service? What steps do we need to take to increase the number of women in senior leadership? What gaps exist in the way we care for patients whose cultural and language needs are different from the majority? What important training was missing in helping our staff learn about the cultural elements of illness, treatment, birthing, or dying? What do physicians need to equip them better to serve their demographically changing patient population? What do leaders need to be thinking about when they are planning the future of the health system?

Even though Bryan had been making allowances for cultural differences in some ways, one of our greatest gaps was gaining insight from the changes in our community's population. To truly understand the needs of the culturally diverse members of a community, it is essential to become actively involved in that community. Building trust takes time and intentional effort. I knew that much, and I began taking a strategic approach to this. One big obstacle was in my way. I was not part of the senior leadership team, so everything I did had to go through multiple layers for approval, and I struggled to find funding.

This made it very difficult to create momentum. Had my position been that of a senior leader, I'd have had a different voice than a program coordinator, who was expected to operate at the level of a senior leader but was shut out of the conversations that could have created the greatest impact. I was fortunate to have direct access to and the respect of the hospital's senior leaders, who were well-informed about what I was doing. But it was still difficult because I was not invited to sit at their table, and I had no budget to work with. I had to be creative.

The cost of my position (my salary) was part of the HR department's budget, so I didn't look there for money. I looked for other ways to fund the activities. For example, I would go to patient care services with a project related to their work and say, "This is what we want to do." If they felt the project would help them reach their objectives, they would agree to fund it. I created content and included it in nursing orientation and new employee orientation. I went to the director of volunteer services and asked for donations to purchase wire-bound bedside books to help nurses care for patients with limited English. I even went to our information technology services and asked if they could justify paying for online access to cultural information, since the material was online.

I formed a council consisting of seventeen employees representing different levels of authority within the hospital. We operated like a mini think tank and achieved goals that had never been thought of before. In many ways, we operated as a separate, cohesive department with a hand in multiple areas of the hospital. It became clear, however, that not everyone felt our work was as important as we did. When I pushed for resources from other departments, I often felt as though I was begging for help, even though I had been hired to do exactly what we were doing. I often felt like I was walking a tightrope.

In one meeting, I voiced my opinion forcefully, too forcefully, it seemed. A senior leader was sent to my office to talk to me. It wasn't the first time. Each of those conversations reminded me that while I had access to power, I was not of it. I was asking people to change the way they were thinking, to expand their idea of patient care, employee engagement, and community involvement. I learned that most humans don't like being challenged. Later, I would learn the neuroscience behind this. At the time, it felt like trying to push a pregnant elephant up a hill during a mudslide.

One year, a vice president position opened. Without any posting, a gentleman was given the role. I couldn't stay silent. I scheduled a meeting with our Chief Operating Officer and told him that the decision undermined everything we had been trying to build. I knew I didn't have the same data or strategic insight he did, but I also knew the impact of this decision.

"If we're serious about this initiative," I said, "this isn't how we show it."

Little by little, honesty and hard work began to open doors. Sometimes I'd have someone stop by my office to engage in honest conversation about what exactly we were trying to do. They thought it was about minority representation. While creating opportunities for growth for our vast minority population in entry-level positions was part of it, it was also about access to jobs and healthcare for individuals with disabilities, ensuring that older staff felt valued as well as younger staff, that veterans could be given the opportunity to return to the work they loved, and so much more. It was about employees whom we often overlooked, feeling seen, valued, and given the opportunity to succeed. Often, I would ask people to think about their great-great-great-grandparents who settled in Nebraska in the mid- to-late 1800s. How would they have wanted them to be treated? And then, I invited them to think about their future great-grandchildren. If they were to have a disability, would they want them to have the opportunity to succeed and to be cared for in the best way possible as a patient?

But truthfully, the work was incredibly difficult and took a toll on my health. I was constantly pushing people to think differently, behave differently, and see the world differently, and many of them weren't ready. There were times their resistance would intentionally sabotage our efforts. I couldn't understand why. I believed so deeply in human beings being treated with dignity and respect regardless of their walk of life. I still do. But if I had known then what the journey would demand of me—the emotional labor, the uphill battles, the intense sense of isolation—I'm not sure I would have had the courage to say yes.

I was already juggling so much: raising a family, supporting my mom and sister, and working through wounds from my past that hadn't fully healed. And yet, I kept pushing forward, one conversation, one meeting, one small breakthrough at a time. Because deep down, I still believed that change was possible. And that I might be the one to help spark it.

Important note: If you are a leader reading this, and the person responsible for driving inclusion and belonging in your organization sits several layers below the CEO, that needs to change. Immediately. Inclusion is not a side initiative; it is a strategic imperative. If that individual has no dedicated budget, correct it. If they lack the authority to challenge the status quo or to align their efforts with your organization's strategic vision, you are, at best, engaging in performative action. At worst, you are undermining your organization's capacity to thrive in an increasingly competitive and diverse global economy. This is not merely my perspective as a practitioner—it is a conclusion drawn from decades of data, analysis, and cross-industry research on what makes organizations sustainable, resilient, and future-ready.

When our oldest son, Jonathan, was in sixth grade, he discovered rap music, which I couldn't understand at all. The beats were loud, the rhythms unfamiliar, and the lyrics—half of which I couldn't decipher—were littered with words I had spent years teaching my children not to say. Every instinct in me wanted to shut it down. I told myself I was protecting him, steering him away from something that might be harmful. To me, it didn't sound like music. It sounded like noise. Angry, defiant noise.

Then one afternoon, during a heated conversation with Jonathan over his choice of music, I said, "I don't get any of it. It doesn't make sense!"

His response struck me like a bolt of lightning, totally unexpected, and deeply impactful. He said, "Mom, things that don't make sense, aren't always bad for you." In that instant, I got it. I saw it not just as a comment about music, but as a message about life. About people. About differences. And suddenly, I understood something that had eluded me in my work.

At Bryan, I had been watching leaders tense up as I spoke about diversity and cultural competence. I saw the discomfort in their body language, heard the hesitation in their questions. My passion and my urgency had begun to feel like pressure. What I thought was clarity had sounded like chaos to them. What I thought was purpose, they interpreted as ambiguity. I was asking them to embrace something that didn't immediately make sense to them, and they were afraid it might be bad for them or at least bad for their departments, their career, or their way of doing things.

Jonathan's words were like a mirror, and I saw myself clearly in it.

I had been trying to force the change, pushing people into thinking differently before they felt safe or ready. And all it had done was build more walls.

That heated conversation between a mother and son cracked something open in me. I didn't need to water down the message, but I did need to make the path into it feel less like a threat. Less like chaos. More readily understandable.

It's true: not everything that doesn't make sense is bad for you. Sometimes, it's the very thing that will help you grow. Sometimes, it's exactly what you need to hear, even if it arrives in a form you never expected. My dad had once told me to be willing to learn from anyone, at any time, and in all circumstances. And I've come to realize that while we as parents are raising our children, God is quietly using them to raise us. I'm grateful for the gift of parenting and now grandparenting, which is helping raise me to be a better person.

The Emancipation Proclamation officially declared the end of slavery in the United States on January 1, 1863. But freedom, real freedom, the kind that allows a person to vote, to drink from the same water fountain and use the same parts of the restaurant, to claim their value, and to walk through the world with dignity, didn't come all at once. It wasn't until a full century later, under President John F. Kennedy's leadership, that laws were finally passed to dismantle some of the barriers that had long kept Black citizens from voting.

Our youngest son, Alan, was in fourth or fifth grade when he connected those dots. One day, he turned to me and asked, "Mom, why did it take so long?" His voice was small, but his question stopped me in my tracks. How could someone so young see so clearly into something so vast and complex? That moment stirred something deep within me. It was the first time I fully grasped a truth I had long sensed: change, especially human transformation and growth, is painfully slow. Not because people are unwilling, necessarily, but because our brains are wired that way.

In their book, *Spiral Dynamics* (1996), Don Beck and Christopher Cowan explore how human consciousness changes in response to life conditions. Not over mere years or decades, but across generations, even centuries. They describe this transformation as a spiral of value systems (vMEMEs, which are color-coded and arranged in a spiral-like hierarchy), each representing a distinct worldview that emerges when the existing one no longer fits the complexity of life. These shifts aren't triggered by wishful thinking or forced agendas. They occur when readiness is present; when both the external pressures and internal capacities align to make transformation possible. In my research, we would see this transformation occur when the leader understood their brain's bent for bias, and how to manage it, developed a level of emotional intelligence, and an intercultural mindset, that enabled them to see their leadership impact in a new way.

I began to see that the process is delicate and painstakingly slow. It's not a straight climb but a spiral, and it is dynamic, uneven, and constantly needing to adapt. Complicating it further is the speed of modern technology and knowledge, which evolves far faster than the human brain can keep up with. The result? We're often out of sync with one another, as I was with the hospital leaders. Some of us are operating from one level of consciousness, while others are shaped by entirely different life conditions and worldviews. We may be sharing space, even mission statements, but not the same internal operating systems.

In institutions, especially ones like hospitals, where hierarchy, tradition, and risk aversion run deep, this uneven development becomes painfully visible. Change doesn't just meet resistance; it gets tangled in power dynamics and legacy mindsets. Some leaders cling to authority, believing, often unconsciously, that for someone else to rise, they must first lose their ranking. That belief, whether voiced or not, slows the evolution of the whole system. When who is in power becomes a zero-sum game, transformation takes not just years but centuries, as observed and questioned by my young son, Alan.

That was when it hit me. If what *Spiral Dynamics* describes is true, then I needed to get radically honest about what was possible, not just at Bryan, but in any institution rooted in traditional systems. I couldn't bulldoze others toward being comfortable with and even inviting differences. I had to shift my strategy from passionately pointing out what was wrong to being present with others' anxiety about the changes they were experiencing. I am not more evolved than other leaders; I was and continue to simply see through a different lens. The words of French American poet Aanïs Nin, "we don't see things as they are, we see things as we are," sank into me in a whole new way. Where I saw opportunity, they saw risk. When I felt urgency, they feared chaos. We weren't adversaries, we were just standing on different rungs of the spiral.

Once I accepted that, I let go of the fantasy of immediate change. I stopped demanding leaps and began inviting steps. I focused on momentum instead of milestones. On connection instead of transformation. On planting seeds that might not bloom until someone else comes along to water them.

Because transformation, as *Spiral Dynamics* reminds us, is not about dragging people into the future. It's about walking with them, honoring where they are, and building bridges between what is and what could be, one conversation, one insight, one act of courage at a time.

I remember September 11, 2001, as vividly as if it happened yesterday. That morning, I arrived at the office early to complete final preparations for a presentation I was scheduled to give at the Goodwill Industries office across town. But before I could gather my materials, my colleague Julie walked into my office and said, "Did you see what happened to the Twin Towers?"

My heart raced as I thought about my family in New York and prayed to God it wasn't the same as what happened in 1979. Someone turned on the television in the conference room. Slowly, my coworkers and I trickled in and huddled around the screen, our coffee forgotten, our mouths open in disbelief as we watched the twin towers collapse into ash and chaos, tears rolling down our stunned faces.

When it was time to leave for my presentation, I paused. I needed to talk to Scott. His voice calmed me and reassured me that we would be fine. I then quickly called my mother in New York City. She was staying with my younger brother, an Orthopedic surgeon in Brooklyn. I wanted to make sure everyone was safe.

"Mom, is Allen okay?" I asked, my voice calm but my heart pounding.

"It's not real," she replied flatly. "It's just people saying these things. It's propaganda." I froze. "Mom," I said gently, "please turn on the TV. See it for yourself. Please call Allen."

At Goodwill, I looked at the waiting audience and knew I couldn't give the talk I'd planned. How could I, a Middle Eastern woman, speak about the value of celebrating differences when hours before, terrorists from the Middle East had carried out an attack on US soil? The pain was too raw for all of us. Instead, we simply talked about what had happened and how everyone would be feeling. To this day, it was one of the most honest conversations I've been part of.

That night, Scott, the boys, and I attended a prayer vigil at our church. One of the things I love about our church is the intentional effort to create an inclusive faith community. People from all walks of life are invited and encouraged to connect with one another. After the gathering, our pastor, David Argue, a Canadian-American, who was the humblest and kindest human I've ever met, approached us. A local news station wanted to speak with a family about how they were processing the tragedy. Would we be willing to share?

The next day, when the news crew arrived at our home, we sat with the boys at our dining room table as we talked through the questions. How do you explain something so enormous, so violent, to your children? How do you balance honesty with hope? For us, there was the added fear of my being from the Middle East.

The next day, back at the hospital in one of the staff lounges, someone made a joke about that day's forecast in the Middle East.

"Monday, Tuesday, and Wednesday: sunny. Thursday: nuclear cloud."

They were referring to the idea that the United States could blow away any Middle Eastern target with a nuclear bomb, if it wanted to. An employee from that department, who was also from the Middle East, came to my office, afraid and apprehensive. Did their coworkers share the same sentiment? How did they feel about us? Would any of us become the target of this hostility? I felt the same misgivings they were feeling. The memories of the hostage crisis began to churn in my gut. The fear, anxiety, and uncertainty rising like smoke from a long-dormant fire. It was a visceral reminder that no matter my citizenship, I was still seen as "one of those people."

We heard more stories of hate toward employees and community members. A Middle Eastern child development employee, who lived in an affluent area of town with her husband, who was a respected physician, told me that someone had set a bag of feces on fire on their front porch and spread their garbage across their lawn. She came to my office, not just for advice, but seeking refuge; a place to make sense of the cruelty and to ask how to respond with dignity when dignity had been so violently denied. We also heard about a local Middle Eastern grocery store that was ransacked, and many other incidents related to the 9/11 attacks. Each one was a gut punch that echoed the crisis in 1979. I couldn't help but think that things hadn't changed much since the Japanese internment camps during World War II.

Something inside me shifted. I realized that no matter how many years we live here, no matter how many flags we wave or taxes we pay, immigrant citizens walk a fragile line. One moment, we are "American." The next, we are "the enemy." Our safety is contingent and conditional. One crisis, one perception, one accusation, and the ground beneath us can disappear.

I was grateful that my family had been spared, but I couldn't shake the question: Why? Why were we being treated differently? Was it because people knew me from my work at the hospital? Was it the respectability of my job? Or was it because I had married a white man who had served in the military? Was our "Americanness" more believable because it looked more familiar? I didn't know. But I wanted to understand. I believed that such understanding could help me bridge the gap, not just between victims and systems, but between people and their pain, between those acting in fear and those living in fear. And above all, because I was being treated with kindness while others were being attacked, I felt a responsibility to be louder, not quieter. I could not afford to be silent.

That moment awakened something in me: a deeper courage, a bolder voice, and a sharper focus on the work I was called to do. My mission had always been clear. But now it was more crucial than ever before.

During the summer of 2000, anticipating a nursing shortage in Nebraska over the next decade, Bryan made a bold decision: we would begin exploring the recruitment of nurses from the Philippines. Their education met US licensing requirements, and most importantly, they had the necessary language skills and a willingness to adapt, enabling them to successfully transition into a nursing position at Bryan. This was a new and ambitious undertaking for Bryan. The hospital assembled a team to travel to the Philippines in the summer of 2001 to conduct interviews and extend offers to those who met the educational, experience, and language requirements.

I wasn't selected to go, but I thought I *should* be on the team. I shared this with my boss, Doug McDaniel.

"I can help," I told him. "I understand what these nurses will need, not just professionally, but emotionally. I can create a mini orientation, prepare them for their life in Nebraska and help make the transition easier for them. I can be the familiar face of someone whose been through a national/cultural transition and guide them through their acculturation process." He agreed, and I joined the team. We also brought along a Filipino employee from Bryan on the recruitment trip so he could share his personal experience working at Bryan; someone who looked like them, spoke their language, and could say, "Bryan will support you." That mattered.

In the Philippines, we interviewed more than a hundred nurses and extended job offers to more than seventy. We expected them to arrive in Nebraska within six to twelve months. But after the attacks on September 11, 2001, everything changed. Visas were delayed, paperwork slowed to a crawl, and, in the end, only thirty-five of the original candidates qualified. This was a setback for the vision to address the anticipated nursing shortage.

Still, we prepared for the nurses' arrival. We knew that coming to Nebraska would be daunting, especially for those who had never set foot in the United States. So, I decided we would assign each Filipino nurse a Nebraska colleague to be a pen pal. Bryan staff volunteered to connect with them and begin a friendship through email. Bryan employees wrote the nurses, offering friendship and a glimpse of what life in Nebraska might look like. My hope was that the connections that formed would help reduce anxiety and build trust long before the first plane ever touched down.

When the nurses began to arrive, they got to meet their pen pals in person. We held a welcome celebration and connected them to Lincoln's growing Filipino community. I had the idea to create a welcome guide, which we called *"Mabuhay* Guide." *Mabuhay* means "welcome" in Tagalog. The guides covered information about living in the United States and Nebraska: everything from housing and transportation to walking on the ice and even how to purchase a used car without getting ripped off.

Traditionally, Bryan provided ninety days of housing for professional-level individuals hired from out of state. We usually placed one person in a house by themselves or with their family. However, knowing the deeply collectivistic nature of the Filipino national culture, we housed same gender nurses together, one nurse per bedroom, under the same roof. We knew they'd need community as much as employment. We hoped this would ensure they had both.

To this day, I keep in touch with many of the nurses we hired through social media. In 2015, I was invited to give the commencement address at a local community college. The daughter of one of the nurses we recruited in 2001 was graduating that day with her nursing degree. She was a little girl when she arrived in the United States. Watching her walk across the stage, I felt a deep, quiet pride. This was what true belonging looked like, measurable in degrees, in hope, in generations.

In the years since, I've realized how innovative our acculturation process was. At the time, no other organization in Nebraska was onboarding international hires as comprehensively and intentionally as we were. Word began to spread. Nizar Mamdani, the director of international healthcare at the University of Nebraska Medical Center, reached out to me. He was developing a global physician exchange program and wanted to learn about our model. We spent several meetings discussing how and why we did what we did. The success of the nurses and our approach was deeply personal to me. I created what I had needed, and in many ways, received from my American family, the Andersons. They guided, protected, supported, and challenged me, while making me feel loved from my very first day in the United States to this day.

During our life in Nebraska, the resettlement of refugees and immigrants, including our Filipino nurses, has been a family affair. We opened our home and invited the nurses and other refugees and immigrants to attend community activities with us. We became more involved with Iranian refugees who were resettling in Lincoln. It was very satisfying for me, as you can imagine. For Scott, Jonathan, and Alan, it was a chance to connect with my heritage in a way that they hadn't been able to before, simply because of our military life and separation from my family, who were either in New York, California, or Texas. We often joked with our family that we are the official "halfway house," and that is what we explained to our new friends coming from different parts of the world to the middle of America.

And somewhere amid all of this, I began to change. I grew more confident. I settled into my role as an advocate, not just at Bryan, but in the community. Nurses, doctors, and caseworkers from the hospital began calling me at all hours to help with everything from birth plans to end-of-life needs, always with the same concern: "We want to do this right. Can you help?" The non-majority community leaders and advocates saw me as someone they could trust. Someone who would explain a baffling healthcare system or help them land their first job.

 I came to understand that real change takes time. Culture doesn't shift because you demand it. It moves because you nurture it, carefully, one seed at a time.

I shifted my strategy. I stopped focusing on what we couldn't do and started building on what we could. I leaned on two incredible mentors, female executives who believed in this work, and figured out where the money was. Who had a budget stake in the project? That's where I made my case. Big policy shifts were still out of reach. But small wins? Those were everywhere.

One day, I overheard a nurse supervisor say she wished her staff had a way to ask patients basic questions in other languages.

"Do you have your glasses?"

"Are you thirsty?"

"Do you need your dentures?"

That small wish became a bedside phrasebook, spiral-bound, simple, and immediately useful.

We ensured that marginalized communities knew when job openings were posted. We took small steps that created ripples. And all the while, I felt something I hadn't felt before; not just hope but purpose. The kind of purpose that grounds you, even on hard days. I started to see the work differently, not just as a challenge to be solved, but as a gift to be honored. The diversity between people, like the contrasting stripes on the tiny flag I received on the day I became a citizen, was no longer something to fear. It was beautiful. It was meaningful. It represented humanity in its fullest.

The pain I carried from my early experiences, the fear, the rejection, the feeling of not quite belonging, hadn't vanished, but it had softened. In its place, a new strength had taken root. A new vision. A voice that wouldn't be silenced. A belief that this work, slow and difficult as it was, could change not only a hospital, but a community. Maybe even the world.

Questions

1. Who gains when we open our hearts, homes, and workplaces to refugees and immigrants? In what ways does the whole community become stronger, more vibrant, and more resilient?
2. What is the difference between performative effort and cultivating deep and lasting inclusion? What does real, systemic change require in time, in leadership, in courage, and how might you play a role in moving that kind of change forward in your workplace or community?
3. Have you ever experienced a moment when being different made you feel like an outsider? What helped you feel seen, supported, or included, and how can you extend that same gift to others?
4. Think of a time when someone advocated for you or made space for your voice. What did that mean to you? How can you do the same for someone else who might not yet feel at home?
5. If you were to take one small step this week toward building a more inclusive environment, at work, at school, or in your neighborhood, what would that look like? What might change because of it?
6. How does your own story, your culture, background, or personal experiences, equip you to be a bridge between people who may not yet understand each other?

Chapter 6

Our Path to Cultural Competence

*'Patience turns stones to rubies,' they say.
Yes! If you work hard and wait long, it may.*
-S.M. Hafiz

As I studied stacks of research while I was at Bryan, I found myself immersed in the intricate, often painful history of health equity in the United States. As the pages turned, a deeper awareness unfolded within me. With each fact, each narrative, each turning point, I began to grasp what it had truly cost to reach the moment we were living through in the wake of 9/11. This wasn't just an academic exercise; it was personal. It was purposeful. Understanding the evolution of *e pluribus unum* (out of many, one) in America—from the battles fought in silence for women's rights to Native American and Black American rights, to the rights of those with disabilities, and to movements that roared across generations—enabled me to develop meaningful and grounded strategies at the hospital. And it gave me something more: a compass. I began to see not only what had been done, but what was missing—that sense of absence, of untold stories, unresolved injustices, and unrealized potential.

If you are someone striving to become a catalyst for change, whether in your place of worship, your school, your company, or your corner of the world, you must understand where we've already been. Progress without perspective is fragile. Without a sense of the ground we've already covered, it becomes far too easy to repeat old mistakes, to misplace our energy, and to lose hard-won gains. So, I encourage you to patiently consume the history I'm about to share, not just as information, but as inheritance. Allow the knowledge to settle in your spirit. Let it challenge you. Let it comfort you to know that the path you're on is one that others have walked before, sometimes stumbling, sometimes triumphing, always pressing forward.

You may find that what you learn gives you the language and insight to help you guide others on their journeys. When they ask the hard questions, when they don't know or fully comprehend what's at stake, or how to begin, you'll provide an encouraging space for them to voice their questions without judgment. I hope the knowledge you gain here helps you feel as hopeful and excited about change as it did me in my evolving role at Bryan. Knowledge with compassion has the potential to lead us to possibilities.

In 1973, the nation could no longer look away. The horror of the Tuskegee syphilis experiment, where hundreds of Black men suffered without consent so researchers could observe the course of untreated disease, burst into public consciousness. The truth, which had been buried for decades, now stood in full view, casting a long, damning shadow over American healthcare. The US government couldn't *not* act! I can imagine the many conversations and meetings that must have taken place to try to understand how this could have happened and figure out what to do about it.

The national shame of the Tuskegee Syphilis study lit a slow-burning fire of reckoning. In 1980, news of the study led to the formation of a task force, which resulted in the creation of the Office of Minority Health (OMH) and an official study of the issues related to racial disparities in healthcare.

Five years later, in 1985, that task force, sponsored by the Department of Health and Human Services (DHHS), released a groundbreaking document: "Report on Black and Minority Health," more commonly known as the Heckler report, named after Margaret Heckler, the fifteenth secretary of Health and Human Services.

This 264-page report was more than an administrative milestone; it was a moral mirror. For the first time, DHHS gathered and synthesized existing knowledge about the health status of Blacks, Hispanics, Asians/Pacific Islanders, and Native Americans. It was the first time DHHS had put minority health issues into a single report. It was a landmark in naming what had long gone unnamed.

In a letter accompanying the report, Heckler did not mince words. She called out the harsh truth that, from the very beginning of federal health data collection, minority Americans had suffered worse health outcomes, marked by higher illness and earlier death. Even as general public health improved, "the stubborn disparity remained, an affront both to our ideals and to the ongoing genius of American medicine," she wrote. To this day, minority Americans continue to suffer poorer health outcomes and earlier death.

The report outlined eight recommendations, ranging from public education and health provider training to increased funding for minority health research. Finally, the government was officially naming the problem. It wasn't the end of the issue, but it was, at last, the beginning of acknowledging it. It opened a door. It invited discussion. It laid the foundation for collaboration between people ready to investigate, understand, and take action.

One year later, in 1986, Congress created the Office of Minority Health by mandate. OMH became a vital hub, a one-stop resource center for literature, research, and guidance on the unique health needs of African Americans, Hispanics, Native Americans, Asian Americans, and Pacific Islanders. It served patients, community organizations, and health professionals alike. This wasn't just about information; it was about visibility. It was about laying the groundwork for a more inclusive healthcare system that recognized that patients, like the Afghani woman I encountered years later, needed care tailored to their unique realities, their stories, their lives.

But understanding alone was not enough. It would take nearly another two decades before the nation was ready to peel back the next layer. In 1998, OMH partnered with the Agency for Healthcare Research and Quality (AHRQ) for a formal study that offered the most definitive picture yet of what was truly happening behind hospital walls. The findings, published in a 2003 report, became a touchstone in the fight for equity: *Unequal Treatment: Confronting Racial and Ethnic Disparities in Health Care*, produced by the Institute of Medicine (IOM). For the first time, we had hard data outlining *why* minority patients were receiving inferior care. A simple yet profound visual chart explained it all: three categories, one based on patient-related factors, and two squarely within the system's control.

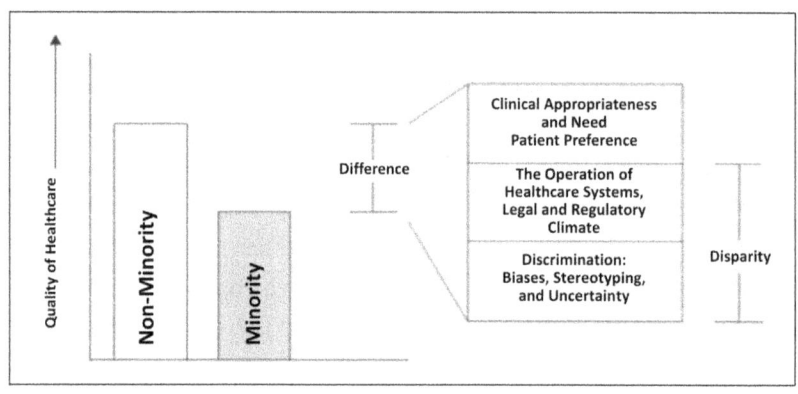

Figure 6.1. *Visual of Findings of IOM Study (IOM, 2003)*

The first category, clinical appropriateness, need, and patient preference, acknowledged differences that could not be externally managed. But the other two? They were where the true disparity lived: in systemic operations and in discrimination, both conscious and unconscious.

This was a reckoning. It was a call to transform the very foundation of the American healthcare system. The IOM didn't just point fingers; it offered a path forward. The study's conclusion was as honest as it was urgent: "The committee finds strong evidence for the role of bias, stereotyping, prejudice, and clinical uncertainty ... and urges more research to identify how and when these processes occur."

It outlined three sweeping recommendations:

1. **Transform health care systems** through legal and regulatory changes.
2. **Train health care professionals** to recognize and eliminate bias and stereotyping.
3. **Adopt patient-centered care**, grounded in understanding the unique needs and values of every patient.

Perhaps the most powerful contribution of the report was this: it *named* the problems. Bias. Discrimination. Stereotyping. Naming these issues made them real. It gave people, patients, providers, and policymakers the language to talk about what had gone unspoken for too long. And with names came responsibility.

The study galvanized change. It reached the right people at the right time, and suddenly the conversations became louder. Clearer. "We need Congress to act," people began to say, and this time, their voices were heard.

This chapter in our national story is built on four critical pillars: the exposure of the Tuskegee experiment, the Heckler report, the creation of the Office of Minority Health, and the IOM's study on unequal treatment. Behind each of these were untold numbers of brilliant, relentless, and compassionate individuals asking questions, analyzing facts, and refusing to settle for silence. The path has never been linear. It has been winding and imprecise, often halting, sometimes maddeningly slow. But that's how we humans seem to move, one painful truth, one brave voice, one policy shift at a time.

The ripple effects of these efforts are still unfolding today. They have reshaped how quality care is defined, how culturally and linguistically appropriate services are delivered, and how medical institutions are held accountable. They have influenced accreditation bodies, reimbursement standards, and medical school curricula.

But the real test is not in the policy. It's in the practice. Will a nurse in a rural hospital recognize implicit bias in her interactions? Will a hospital administrator understand how to track and close gaps in care? Will a physician truly hear the story behind a patient's symptoms? These are the questions that remain. Because the transformation of healthcare will not be measured solely by legislation or reports, but by what happens in the quiet, everyday moments where care meets the human soul.

When the Afghani woman entered Bryan hospital, flanked by her daughter and son-in-law, she was seeking healing. What she found instead was a system that was unprepared for her, even though the people within the system deeply cared *about* her. And that, perhaps, is the most painful truth of all. In medical institutions across the country, just like in the history books that tell the story of Tuskegee, the blindness to acknowledging the treatment of people who are different from us continues to shape outcomes.

 We want, and often assume, that fairness and righteousness are baked into our care, yet, too often, we fail to see the barriers we've unconsciously built.

Most healthcare workers I've known are compassionate and devoted. But there are those whose hearts have grown calloused, not out of cruelty but from exhaustion, overwhelming demands, and persistent frustration. This often triggers a self-protective shift into System 1 thinking, driven by the amygdala, where instinct overrides empathy. I remember vividly the day my father's nurse vented her frustrations, thinking we didn't hear her. Instead of seeing our grief, she saw only that the language slowed her down and required extra time to do her job. She judged my father's inability to comprehend English, assuming he didn't want to learn the language. That assumption, instead of compassion, led to anger, perpetuated misunderstanding, and eliminated any chance of connection. This is disparity in its rawest form.

When we pause and look more closely, we see that healthcare disparities go far beyond personal interactions. It is embedded within the scaffolding of the system itself. Think about how healthcare is funded. Research has shown that if you are struggling financially and have little education, you likely will have more serious health issues than someone with affluence because you don't have the privileges that help maintain wellness.

For someone living paycheck to paycheck, preventative care becomes a luxury. They delay medical visits until the pain becomes unbearable or life-threatening. What might have been prevented with early treatment becomes a desperate trip to the emergency room as a last resort, where they incur higher costs and receive fragmented care. And when addiction or mental illness are part of the equation, as they often are in underserved communities, the need for long-term support grows. But without insurance, or with only minimal coverage, these patients are left without options. The system closes in on them like a fist.

Now compare that to someone with means. They can schedule a doctor's visit at the first sign of a problem. They catch illnesses early, prevent them from progressing, and pay less in the long run. They have access not only to better care, but to care at all. This is the cruel irony of our system: the people with the greatest needs often have the fewest resources, while those with the most resources require the least urgent care. And yet, the solutions we offer don't match the complexity of the problems. We try to fix deep wounds with surface-level treatments. We slap on policy bandages and hope for healing.

Take language, for example. We say, "Immigrants should learn English," as if fluency alone would erase every barrier. We offer interpreters, an important tool, yes, but rarely do we stop to ask what psychological, cultural, and systemic hurdles must be cleared before a person can even begin to learn a new language. We ignore the trauma, the shame, the isolation the person has or is experiencing, and how that impacts learning anything, much less working seventy hours a week, and then trying to go to school to learn a new language.

Or consider the person who arrives at the ER, intoxicated and broken. We detox them, discharge them, and direct them to outpatient therapy. But what if their reality, the one that led them to self-medicate, feels hostile and hopeless? What if they need not just sobriety, but healing of identity, of community, of soul? Until we acknowledge these deeper needs, our interventions fail. Or, at best, they'll offer temporary relief without real resolution, and the pain continues into the next generation. The full complexity of our healthcare system is beyond the scope of this book. But what must be understood, what must be *felt*, is that people are slipping through the cracks. Some never even reach the system in the first place. And the price isn't just measured in suffering or lives quietly lost. It is paid in our collective erosion, a society fraying at the seams as we turn away from one another and fail to confront the deeper wounds that demand shared responsibility and courageous collaboration.

This isn't just a healthcare problem. It's a national problem affecting every segment of our society. Disparities like these show up in classrooms, courtrooms, police departments, housing applications, and even at restaurant tables. Anywhere bias and broken systems intersect, inequity takes root.

However, there is hope because awareness is a starting point.

If we can pause and acknowledge that the issues run deeper than we've realized, that the gap between intention and impact is wide and real, then we have already taken the first step toward healing, not just of bodies, but of the very systems meant to protect them.

Let's zoom in on the quiet tension that followed the public reckoning of the Tuskegee experiment. One might imagine that such a devastating revelation would spark immediate and sweeping reforms across every corner of government and healthcare. But it didn't. The wheels of change turned achingly slowly. It took seven long years before a national task force was even formed.

Seven years.

What held us back? Surely, there were people who cared. People who felt the weight of Tuskegee in their bones and wanted to do something. And yet, despite the passion, the facts, and the moral urgency, meaningful change took years to take shape. Why? The answer, or at least part of it, lies in what was still missing.

The Heckler Report had laid crucial groundwork. It highlighted disparities, named them, and gave them a voice in the national conversation. The creation of the Office of Minority Health was another leap forward. But even those groundbreaking efforts failed to answer one essential question: **How can we accelerate sustainable change?**

That question has echoed through the 1990s and early 2000s as researchers, policymakers, educators, and clinicians wrestled with the realities of disparities in health outcomes. They built upon each other's insights, adding layer after layer of understanding. I remember what it was like around the turn of the new century. There was a shift happening. It became not only acceptable but also admirable to be a believer in healthcare equity. To speak up. To question. To strive for solutions. Cultural competence and health equity were no longer whispers in the corner; they were becoming part of the conversation, and in some places, even a personal mission.

And then, the research began to tell a more complete story:

- We cannot transform a massive system (for example, healthcare, education, legal, etc.) without first transforming the smaller systems within it (hospitals, clinics, schools, police departments, etc.) (Bass and Avolio 1994).
- And we cannot transform an organization without first transforming the individuals who run it (Bass and Riggio 2005).

- That kind of individual transformation, especially in mindset, isn't fast or simple. It is typically a result of intentional and consistent self-examination, learning, unlearning, and a willingness to shift perspective (Fagan, Guenther, and Wells 2022).
- As individuals deepen their understanding of cultural complexity, they develop intercultural sensitivity. They become more aware of how beliefs, attitudes, and assumptions are shaped by culture (Bennett 1993).
- Development requires intentionally taking a deep dive and evaluating one's beliefs, values, biases, stereotypes, and assumptions held as truths on multiple levels: macro cultural (national or regional), micro cultural (organization or educational institution), and individual (familial). This developmental work takes time, can be painful, and requires a willingness to accept ambiguity with the ever-changing patient population (Gardenswartz, Cherbosque, and Rowe 2010).

In 2001, I came face-to-face with a truth that rocked me to my core. I began to gain a deeper understanding of the impact of the intercultural developmental mindset and its relationship to cultural competence, health equity, and inclusion. It happened during the conversation when I learned the results of an assessment I'd recently completed, along with others on our diversity council. The Intercultural Development Inventory (IDI) is designed to measure how you process differences. I didn't expect to be surprised. After all, I had built a program from the ground up at Bryan Health. I had lived in three countries and five US states. I spoke Farsi and English fluently, as well as conversational French, Spanish, and Latin. I had traveled to more than twenty countries and forty-three states in the US. I had worked with people from every walk of life. I had mentored immigrants and refugees, embraced international students, and spent years in the heart of cross-cultural service. In other words, I was confident I had this.

So, when the results came back and said I was operating in Minimization on the Intercultural Development Continuum, my initial reaction was disbelief.

Minimization? Me? That must be a mistake.

I stared at the page, stunned. My heart raced with fear. *If anyone finds out about this,* I thought, *I'll be discredited. Fired. Everything I've worked for will be undone. How can this be? Minimization wasn't a place I belonged, not after all I'd seen, all I'd done, all I'd lived.*

I convinced myself the assessment was flawed. Or maybe I had taken it wrong. Maybe I had broken the tool. That had to be it. But then I did what I've always done when something doesn't make sense. I started exploring to learn more. I turned to the theory behind the assessment: the Developmental Model of Intercultural Sensitivity (DMIS). And as I unpacked its framework, I slowly began to unpack myself.

I revisited painful moments, like the time the nurse misjudged my father in his final hours because we spoke a different language, and my anger as I lashed back in response, shutting down any chance for connection. I thought about the Native American family who donated their son's organs, a first in Nebraska history, and the choices made by medical staff who misunderstood the cultural weight of that decision. I thought about the moments that had haunted me, and I saw them with new eyes.

That's when it hit me:

 Having cultural experiences is not the same as having a developmental mindset.

Traveling the world didn't mean I had transcended bias. Speaking other languages didn't mean I truly understood the cultural frames of those around me. I had mistaken exposure for growth and development. And then came the revelation that made everything personal: Minimization looks different for people like me—those from nondominant, marginalized backgrounds. Our Minimization isn't about denying others; it's about denying ourselves. We learn to shrink our differences to survive. We assimilate to fit in. We downplay who we are to be accepted, to be safe.

I had done exactly that. I had kept my Iranian identity hidden for years, too afraid of the judgment it might bring. I had chosen American-sounding names for my sons, hoping to spare them the ridicule I'd endured. I hadn't taught them Farsi, not because I didn't cherish it, but because I didn't want them to be teased for sounding foreign.

I had lived in Minimization, not out of malice or ignorance, but out of necessity. It was a "go along to get along" strategy, and I hadn't even known I was doing it. That realization cut deep. It was painful. But it was also freeing. It gave me language for a struggle I had never quite understood before.

As I immersed myself in the research on the Developmental Levels of Intercultural Sensitivity (DMIS as created by Dr. Milton Bennett), I began to understand the limitations of our conventional approach in healthcare. We taught people *about* other cultures. We encouraged them to learn *facts* about diets, dress, and customs. But we didn't teach them to confront their *own* cultural beliefs. We didn't help them examine how their familial culture, national culture, and even healthcare culture shaped their perspectives and expectations of others. That kind of growth and development doesn't happen in a two-hour training. It must be lived. It must be *felt*.

The more I learned, the more I knew I had to go through the developmental process myself, not just for my personal growth and development, but to guide others on their journeys. I wasn't content to simply understand cultural competence anymore.

I wanted to build a bridge to it for everyone still standing where I once stood, thinking they'd already arrived.

That was the missing piece: cultivating cultural self-awareness on the part of healthcare practitioners, administrators, and educators. People like me. To close the gap in cultural competence and equity, we must begin by looking within.

What is the culture of healthcare? How does it become an invisible expectation, a lens through which care is delivered, often without question? There is an implicit assumption that clinicians are the unquestioned experts and that patients must trust them implicitly.

The words of Dr. Edward T. Hall, the father of intercultural communication, echoed in every fiber of my being as I considered this gap. In his seminal work *The Silent Language*, Hall wrote,

> "Culture hides more than it reveals, and strangely enough, what it hides, it hides most effectively from its own participants. Years of study have convinced me that the real job is not to understand foreign cultures, but to understand our own."

This insight strikes at the core of the challenge in healthcare: practitioners often operate within an invisible cultural framework that must first be uncovered and examined before authentic cross-cultural care can be delivered.

In 2013, the Office of Minority Health (OMH) named cultural competence as a cornerstone for eliminating health disparities. On their website, they offered a definition that cuts to the heart of it:

"Cultural competency is the way patients and doctors can come together and talk about health concerns without cultural differences hindering the conversation but enhancing it."

It's a simple idea with profound implications: when healthcare is delivered in ways that honor the beliefs, practices, and languages of numerous communities, outcomes improve. Trust grows. Healing happens. I think of the Afghani woman and her family at Bryan. Their needs were not just medical; they were cultural, spiritual, and relational. By recognizing the unique layers of their experience and having the cultural competence to meet them with dignity and respect, we did more than avoid misunderstandings. We created a space where healing could truly begin. That's what cultural competence looks like in action.

OMH went further, listing specific ways culture and language influence healthcare:

- People's beliefs about health, healing, and wellness
- How illness and disease are perceived, not only by patients, but by providers
- Attitudes and behaviors surrounding when and how patients seek care
- Provider worldviews shaped by narrow cultural norms that limit access for others

To reach equity in health care, OMH says, both the provider and the patient must be willing to transcend the learned cultural patterns they bring to the table. That is where health equity begins, not in systems alone, but in relationships. In the courage to ask better questions. In the humility to listen. In the commitment to see one another not through the lens of difference, but through the shared hope of caring as humans.

In 1993, Dr. Milton Bennett introduced what would become a quiet revolution in how we understand human interaction across cultures: the Developmental Model of Intercultural Sensitivity (DMIS). Rooted in his research in intercultural communication—a field that, at the time, had little overlap with healthcare or cultural competence—Bennett's work offered a developmental lens for how individuals engage with cultural differences.

For decades, Bennett studied and taught strategies for effective communication in multicultural environments. He defined culture broadly—not just ethnicity or nationality, but any group united by shared meaning systems. That framework made his model highly adaptable, relevant not only to global contexts but also to systems shaped by religion, socioeconomic background, education, and profession.

At the heart of his theory was a structured continuum—a scale of increasing complexity in how we perceive and respond to cultural differences. The core idea is that when faced with intercultural challenges, we either simplify to protect ourselves or expand to understand more. Our capacity to grow along this scale depends on both exposure and reflection. As we accumulate experiences, our awareness deepens—and with it, our ability to engage across cultural lines becomes more nuanced and intentional.

In 2003, Bennett and Dr. Mitch Hammer operationalized the model by creating the Intercultural Development Inventory (IDI), a validated assessment tool used to identify where individuals or organizations fall on the developmental scale. (This is the same tool that once placed me in the stage of Minimization.) While the IDI offers powerful self-awareness, Bennett was clear: growth isn't guaranteed. Development is neither automatic nor linear. We don't simply "graduate" to the next stage and stay there. True progress requires us to reshape the way we organize perception—to build internal patterns that allow us to process new experiences with complexity and compassion.

"We do not perceive events directly. Rather, our experience of events is built up through patterns or categories that we use to organize our perception of phenomena" (Bennett, 2004, 72-73).

For me, this insight was revolutionary in its simplicity. Cultural awareness doesn't begin with exposure. It begins with noticing. The shift happens the moment we stop judging differences as better or worse and start seeing them simply as different. That moment of awareness is the spark. It's the beginning of seeing our own beliefs, behaviors, and assumptions as shaped by a particular lens—and recognizing that others move through the world with lenses just as vivid, valid, and layered as our own.

Bennett's model describes a journey from a monocultural mindset —where our own culture is the lens through which we see the world —to an intercultural mindset, where we hold space for many perspectives and measure our own in context. In practice, though, this journey is rarely smooth. In our research, we've seen that knowing your developmental stage (like Minimization) doesn't automatically translate to operating from a higher stage (like Adaptation). That transition takes intentional effort, especially when we're emotionally triggered or facing discomfort.

In those moments, our fast-acting, protective System 1 brain kicks in. It's efficient but reactive, and it often overrides our more thoughtful System 2 brain—the one that could help us respond with empathy and adaptability. As a result, we fall back into Minimization, not out of malice, but out of instinct. It's ironic: the moments when we most need intercultural sensitivity are often the times when it's hardest to access.

Bennett's theory gave shape to something I had long sensed: cultural differences are layered, enduring, and deeply internalized. We rarely acknowledge just how much our worldview is a product of our upbringing and surroundings. His work didn't just expand my thinking, it shifted the very foundation of how I understood the success or failure of diversity efforts.

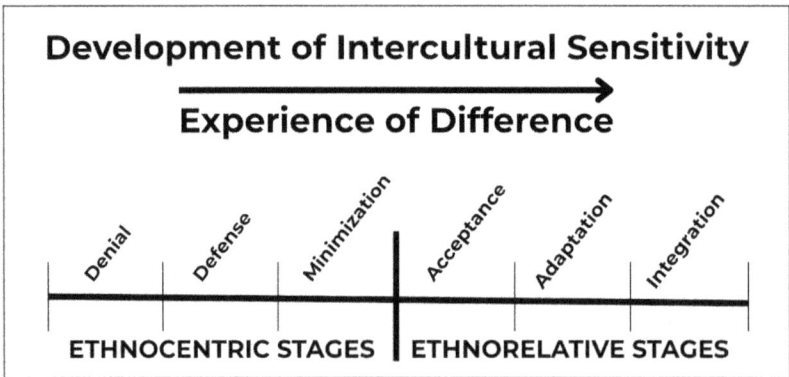

In other words, how we experience cultural difference is largely determined by the developmental stage we're in. What once felt threatening may, in another stage, become a source of curiosity and learning. What we once dismissed becomes a new lens for connection.

Armed with this understanding of human development, I was finally ready to ask a deeper question: What impact does a leader's developmental mindset have on the teams they lead and the decisions they make?

My doctoral research findings closely align with what Acheson and Schneider-Bean shared in their 2018 article, which proposed that development isn't linear—it moves like a pendulum. When we enter unfamiliar cultural terrain, our perspectives can become destabilized. Like a pendulum swinging from a clock, our worldview can shift—sometimes progressing, sometimes regressing—depending on internal and external forces.

The *2003 Unequal Treatment* study by OMH was a signal to every hospital, clinic, doctor's office, and welfare agency that the time for complacency was over. It reflected the mounting pressure on the government to respond decisively to the widening cracks in our healthcare system that left countless people vulnerable to mistreatment. And not just those from racially or ethnically diverse backgrounds, but anyone outside the dominant population: women, elders, non-native speakers, LGBTQ+ individuals, and those with disabilities. The study gave voice to what so many had experienced in silence.

At our hospital, the study was a long-awaited affirmation. We had already taken many of the actions the report recommended. For us, it was energizing proof that the steps we'd taken, sometimes against resistance, sometimes on sheer conviction, were the right ones. We hadn't waited for permission. We'd acted on principle.

For years, I'd poured myself into building a more inclusive and culturally competent hospital. What I longed to do, it turned out, others were doing across the country, in communities big and small. My friends used to tease that I was ahead of my time. The irony wasn't lost on me. I'd always considered myself a late bloomer, still catching up after a slow and sometimes painful process of acculturation. But in this one area, I wasn't behind; I was ready. Perhaps it was the long road I had walked. The pain. The otherness. The fight for belonging. All of it had shaped my vision in ways theory never could.

When the time came to lead, I knew what needed to be done. I had proposed a three-pronged strategy for our hospital, each one intentionally aligned with our overarching strategic vision as an organization:

1. **Foster an inclusive organization**: a place where all employees and volunteers are given the opportunity to learn and grow and provided the resources necessary to be successful.
2. **Elevate patient care**: ensuring people from all backgrounds had access to and were treated in ways that honored them, their dignity, their culture, and their need for healing.
3. **Engage with the community**: to understand and meet the evolving needs of our population with empathy, innovation, and responsiveness.

Then, in 2006, a third major study was launched, this one by The Joint Commission. It aimed to create a more detailed roadmap for eliminating health disparities. By what felt like divine coincidence, I learned about the study just as they were searching for institutions to participate. At a health conference in Washington, DC, I met the lead investigator. We spoke, exchanged contact information, and not long after, she invited Bryan to join the research. I was thrilled for us to participate.

The research team came to our facility and interviewed our CEO, clinical staff, non-clinical workers, and me, as the leader of our diversity and cultural competence efforts. Watching their process up close was like peering behind the curtain of what my future would hold. I saw how they gathered data, validated stories, and identified patterns. Their approach wasn't just academic; it was deeply human. And it would later inspire much of my research. Those were heady days.

Everywhere I turned, I saw glimmers of hope, new ideas taking root, brave conversations taking place, people willing to lean in and *listen*. The work was far from over. Disparities persisted. But for the first time, it felt like the winds were shifting.

For me, those years carried a strange duality: the weight of past wounds and the thrill of forward motion. The stress hadn't disappeared. I still bear the invisible scars of being part of a "hated" group, of years spent trying to prove my worth in spaces that didn't always welcome difference. But now, finally, those experiences had a place. A purpose. People were talking. People were *trying*. And I was there, in the thick of it, not on the sidelines, but front and center. I had a seat in the theater of change, and the curtain was rising. There was still so much work to do, but I believed in the story we were writing, in our hospital and in our community. I believed it could have a hopeful, just ending. I held onto the quiet conviction that maybe, just maybe, I had what it would take to help see it through.

Questions

1. In what ways do the healthcare disparities discussed in this chapter mirror the diversity challenges you've encountered in your own life, community, or workplace?
2. Can you recall a personal experience where cultural misunderstanding or bias affected the quality of care or connection you received from a healthcare provider? When that happened, did you expect the system or an individual to take responsibility? Why?
3. Just as the government took years to shift from identifying the problem to implementing solutions, where are you on that path toward cultural competence? Are you ready to act, or are you still in a season of learning and unlearning?
4. Have you ever minimized cultural differences, your own or someone else's, to avoid conflict or fit in? What were the consequences of that choice?
5. What assumptions have you held about people from different cultural backgrounds that you're now beginning to question?
6. Who in your life has modeled cultural humility or inclusive leadership? What did you learn from their example?
7. What is one small step you can take this week to grow your intercultural sensitivity, whether in conversation, reading, or reflection?

Chapter 7

Courage and Humility

If you lose your head but gain a kingdom,
It's a silly bargain, far from wisdom.
   -S.M. Hafiz

During my time at Bryan Health, we considered expanding our women's and babies' units. As part of our process, we conducted focus groups with women. Unsurprisingly, the results confirmed a pressing need for expanded services. Our community was growing, and so were the needs of its families. But as I reviewed the findings, one question kept surfacing: *What about the voices we haven't heard?*

I requested a meeting with the vice president in charge of the initiative and asked, "Has anyone considered reaching out to our rapidly growing immigrant and refugee communities?" Her eyes widened. Clearly, no one had ever posed the question. Rather than dismiss it, she did something extraordinary: she leaned into the moment with humility and resolve.

"No," she admitted, "but we should."

Then she gave me both the green light and the funding to conduct a series of focus groups with the singular mission of ensuring that the new women's and children's health services would include *all* women.

I conducted focus groups with Hispanic, Middle Eastern, Asian, and Black women. Each conversation was rich with truth and vulnerability. Together, we gave voice to the unseen and too often unheard. I wrote the findings in a report, which I presented to our Senior Leadership team. "Understanding the Health Care Challenges and Needs of Women of Marginalized Groups in Our Community" helped shape the design, structure, layout, and even the staffing model of the hospital's new wing. When the hospital hired someone to head the new neonatal division, they kept the needs that our study illuminated in mind. The neonatologist, originally from Ghana, told me decades later that the reason he said yes to Bryan was because he met me and saw what I was doing. I was deeply humbled by his words because the transformation he saw involved so many others. Leaders who dared to listen and act made our efforts possible. And because they did, we took numerous steps forward in building a hospital that would truly care for a diverse and changing community.

The longer I have worked in this space, the more I understand a truth that is both sobering and hopeful: developing the necessary mindset to lead like people matter is not a destination but a journey. One that is lifelong, often uncomfortable, and always deeply human. It demands not just willingness, but *courage*. The sobering part is that most people I encounter want the journey to be quick and painless. But real mindset shift often begins with a personal disruption: an interracial marriage in the family, a new disability diagnosis, or the loss of a job triggered by resistance to growth. That's when the work truly starts.

I've heard it said that "pain pushes us until inspiration pulls us." Most people I've encountered invite transformation only when the pain of staying the same is greater than the pain of change, and once they do, the impact inspires them and keeps them going. I worked with an executive whose CEO required him and his entire team to go through a leadership development journey with me. During his first coaching session, he said, "I'm going to be retiring soon. I don't know why I have to do this, but I'm doing it because we are doing it as a cohort." During his last coaching session, he confessed, "I was not willing to engage, but I'm so glad I did. The impact on me has been remarkable. I wish I had known this stuff fifty years ago when I started my career, or even thirty years ago when I was promoted to a leadership position. I would have been a better boss. I think I would have even been a better husband and father. Now that I know it, I know I will be a better grandfather."

The transformation of the leader often precedes any group change, yet the effort it demands is more intricate than most people realize. We live in a world that is fraying at the seams because we struggle to navigate our differences. Turn on the news and see racial violence, religious persecution, ethnic cleansing. Or sit in a coffee shop and overhear the offhanded remarks that are painful reminders of how casually we diminish each other. We are running out of time. The unwillingness to embrace our human differences at the same time as embracing our shared humanity is threatening the very fabric of our society. And unless we collectively begin to do the work internally, the challenges of our future will become insurmountable.

I do not write these words as someone who has it all figured out. I am not an expert. I am a student of life and of this work. My mother once told me, "As long as you're breathing, you must be open to learning." And I breathe that truth every day. I am still discovering new layers of myself, still uncovering blind spots, still learning how to listen better, how to *be* a better human. The more often and more deeply we engage with people different from ourselves, the more complexity we must learn to embrace.

There are no shortcuts. We cannot outsource this work to machines or policy. It is personal. It is intentional. And it is essential.

A translation app can instantly convert foreign words during a virtual meeting, yet it cannot translate context. It cannot decode the cultural lens through which someone views the world. That's our job, to lean in, to listen, to *understand*. To lead like people matter begins with a deep awareness of both self and other. Even when we have the chance to connect, we don't always rise to meet the moment with grace.

It may sound dramatic, but I believe our survival as a species depends on our ability to embrace one another, not despite our differences, but *because of them*. Cultivating that ability starts at the individual level with the humility, courage, and patience to sit still long enough to meet ourselves.

Authenticity is the root of every real connection. But to be authentic, we must first have the guts to confront our own stories: the beliefs we inherited, the values shaped by our childhood, and the wounds we've ignored. That kind of digging is not easy. Most of us are taught to "get over it" or "keep moving." But healing does not happen at a sprint. It requires stillness. Solitude. Reflection. I think back to my reaction to that nurse years ago when my father was sick. I had spoken without thinking, an unfiltered response rising from unresolved pain. That pain was born in my earliest days in the US when people told me, explicitly and implicitly, that to belong, I had to erase who I was. That I must assimilate, not acculturate.

Hospitals are sacred spaces. Often, they hold us during our most vulnerable seasons, when we are sick, afraid, or watching someone we love suffer. And because we will all pass through the doors of a clinic or a hospital at some point in our lives, healthcare offers a rare and potent opportunity to see compassion for those whose lives are different in action. For me, healthcare was a doorway. It's where I started to unravel the threads of my own identity and purpose. It's where I began to understand that cultural competence is not a checklist; it's a way of growing and becoming for a lifetime. Over time, I took what I learned in hospitals and applied it to classrooms, boardrooms, congregations, and communities. But healthcare was the spark. The mirror. The beginning.

You may not be a healthcare provider. Perhaps you are a community leader guiding your growing community, a teacher shaping young minds, a CEO steering an organization, or a parent raising the next generation. Maybe you're simply someone who cares enough to want to understand. Whoever you are, these lessons are yours, too. Being inclusive is not part of a job. It's a way of living, thinking, and relating. As you contemplate your experiences while reading this chapter, you will likely begin to identify areas in your own life where this work matters. The challenges of navigating human differences with empathy and grace are universal, and so are the opportunities.

My hope is that you allow this chapter to serve as a guide. A reminder that it all starts with an important and courageous step: *the decision to care.*

July 25, 2007, began like most other days, except I wasn't doing well. I hadn't felt good for quite some time. Sleep had become elusive, headaches persistent, and dizziness unshakable. My body had been whispering for months, maybe years, but I wasn't listening. I had learned to ignore the warning signs. I had too much to do, too many people to serve, too much to prove.

My pace was punishing. I believed my worth lay in my ability to accomplish, produce, and perform. I had perfected the art of being a *human doing*. The concept of simply living as a human being was foreign to me. That morning, I pushed through the fog and went to work at the hospital. Serving others had always been my comfort, my escape, my anchor.

By 1:30 p.m., the weight of it all came crashing down. I was nauseated, dizzy, and my head throbbed violently. I walked out of my office and told my assistant I needed medicine from the employee health nurse. It seemed simple enough. Within minutes of checking my blood pressure, the nurse looked me in the eye and said, "We're going to the Emergency Department. Now."

She placed me in a wheelchair and wheeled me quickly through the hospital corridor. The elevator ride was a blur. The emergency room doors opened with urgency, and suddenly I was on a gurney, surrounded by beeping monitors and a flurry of nurses and doctors. A pill was slipped under my tongue. The medical staff moved quickly, their voices calm but urgent.

I must be having a heart attack, I thought, breathless with disbelief. *What would Scott and the boys do without me?*

I felt powerless. But even in that helpless moment, I turned to the one thing that had always brought me peace. "Okay, God," I prayed silently, "If it's my time, please take care of my family. Let them know how much I love them. Help them make it through this." In the quiet of my heart, I sensed the words: *"Be still and know that I am God."* It felt like a lifeline. I sank back into the crisp hospital pillows and surrendered.

It wasn't a heart attack. It wasn't anything—physically, at least. Months of tests came back normal. But I wasn't okay. My mind was foggy. I was constantly tired. The headaches and stomachaches persisted. I felt like I was choking on my own life. Eventually, I reached out to my psychologist friend, Dr. Maria. If my body wasn't sick, maybe my mind was. After multiple visits and assessments, she looked me in the eyes and gently said, "You have post-traumatic stress disorder (PTSD) and major depressive disorder (MDD)."

I was stunned, grateful for a name, but confused. PTSD? I wasn't a soldier. I hadn't seen war. Or had I? Dr. Maria, an expert in refugee and immigrant trauma, explained that PTSD and MDD were even more prevalent in immigrant populations than among veterans. The dissonance of leaving home, especially at a formative age, creates deep, lasting fractures in one's identity.

She walked me through her research: those displaced before age ten typically adapt by internalizing their new environment into their identity; those who leave after eighteen retain a strong sense of identity with their origin. But those who migrate between ten and eighteen, when identity is still forming, often live in a kind of identity limbo. That in-between space is where I had lived for decades. I would later learn this was similar to the experiences of third culture kids (TCKs).

Third culture kids offer a valuable lens for understanding the identity development and challenges faced by immigrant children. TCKs are individuals who spend a significant portion of their developmental years in a culture different from that of their parents, often blending the values of their home and host cultures to create a unique "third culture." Although this concept initially applied to the children of globally mobile families such as diplomats or international businesspeople, its relevance extends to immigrant children, who must also navigate multiple cultural frameworks. Both groups often develop cultural fluidity and intercultural competence, but also wrestle with questions of belonging and identity.

A central theme in the TCK and immigrant child experience is the complexity of identity formation. These children frequently find themselves caught between cultural worlds, leading to feelings of marginalization and confusion about where they belong. While they may acquire adaptability and global awareness, they are also at risk of developing fragmented identities. Erikson's theory of psychosocial development, particularly the stage of identity vs. role confusion, can be complicated by these cross-cultural experiences. Children may delay solidifying their identity as they try to reconcile often conflicting cultural expectations from home, school, and society. Ambiguous loss—missing people, places, or a way of life without closure—is another emotional challenge they often face. This can result in a deep sense of rootlessness, as neither the home nor the host culture fully embraces them.

Despite these challenges, both TCKs and immigrant children can develop significant emotional and social strengths. With appropriate support, they often become resilient, empathetic, and skilled at navigating diverse social settings. Their exposure to multiple worldviews fosters open-mindedness and adaptability, qualities that are increasingly valuable in a globalized world. These strengths, however, can only flourish when emotional needs are acknowledged and addressed. Children who face racism, cultural dissonance, or isolation without guidance may experience increased anxiety, depression, or identity confusion.

At twelve, I left Iran. At fifteen, I was dropped into an American boarding school, months before the Iran Hostage Crisis erupted. I became the target of cruel jokes, the subject of suspicion, and the symbol of something many people hated. I was told, with words and without, "You don't belong here," which solidified the feeling of isolation and dissonance I'd begun to feel.

By the time I reached forty, I had moved thirty-two times. I had survived separation from my family in Iran, from my husband and family in the US, from my cultural roots. I had endured the loss of pregnancies and the deaths of loved ones, including my father, Ahga, whose passing left a hole I never truly acknowledged. And I carried the invisible weight of needing to be everything my parents hoped for, while also proving my worth to a society that too often saw immigrants as burdens.

I wore my strength like armor. "What doesn't kill me makes me stronger," I repeatedly told myself. But the truth was, I was tired. My mind coped. My body bore the brunt. And my heart was still grieving. That fifteen-year-old girl inside me felt lost.

Months passed. Healing didn't come quickly. It never does. It came in quiet moments, when I gave myself permission to admit I needed help. It came in therapy with Dr. Maria, in prayer, meditation, and always in stillness. I began to process some of the deepest pain I'd long buried:

- The heartache of leaving Iran at twelve, my family waving goodbye.
- The loneliness of being left in a boarding school in America at fifteen.
- The years of separation, the miscarriages, the grief that never had space to speak.

- The loss of my beloved father and the guilt of not truly saying goodbye.

And slowly, I let go. I let go of the need to prove. I let go of the story that I had to be either Iranian or American. I allowed myself to be *both*. I realized I didn't have to choose. My identity could be layered, complex, whole. My father's words echoed: *"You may be the only Iranian these people will ever meet. Represent us well."* My mother's voice rang strong: *"You are from a people of courage. Be a woman who stands tall."* And so, I stood, tender and tall.

With the support of family and close friends, I began to accept all of me, even the frightened teenager. I stopped shaming her for her fear and started listening to her. She mattered. I realized that authentic connection with others only happens when we are connected to ourselves. That connection spans oceans, cultures, languages. I am rooted in my ancestors in Iran *and* in the life that I've built in America. I don't have to choose. That is the gift of *and/both*. Sometimes I still retreat, afraid of rejection. I still feel the old pull to blend in. But I now know fitting in is not the same as belonging. Belonging requires truth, vulnerability, and presence. True belonging begins within. We cannot find belonging externally until we uncover it and nurture it within. Peace comes when we feel seen for all of who we are. My pain, while once my purpose, is now a singular part of my complex whole. The struggles I once tried to bury are now the soil from which my voice grows. I write, teach, and speak about creating space for belonging, identity, and leadership, not just from theory, but also from lived experience. Louise Anderson and her entire family's support of the fifteen-year-old me played a vital role in my resilience and identity development during those formative years. Their care planted seeds of belonging that took root when I needed them most. The enduring love of Scott and his family deepened that sense of safety and connection. Our sons, both gifts from God, came into our lives at a time when I most needed to feel unconditional love.

Over the years, countless others have crossed my path and expressed love, acceptance, and belonging in ways that words can barely capture. The African philosophy of *Ubuntu*—I am because you are—beautifully encapsulates the essence of what I have experienced. It lives in every fiber of my being and shapes every interaction. Through their love, I learned I didn't have to walk alone. And now, I carry forward their legacy by creating spaces where others feel they belong, too.

If you've ever felt like you didn't belong, I see you. If you've ever wrestled with who you are in a world that asks you to be simpler than you are, I hear you. There is healing in the telling. And there is freedom in living our truth. Let's keep telling our stories. Let's keep listening to others. Let's embrace the hard things, the brave things, the *real* things, because we are more powerful when we bring all of ourselves to the table.

Butterflies go through four stages of life: egg, larva (caterpillar), pupa, and finally, adult insect. A miracle of transformation unfolds in those stages, but it's the third stage, the chrysalis, that holds the deepest mystery.

When the larva is fully grown, it stops feeding and begins to search for a quiet place to undergo its metamorphosis. Some spin a cocoon, attaching themselves to a leaf or twig. Most simply hang suspended, still and silent, allowing the metamorphosis to begin. What happens next is not gentle. Inside the pupa, there is destruction. The caterpillar releases enzymes that dissolve its form and identity, digesting itself from the inside out. Organs disintegrate. Muscles melt into unrecognizable clumps of cells. Some parts remain intact, others become a kind of raw biological clay. From this chaos emerges what biologists call imaginal discs, the hidden blueprint for wings, antennae, and all the breathtaking structures of the butterfly.

It is nothing short of profound: to become something new, the caterpillar must first fall apart. This process is not unlike the human experience of suffering. Our lives, too, are shaped by struggle, then reconfigured by the dark and necessary work of transformation. We see it even in the gym. Physical strength doesn't come from ease, but from resistance. Muscles are torn, rested, repaired, and slowly rebuilt, stronger than before.

Emotional maturity follows the same law. In times of pain or crisis, we encounter the raw materials of growth: insight, resilience, empathy. Struggle can deepen our understanding of ourselves and sharpen our perception of others. It stretches our hearts open, if we let it. And yet, we recoil from pain. We look back at our struggles with regret. We try to sidestep anything that threatens to shake our peace. Especially when pain comes to our children and those we love, we feel the urge to protect, to rescue, to swoop in and save them from discomfort. But in doing so, we can inadvertently rob them of the very thing that would make them whole. Naturalists tell an old cautionary tale that if someone splits open a chrysalis too early in an attempt to help a butterfly emerge, the butterfly cannot survive. It emerges deformed, underdeveloped, unable to fly. The struggle inside the chrysalis is not a design flaw: it's essential. The same pressure that breaks down the caterpillar's form is what pumps fluid into its wings, giving them shape and strength. Without the struggle, the butterfly dies. And so it is with us.

Supporting someone in their pain does not mean sparing them from it; it means bearing witness to their experience. It means standing near, not taking over. The transformation must be theirs to complete. When I was diagnosed with PTSD and major depressive disorder (MDD), I entered my chrysalis, a dark, disorienting space where nothing made sense, and everything hurt. But I wasn't alone. My husband and children, friends, mentors, and coworkers showed up for me in quiet, consistent ways. They made meals, offered prayers, sent messages, or simply listened.

They became my scaffolding. But the internal work? That was mine. Like the pupa rebuilding itself from within, I slowly began reassembling my life, piece by piece, memory by memory, purpose by purpose. I began to see my past in a different light. Helping Filipino nurses adapt to American culture. Welcoming immigrants and refugees into our city. Taking in an exchange student from South

Korea in 2005. All these acts of service became threads in the new wings I was forming. And then one day, the pain didn't feel like a prison anymore. It felt like a passage.

I emerged from my dark chrysalis into a life of deeper meaning. My pain had refined me, not ruined me. And it had taught me this: the struggle is not a detour, it's the path. If I could use what I had been through to ease another person's pain, to light someone else's way, then perhaps none of it was in vain. Each of us is transforming, even when it feels like we're falling apart. Especially then. We are not meant to be spared from struggle, but to be supported through it. And if we allow it, struggle has the power to reshape us, not just into something beautiful, but into something true.

After being diagnosed with PTSD and MDD, I had no choice but to stop everything. Life, as I had known it—constant motion, achievement, pushing through—had to pause. I had to surrender to what my mind and body had been quietly screaming for years: I was carrying wounds that needed tending. Deep, unhealed, devastating losses had left scars that were no longer content to stay hidden.

So, I made the difficult decision to resign from my full-time position at Bryan Hospital. Walking away from work I loved, from a team I respected, from a mission that mattered deeply to me, felt like tearing off a piece of myself. I feared disappointing others. But even more, I feared what would happen if I didn't make the change. My health was unraveling, and I knew the cost of ignoring it would be far greater than the temporary pain of letting go.

I also put my master's degree on hold. I had been chipping away at it slowly, one class at a time, since 2003 through Doane University. It had become a steady thread through the chaos of life. But now even that had to wait. Later, when the fog began to lift and I could see clearly again, I returned to finish the degree. And when I walked across that stage, I received a special award for perseverance through hardship, an honor that felt like an embrace for the woman who had nearly lost herself in the struggle.

Therapy with Dr. Maria became a lifeline. Healing wasn't just about rest or reflection. I needed something else, something forward-looking. A reason to wake up. A way to reengage my heart and mind. I needed something that reminded me of who I was beyond the pain. We explored possibilities. Small steps, quiet hopes. Eventually, one idea kept rising to the surface: Teaching. It made sense. I had spent much of my career in human resources doing just that. Teaching, mentoring, and developing curriculum. Helping others grow had always been a source of deep joy and meaning for me. Watching someone light up with new understanding or confidence was like witnessing a miracle. It was, in its own way, sacred. Before I stepped away from Bryan Hospital, the President of Bryan College of Health Sciences invited me to create and teach a course in cultural diversity. At the time, I had filed the idea away, uncertain of what the future would hold. But now, with a bit of clarity returning, the memory resurfaced. Maybe I could still do what I loved in a different way. Perhaps creating and teaching this course, helping future health practitioners understand the rich, complex layers of human identity, was not only something I could do, but something I needed to do. It could be both purpose and medicine. It felt right.

The thought of sharing what I had lived and learned, especially after walking through a dark valley, gave me hope. It reminded me that even broken things can be used to build beauty. And maybe, just maybe, my healing could help someone else along the way.

Since 1992, the more I interacted with people struggling to navigate differences, the clearer it became: I was meant to be a bridge. Something inside me was drawn to those uncomfortable, often tense moments, and I could see myself standing in the gap, helping others find their way across.

At first, I was fueled by anger. I wanted to show people like the nurse who had berated my father for not learning English that they were wrong. But life and experience softened that edge. Through years of study and countless conversations, I came to understand what sits beneath such behaviors: fear, uncertainty, and the panic of feeling incompetent, especially in high-stakes environments like healthcare. I had come to appreciate how deeply human it is to resist what we don't understand.

Instead of allowing these moments to hijack me emotionally, I began asking different questions. *Why did she act that way? What was she afraid of? What tools was she missing?* Over time, I came to view that infamous interaction with the nurse not with bitterness, but with understanding. What I wanted now was to teach others what I had learned. I realized that to teach in higher education and consult at the level I aspired to, I would need to pursue a doctoral degree. Applying meant identifying a research topic—one big, guiding question that could carry me through years of study and ultimately become my dissertation. So, I asked myself: *What's still missing? What remains unanswered, not just in the work, but in me?* Two questions echoed louder than all the others:

- Is it possible to develop the mindset of leaders to be like that of our chaplain instead of the nurse, and even myself, who'd responded to her comment so vehemently?
- How can we create more healthcare outcomes like the one with the twelve-year-old Native American boy and fewer like the one my father endured?

I believed that if we could answer these two questions, we could help healthcare workers develop the internal capacity, the insight, the empathy, the tools, to drive real, systemic change. But I knew I couldn't answer that question alone. I needed research. Rigor. A path.

I chose the University of Nebraska–Lincoln's PhD in human sciences with a specialization in leadership. It was the right fit for two key reasons. First, the program allowed me to design a course of study tailored to my passion. I could draw from disciplines that truly mattered to my work: medical anthropology, organizational behavior, psychology, public health, and leadership, all converging around my core interests in human differences, cultural competence, the neuroscience of inclusion, and the transformative power of leaders. Second, and perhaps more importantly, I was drawn to Dr. Gina Matkin.

Her research, like mine, centered on developing leader competencies to create the inclusive mindset I believed was critical to creating change. She believed, as I did, in the developmental power of the IDI, a tool I had used extensively. She didn't just understand my vision, she *shared* it. She was the kind of mentor who could both challenge and champion me. For the first time in a long while, I felt both direction and alignment. And then, the other shoe dropped.

Questions

1. Where in your life is courage asking to emerge? What would it look like to step into that space with boldness, even if your voice shakes?
2. Where might greater humility open doors to growth, healing, or connection? What would it take for you to listen more deeply to yourself or to others?
3. How could the courage and humility you've named be channeled into your efforts to foster inclusion in your workplace, your community, your school, or your faith space?
4. In what ways are you honest with yourself about your pain, needs, or limitations? What support systems or boundaries could help you protect your well-being and avoid burnout?
5. What parts of your story have you been afraid to acknowledge or share? How might embracing those hidden chapters empower you and others?
6. Who around you needs to know they are safe, seen, and valued? How can you be a bridge for belonging?

Chapter 8

The Rewards of Struggle

Go learn a lesson of the flowers;
Joy's season is in life's young spring,
Then seize, like them,
the fleeting hours.
-Omar Khayyam

I had been sick for weeks with a cough and cold. Nothing serious. I kept insisting I only needed a little more time to heal. But I was always exhausted. Bone-deep tired. I chalked it up to the PTSD and MDD, convinced I just had to power through. I was still learning what it meant to listen to my body. I had promised Scott I'd see the doctor after I took the Graduate Management Admission Test (GMAT), the final hurdle in my PhD application. True to my word, I went to our doctor's walk-in clinic that very afternoon. He diagnosed me with pneumonia.

Ten days of oral antibiotics followed by three days of antibiotic infusions. But I didn't get better, and he admitted me to the hospital. On January 18, 2009, I had a CT scan of my lungs. The next day was

Dr. Martin Luther King, Jr. Day. Scott and I sat together in the hospital room watching history unfold: the inauguration of President Barack Obama, when a physician walked in.

He didn't hesitate. "You have a mass on your pancreas that has woven itself around your spleen."

The room stilled.

"You have two options: biopsy it or go straight to surgery to remove it. Either way, you'll need a specialist." Scott and I looked at each other, shocked by the magnitude of what he was saying.

"If I was your sister," I asked, "what would you tell her to do?"

"I'd recommend removing it given its size and location. And I'd tell her to go to Dr. Are, at University of Nebraska Medical Center."

Suddenly, I wasn't just navigating the dark waters of PTSD and MDD, but recovery from pneumonia and possible cancer. While the air around us felt unreal, there was a strange peace in that hospital room. Maybe it came from the hope sparked by the inauguration of our country's first Black president, or maybe it came from the hard-won resilience we had earned through years of struggle. Whatever it was, that peace carried us as we took our first steps into the unknown.

That night, after Scott left, I turned to the place I always found solace: my faith. I opened the little pocket Bible I took with me everywhere, not seeking anything in particular, just wanting to talk to God. There, in the silence of that sterile room, the first words I saw were: "Jesus said to the woman, your faith has saved you. Go in peace."

I whispered those words over and over until I fell asleep, the Bible still open in my lap. The next morning, as the nurse changed the calendar hanging in my room, I asked if I could keep the torn page from the day before. "Yesterday changed my life," I told her. "That calendar page, it's like a souvenir. A reminder that all my hard work mattered."

I still have that page. It hangs on the dream board, right above my desk.

A second CT scan revealed the mass was 4.5 by 4 centimeters. It was mucinous, which the doctor told us meant that if it was not cancer now, it could become cancer later. The surgeon recommended we move quickly. They would remove one-third of my pancreas, my spleen, and two lymph nodes sitting on top of my stomach. But first, the anesthesiologist wanted my lungs to get stronger. Surgery was scheduled for March 16th. Scott and I looked at each other in amazement. They would remove the tumor on the exact day I had become a US Citizen seventeen years earlier.

At 4:00 a.m. on the day of surgery, we arrived at the University of Nebraska Medical Center. My little sister had flown in from New York. Our youngest son was with us, along with a few close friends. I had quite the entourage. Dr. Are warned us that it would be a long surgery, five to six hours, and recovery would be grueling. He wasn't wrong. I spent six days in the hospital. Recovery at home lasted three months.

On the fourth day in the hospital, my phone rang. It was Dr. Gina Matkin calling to interview me for the PhD program. We talked for a while. Then, she said the words that filled my heart: "Congratulations, Helen. I want to be the first person to welcome you to the program." Tears welled up. I was elated. I hadn't even received the lab results on the tumor yet, but here was this shining light.

I'd had other successes over the years: a master's with a 4.0 GPA, the Keith Berlage Award for perseverance, a Key to the City in 2004, and a Tribute to Women Award in 2005. But this? This meant something different. This was for the girl who once believed she was not smart. Who had been mocked because of her accent in England, who was made to feel like an outsider in every school hallway in Florida.

I didn't know if I'd be able to start the PhD program, but I'd been accepted, and that alone was a victory. Before hanging up, I asked Dr. Matkin if she had any advice for a non-traditional student like me. She had earned her PhD while married and working full-time. She understood where my question was coming from. "Two things," she said. "Create a space at home that brings you energy. Make it your sanctuary. And second, appreciate the journey. Don't lose focus on today by worrying too much about the future." I still live by that advice.

On Sunday, March 22nd, Dr. Are and his team walked into my

room. Family and friends surrounded my bed. He smiled. "You do not have cancer." Cheers erupted. High fives flew. It sounded like Nebraska had scored a game-winning touchdown. I lay there in tears, overwhelmed by joy and relief.

That evening, I opened my journal and tried to find the words to capture my gratitude.

Now, here I sit today by the window, sobbing. I don't know what is causing me to cry. I think a deep sense of gratitude. I don't want to feel guilty that I have been spared from pancreatic cancer, yet I do. And, because I have been spared, I want to continue the rest of my days always seeking you first, oh God. I want more than anything to trust in you. I want to love graciously and generously the people you put in my path. To give and serve others because you've called us to love others as we love ourselves.

The memory of that day still brings me to tears. It is the reason I have devoted myself to creating a society that values humans, in all our differences, and the reason I want to equip people to lead in a way that expresses that people matter.

Yes, the pain in my heart was still there, but now, I understood it. I could work with it. Integrate it into my life. Pain gave me the gift of resilience. It shattered the illusion that I was powerless. I began to believe in myself again, to meet each new challenge with a quiet mantra: "I can face this. I have done harder things before." Every difficult memory became a reservoir of strength.

And because of all that pain, because of every step, I had found my direction. I could finally answer the question that had always haunted me: Do I belong in this work? Do I dare help leaders navigate change and challenges beyond their control? The answer is yes. Unequivocally yes. I could tell my story. I could help others navigate their own. I could shape a legacy of hope and transformation.

The dreams I had tucked away in the corners of my heart were beginning to bloom. And that, more than any title, award, or accolade, was the breathtaking reward of my struggle.

My mindset was shifting. Not through willpower alone, but through the weight of experience, the power of education, and the sometimes-uncomfortable clarity of self-reflection. I was changing, and I began to wonder what research says about the connection between life experience and the deep internal shifts that shape human development. Could we enhance our ability to connect across cultural differences, not just in terms of race, ethnicity, religion, or nationality, but in the full spectrum of human identity?

In the early 2000s, researchers were chasing the same question. Scholars like Milton Bennet and Mitch Hammer had laid the groundwork, but others were now pressing further. Ayas's (2006) mixed-methods study of third-year medical students found something surprising: international experience didn't correlate with the development of intercultural sensitivity. But the students did agree that what mattered most were the tasks assigned to them during the experience: active participation, reflection, dialogue, and openness to difference.

Lundgren (2007) discovered that teachers made the greatest developmental strides when learning in groups, particularly when supported by their school's administrators. Learning, it turned out, is a relational, shared experience.

In Moodian's 2009 study, some participants regressed in intercultural sensitivity. Their scores dropped between the two assessments. The explanation? Stress. Stress contracts our perspectives, dimming the very openness we seek to cultivate. I saw this reflected in my research at Bryan College. This is the very reason the Pendulum Model of Intercultural Sensitivity was born in the work of Acheson and Schneider-Bean (2018).

Acheson and Schneider-Bean explained that a "linear representation" of the DMIS "often doesn't resonate with the lived experiences of their clients, colleagues, and students." They saw development as points along the arc of a pendulum. The stress of moving into unfamiliar territory could and had resulted in destabilizing a person's perspective. Similar to what Moodian described in his study. They described it as being "like over-correcting a vehicle with sensitive steering, people swing too far toward the opposite of their current orientation before (hopefully) finding balance between seeing cultural similarities and differences between themselves and others." The job of educators, practitioners, and coaches is to help our clients identify the factors that caused the destabilization and cultivate internal emotional and physical resilience to balance themselves. What helped each person regain balance varied. For example, for me, activities such as playing with my grandkids, taking a walk in nature, taking a nap, or sometimes practicing meditation, prayer, yoga, and mindfulness are essential during times that I become destabilized.

Li's 2010 study of Canadian healthcare executives unearthed something sobering. These competent executives were highly motivated, but they could not make progress on personal or organizational intercultural development. Worse still, their fear increased after IDI assessment and training. The lesson from this was clear: It's not what happens to us, it's the meaning we make of it that shapes growth. The development of an intercultural mindset requires more than being exposed to difference. It requires the internal capacity to reflect, to question, to unlearn, and to expand. As Bennett (1986) wrote, development isn't marked by *what* we think about difference, but *how* we think about it.

That realization hit me hard. Christopher and Hickinbottom (2008) warned that individuals are "doomed to being narrow and ethnocentric as long as they remain unaware of the cultural assumptions underlying their work." That word *doomed* struck something in me. I didn't want to be doomed. I didn't want my work, or my worldview, to be limited by blind spots I didn't even know I had.

In the spring of 2007, I attended the IDI qualification training. When I took the assessment, my results placed me in the Acceptance stage. That was progress from where I'd once been, Minimization in 2001, but it also revealed unresolved pain. My identity as a multicultural woman, layered, complex, and bruised, still shaped how I made sense of the world. The political rhetoric surrounding Iran, my country of birth, stirred old anguish. The fear wasn't theoretical. It was real. It was daily.

During that three-day training, I learned from giants in the field:

Dr. Mitch Hammer, Dr. Michael Paige, and Akiko Maeker, one of Dr. Paige's graduate students. I felt an instant connection with Akiko. Like me, she was an immigrant. She is a Japanese American woman married to a white American man. We were both mothers of two sons (hers still young, mine nearly grown), and we both believed in the transformational power of coaching. Over lunch, we swapped stories about motherhood, about identity, about our shared passion for mindset change. That conversation echoed through my PhD journey like a steady guiding voice.

The IDI captivated me. Here was a tool, grounded in solid psychometrics, that could actually *measure* how people thought about cultural difference. Even better, we could use it to help them grow. Whether in academia, government, business, or beyond, the IDI offered a roadmap to meaningful connection.

I saw its power firsthand at Bryan College. I agreed to develop a course on cultural diversity on one condition: I wanted to use the IDI to assess students' ability to make meaning of difference. The college president agreed. The college had already committed to a strategic initiative to grow students' intercultural competence from the time they entered until graduation.

This wasn't just one class; it was a paradigm shift at the college, which I was invited to help facilitate. The deans of students, nursing, and allied health all stepped in to help. The dean of students, in particular, became a fierce champion of the college's vision.

As I taught students and met with them individually to review their IDI results and help them understand how it could impact their personal and professional lives, they began to ask, "Are our faculty and staff learning about the IDI too?" When I told them no, they asked, "Why not?" I brought their concern to the college's leadership, and, to their credit, they listened. Soon, faculty and staff began taking the IDI and engaging in their own individual development work while weaving the concept into their courses and programs. That shift marked a turning point for Bryan College. The ripple effects of infusing the IDI and intercultural mindset into student, faculty, and staff development continue to shape the campus, its graduates, its educators, and its mission to this day.

At the same time, I found myself returning to the principles of positive psychology. I began exploring positive psychology during my sessions with Dr. Maria. Each week, she would bring a new article or reading for me. While she never said it, I believe deep down she knew the intellectual stimulation would be important to my healing journey. That insight into the world of positive psychology expanded during my doctoral coursework. I wanted to understand what compels a person to want to learn and grow. What is the inner state, the mental or emotional tipping point, that pushes someone along a path of ongoing development?

By then, I had already logged years in the trenches of teaching and learning about cultural competence. I had seen glimpses of what worked and what didn't. I had witnessed moments of breakthrough and moments of fear-fueled resistance. Now, I had the question that would drive me forward:

What does it take to make a shift, not just in behavior, but in mindset, heart, and soul?

Scott and our sons had never met any of my extended family from Iran. Over the years, I'd been invited to visit many times, but I always declined. The timing never felt right. In truth, it wasn't only about calendars or money. It was about fear. I'd experienced a deep personal faith conversion. I didn't know how they would react, or if they would reject me outright. I wasn't sure I could bear the tension, the silence, or the conflict that might arise between the faith I had chosen and the one I was born into.

Then, in 2009, my mother's side of the family organized a reunion in Turkey. My uncle rented a villa in the ancient seaside town of Silivri, just outside Istanbul, overlooking the Sea of Marmara. For the first time, I felt drawn to being with my extended family, so we went.

It was the first time I'd traveled that far internationally with Scott,

Jonathan, and Alan. We'd traveled to Mexico and Canada but not anywhere else together. Separately, Scott and I had traveled to different places for work, but as a family, this was a first. Jonathan was twenty-three, fresh out of college with a degree in audio engineering and entertainment business. Alan was nineteen and had completed his freshman year of college.

My grandmother, Naneh Shahree, was eighty-three and brimming with excitement to finally meet my husband and sons. I had visited her in England in 2006, and she'd beamed with pride as she said, "I have grandchildren who live in different countries and don't speak the same language as me. That makes me an international grandmother, right?" Before that meeting in England in 2006, we hadn't seen each other since 1978, when I last visited Iran. I was a child then, but I had made a silent promise when I visited her in England, that someday, at least one of my grandparents would meet Scott and our sons.

When our taxi pulled up to the villa, the air was already thick with emotion. Family from Iran, England, and Malaysia had arrived before us. As we stepped out, hugs and tears flowed freely. Laughter echoed between the tiled walls and stone courtyards. The years we'd lost dissolved in a single, shared breath of reunion. Then came a moment I'll never forget: the men of the family gathered around Scott and the boys, showering them with kisses on the cheeks and firm, brotherly embraces.

Later that night, as we lay in bed, I turned to Scott. "So … how did you feel about that?" I was bracing for a reaction. After our wedding, Scott had fervently declared that the kiss on the cheek from my father had been a one-time courtesy. "If either of your brothers ever tries that," he'd joked, "I'll lay them out." But in Turkey, something shifted.

He turned to me and said, "Just because I'm okay with it here doesn't make me any less of a man or less American. Like your dad used to tell you, maybe I'm the only American man they'll ever meet. I want to represent our country, and our family, well." In that moment, I fell in love with him all over again.

And I felt that yearning to understand how and why change

happens in humans. How did the man who once proudly sang "My baby is American made" become someone who accepted and honored a custom that once felt foreign, even threatening? Scott wasn't perfect. But he was growing. He had developed an intercultural mindset. I wanted to understand how. How do people move from resistance to acceptance? From fear to openness? From disconnection to belonging?

At the airport on our way home, I turned to our sons. "Did being there help you understand me better?"

"Mom," Jonathan said, "it helped me understand *myself* better."

That was it. The gift of the whole trip wrapped in one sentence. No souvenir could match the power of that moment of self-awareness handed from one generation to the next like an heirloom. Both Jonathan and Alan left Turkey frustrated by only one thing: they wished I had taught them Farsi.

While everyone spoke English, except my grandmother and a few aunts, our sons wanted more. They wanted to belong. After years of trying to hide my accent, trying to blend in, our sons yearned for the very heritage I once tried to erase. Family bonds, I learned, run deeper than language, deeper than borders, deeper than difference. They survive time, silence, and separation. They wait for us.

When we returned home, I began my PhD program. It was time to walk the talk, to "put my money where my mouth is," as the idiom goes. (Though I always picture someone literally trying to shove dollar bills into their mouth when I hear it.)

I was eager to finally find answers to the questions that had lingered for years. Gina, my program chair, became a key figure on that path. I can't overstate how much her support mattered. She was a fierce advocate and a gentle guide, nonjudgmental, always encouraging, and never afraid to challenge me to see the bigger picture. We often joke that we are sisters from another motherland, religion, and sexual orientation, but sisters, nonetheless. SFAML is how we sign off from messages to one another. We had enough in common to connect deeply, and enough differences to stretch one another. That was the magic.

At UNL, a full-time graduate load was three courses per semester. Because I was recovering from major surgery and teaching at Bryan College, I enrolled in two. My first class, Theoretical Foundations of Leadership, took us on a sweeping journey, from Lao Tzu and Weber to Bennis and Stogdill. We explored transformational leadership, authentic leadership, servant leadership, and more.

On the first day, our professor asked, "What did you do this summer, and why this program?"

I told them about the surgery, the reunion in Turkey, and the burning question I wanted to explore. During break, he pulled me aside and said, "I'm so glad you're here. Speak up in class. You have experiences these students need to learn from."

That semester stretched me. Every week, we read eight to ten peer-reviewed articles, wrote critical reflections, and discussed them in class. For the first time, I wasn't just doing leadership, I was studying it. And it changed me.

In *Dare to Lead*, Brené Brown writes, "Studying leadership is a whole lot different from teaching and researching leadership." She's right. Before academia, I'd spent nearly three decades leading people and programs, but I never saw myself as a leader. I saw myself as a servant, called to help others. Only when I began to study leadership did I start to understand how others viewed me. Leadership isn't about titles or power or paychecks. As Peter Northouse reminds us in *Leadership: Theory and Practice*, there are as many definitions of leadership as there are people trying to define it, but the one that resonates most with me is from Kevin Cashman:

 Leadership is authentic influence that creates value.

That's the kind of leader I aspire to be. Not just in boardrooms, but in hospital rooms. Not just in speeches, but in reunions by the sea. Not just in theory, but in the way I live, love, and leave a legacy. Real leadership isn't about where you sit. It's about who you become, and who you help others become along the way.

In May of 2010, I began conducting IDI assessments with faculty and staff at Bryan College. We started together in a group session, where I explained how the results were interpreted, what the data meant, and more importantly, how it could be used to inspire change. Afterward, each person met with me one-on-one to review their results and craft a personal development plan. It wasn't just about numbers. It was about growth. It was about owning where we stood and choosing where we wanted to go.

When we shifted our focus to faculty and staff development, I recommended that a few key individuals go through IDI certification training before the rest. I wanted them to understand the instrument and become champions of the work. The dean of students and two faculty members agreed. Their leadership added critical momentum. Soon, we established an Advisory Committee, composed of respected leaders from across the community. We launched a faculty and staff Council and increased the training opportunities around cultural competence and inclusion. Slowly and purposefully, the culture began to shift.

As faculty and staff grew in their intercultural competence, students began to follow. It was subtle at first, then steady. Year after year, following 2010, the IDI results for graduating students inched upward. It was small, measurable progress. But more than that, it confirmed what research had already shown: *we cannot help others grow beyond where we've grown ourselves* (Bennett 2004; Long 2012). We teach not just by what we know, but by who we are.

Three years later, in May of 2013, every faculty and staff member at Bryan College took the IDI again. We gathered once more to review the collective data, and I opened my calendar for anyone who wanted to revisit their individual journey with me. The results were surprising. Despite being on the same campus, engaged in the same programming, with the same access to tools and resources, developmental paths looked vastly different.

Some people had grown. Their developmental orientation scores had moved upward, reflecting deeper intercultural sensitivity and an increased ability to navigate differences with empathy and understanding. Others had remained at the same level. And some had regressed. I remember sitting with those results, the silence around them almost sacred. This wasn't just data. These were colleagues and friends who had embarked on the same journey but arrived at different destinations. Why? Why didn't everyone see a positive shift in their developmental level?

The question haunted my curiosity. If we could answer it, we might find a roadmap for change not just in schools, but in workplaces, communities, and nations. If human development is not just about exposure but about *how* we make meaning from our experiences, then perhaps the real work lies not in creating better programs but in helping people ask deeper questions of themselves. Perhaps transformation doesn't begin with strategy or policy, but with soul-level reckoning. The kind that whispers:

Am I willing to be changed by what I encounter? Am I open to seeing myself in the face of someone I've been taught to fear, ignore, or judge? Am I brave enough to grow, not just for myself, but for the world I help shape?

The journey at Bryan College taught me that real development isn't linear. It's layered. Personal. Messy. Sacred. And it reminded me that the most important measurements in life aren't the ones we print in reports. They're the ones that show up in how we treat each other, how we sit in discomfort, and how we choose to become more human.

When I first began working with the IDI, one of the biggest surprises was hidden in plain sight. Roughly 60% of the general population falls into the category of **Minimization.** I had assumed, naively, that people engaged in higher education, healthcare, or leadership might be further along. I have now assessed more than 13,000 people from all walks of life, and my experience aligns with the research findings. Most people, regardless of their level of education, or profession, or good intentions, sit squarely in Minimization.

The irony is that these people often want to build inclusive workplaces, classrooms, and communities. They don't want cultural differences to be stumbling blocks; they want them to become sources of synergy and innovation. But sadly, we live in a time when we're often also looking for shortcuts and quick fixes.

"Just tell me what I need to know," they say. "Give me a checklist for working with *that* group. Show me the magic of how to make my team work better together and do it fast."

They don't realize that the very nature of Minimization is this desire to reduce difference, to flatten the complexities of identity into something manageable, digestible, and comfortably universal. Minimization isn't bad, it's just not enough.

We're trying to lead humans, in all their layered, lived complexity, to appreciate one another, while the world is screaming that anyone who is different is bad, wrong, or harmful. Political differences = bad. Religious differences = fear. Value differences = shameful. Socioeconomic differences = challenging. So why does most of the population fall in Minimization? I believe it's because we've been taught, formally, informally, and legally, that equal treatment *is* fair treatment. That treating everyone the same is the moral high ground.

I'll never forget an Equal Employment Opportunity Commission (EEOC) training I attended in the mid-1980s as a young HR professional. The attorney leading the session said, "I don't care if you lock your employees in the closet and beat them, as long as you do it equally, regardless of race, ethnicity, religion, or age." (Disabilities weren't even protected until the Americans with Disabilities Act passed in 1990.) It was meant to be sarcastic. His idea was that he could use the asshole defense to defend you for being an asshole, but if you treat people differently, he couldn't defend you because then there's a bigger issue at play. But the message was painfully clear: **equality**, not **equity**, was the goal. Thankfully, slowly, we're beginning to understand that **equitable** treatment, providing people with what they need to succeed, is the true path to fairness.

The best example of equity I've seen was depicted in a short video about a kindergarten teacher. She began the morning by welcoming all the kids and telling them that today, she would only put Band-Aids for boo-boos on elbows and nothing else. The children listened and smiled, clueless about what she meant. Later, during a shuffle to get outside, one of the kids fell and skinned his knee and came crying to her. She said, "Oh no, I'm so sorry you hurt your knee, here's a Band-Aid for your elbow." The child left bewildered. A few minutes later, two kids collided heads while reaching for a ball. She responded the same way, "Oh no, I'm so sorry you hurt your head, here's a Band-Aid for your elbow." And so it went that way for the rest of the day. None of the kids' needs were met, but she handed out many Band-Aids for elbows. The story ended with a simple message: equity is not our enemy.

Equity acknowledges that people come from different places and are shaped by distinct cultural inputs, life circumstances, and barriers. But deeply embedding that into our collective psyche will take decades.

Another reason I believe Minimization is so common is assimilation. The United States has a long history of pressuring people to be like us, to speak like us, worship like us, dress like us, think like us. From the first forced assimilations of Indigenous peoples to more subtle expectations placed on immigrants and minorities today, the pattern remains. We reward sameness. We fear difference.

Now, we have a whole generation that is asking something different of us. They're asking if we can walk alongside those who are different, not to fix them or teach them, but to support them as they adapt and thrive in their own way. Can we be scaffolding instead of a zapper? Encouragers instead of enforcers? Can we move beyond mere tolerance into **celebration**?

We teach children to be brave and unique and to honor the things that make their classmates different. But somewhere along the way, as adults, we forget. We trade wonder for wariness. Inclusion becomes compliance, not connection. I've found that **students** are often more willing to do the hard work of development than seasoned leaders. Why? Because their grade depends on it. They invest the time. They wrestle with the content. They allow the struggle.

Organizational leaders, on the other hand, are pulled in a dozen directions. And unless they have personal skin in the game, developing an intercultural mindset feels like a nice-to-have, not a necessity. It's easy to believe we already know what we need to know to be effective leaders. But human beings are the most complex organisms on the planet. There is no *one-size-fits-all* formula for navigating human differences. That's why creating a just and equitable society hasn't happened yet. It won't happen until individuals choose transformation. Until they struggle for it. Until they earn the growth.

 Leading like people matter is an inside job.

Until individuals are held accountable for that inner work, most won't do it. For many, the developmental level of Minimization is good enough to get by.

But it wasn't for me. I kept learning, kept seeking, and kept working on myself. Still, I noticed something sobering: the struggle simply isn't worth it for some people. I saw it in my clients, in my coaching sessions, and in the assessments. Some people would rather remain comfortably unaware than risk the discomfort of growth. When I entered the second semester of my PhD program, I took the IDI again. I had moved from Acceptance to **Adaptation.** I didn't believe it. Surely the test had malfunctioned. Growth that profound in just two years didn't seem possible.

But Dr. Matkin helped me understand what had happened. Together, we unpacked my experiences and the meaning I was making from them. We looked at my desire to be a bridge, to create space where people feel seen, valued, and celebrated for who they are.

She reminded me that **growth never ends**. No one is ever truly done. She quoted my own words back to me, gently, lovingly, like a mirror: "You're in Adaptation, Helen, but you're still growing. You still have more to learn."

And she was right. Because growth isn't a destination, it's a discipline. A way of living.

Questions

1. How have you seen equal treatment fall short in your own life or community, and what might change if we embraced equitable treatment instead? Consider moments when "treating everyone the same" didn't lead to fairness. How might tailored support have created more meaningful outcomes?
2. What personal challenge are you currently navigating, and what deeper growth might be hidden within it? Struggles often carry hidden wisdom. What lessons might your current season of difficulty be trying to teach you?
3. When others are hurting, how do you show up? What does empathy look like, not just in words, but in action? What does it mean to *walk alongside* someone in their pain?
4. In what areas are you still operating from Minimization, seeing differences as inconvenient instead of invaluable? Reflect on any desire to "keep it simple" when it comes to cultural or human complexity. Where might you need to do the deeper work of understanding?
5. What cultural assumptions are you still holding that could be limiting your growth or relationships? We all carry blind spots. What beliefs or biases might you need to challenge to develop a more inclusive mindset?
6. What's one intentional step you can take this week to grow your cultural competence or help someone else feel seen and valued, whether it's learning, listening, apologizing, or amplifying? Growth begins with action.

Chapter 9

Wired for Connection

What we speak becomes the house we live in.
- S. M. Hafiz

One of our previous homes in Nebraska bordered a quiet stretch of state land dense with trees. We lovingly referred to it as "our forest." In winter, the forest transformed. The trees, stripped bare by the cold, stood like silent sentries, skeletal and still. Their limbs stretched skyward like bony fingers, and the forest took on the haunting beauty of a boneyard. There was something otherworldly about it, especially when it was under snow or shrouded in fog.

When I was growing up on Kharg Island off the southern coast of Iran, I never saw trees lose their leaves. Though Iran spans diverse climates and landscapes, and some regions experience all four seasons, our region does not. It wasn't until I moved to England that I experienced autumn's quiet alchemy. At Stanborough Academy in Watford, I would walk through the woodlands on my way to chapel, and our art teacher would take us out to collect leaves for class projects. I was enchanted. The air turned crisp, the trees glowed in golds and scarlets, and I fell in love with the woods, with wandering, with the act of witnessing change.

At first glance, winter trees appear lifeless, dull, even mournful. Under certain skies, they seem almost dead. But some people describe them as beautiful. I used to wonder how anyone could see beauty in such starkness. Now, I get it. That beauty comes from knowing what's unseen. Inside those lifeless-looking trunks, life is quietly unfolding. Roots are stretching, cells are preparing, and the blueprint for spring is already being drafted. People who love bare trees aren't seeing just what is; they're holding in their minds what will be. They respect the process, even when it doesn't look like progress. Some say the trees look like lace, while others liken them to dancers frozen mid-pirouette. I say they're a lesson in trust.

We often see people the way we see bare winter trees, through the lens of what is missing, what is strange to us, or doesn't "look right." When someone behaves in ways we don't understand, often our human instinct is to judge. We might even convince ourselves that their actions are wrong or that they are somehow less than. It's easier for our brain to categorize. Operating on autopilot limits our ability to respond with empathy. And we do this not just to others, but also to ourselves. Think of the last time you made a mistake. Did you mentally kick yourself for being, saying, or doing something "stupid," all the while forgetting your worth, all the wonderful things you've done, and how amazing you are on the whole? We all do it. It's deeply human.

The work of engaging with non-judgment and greater understanding starts with questioning those instinctual responses. It requires us to pause, to look again, to imagine the spring inside the winter. How can we learn to see beyond the surface? How do we overcome our fear of the unknown and begin to celebrate each other in all our seasons?

That question has guided my work for the last twenty-five years. I've devoted my career to helping people shift from monocultural to intercultural mindsets. Through study, teaching, personal experience, and constant inquiry, I've pieced together a framework for understanding and growth. The stories of Henrietta Lacks and the tragedy of Tuskegee show the devastating consequences of getting it wrong. *The Spirit Catches You and You Fall Down* reveals the cultural chasms we must cross and the grace that awaits when we do. Scholars like Bennett and Hammer offer pathways through the stages of cultural competence. Daniel Kahneman's *Thinking, Fast and Slow* helps us understand how our brains trick us. Our fast-thinking brain, built for survival, often overrides our capacity for empathy and logic. But our slow brain, our prefrontal cortex, offers us the space to suspend judgment, to reflect, and to choose a better response.

I've learned this through conversations with my sons about rap music and hip-hop culture. The beats, lyrics, and defiance are all part of a cultural shift that I hadn't given space to understand and appreciate fully. We've discussed generational shifts in the perception of tattoos, perceptions based on level of education, and socioeconomic status.

What surprises me the most is that the answer has always been in us. Human beings are wired for connection. It's not just a psychological concept; it's a biological essence woven into every cell of our body. We long to be seen, understood, and loved. That same longing can help us see and understand others. It's what makes family reunions in Turkey so powerful. Gathered in the warmth of shared history, we remember who we are and how deeply we belong to one another. We honor our ancestors, whose sacrifices shaped our present, and we pass those stories down like sacred heirlooms. That kind of emotional intensity—the kind that roots us to something greater than ourselves—can catalyze change. It can motivate us to build bridges, to lean into differences, to stay curious instead of fearful. Our need for connection, so often overlooked, may be what saves us from our worst selves.

I continue to make the case that in healthcare, becoming culturally competent is essential for providing quality care. Yet, in our efforts to prepare future professionals quickly and efficiently, we often rush the developmental process by exposing students to surface-level differences such as religion, nationality, race, and beliefs about health and illness. While this exposure is valuable, it may be putting the cart before the horse. What if we began by guiding students inward to explore their own cultural identity and the unique culture of healthcare itself? What if we first nurtured the mindset that fosters cultural self-awareness, even as they begin to learn about others?

In *The Silent Language*, Dr. Edward T. Hall observed, "One of the most effective ways to learn about oneself is by taking seriously the cultures of others. It forces you to pay attention to those details of life which differentiate them from you." When students develop this kind of self-awareness, it lays the foundation for deeper, more sustainable growth. And this isn't just a strategy for healthcare, it's a universal approach to navigating the complexity of human differences with empathy, clarity, and skill.

Of all the frameworks I've studied, Dr. Campinha-Bacote's Model of the Process of Cultural Competence in the Delivery of Healthcare Services stands out as the most profound and practical. What resonates most deeply with me is her foundational principle: desire. Desire fuels the journey. It's the inner engine of Adaptation, the birthplace of intercultural mindset in the IDI. To reach that mindset, one must develop not only awareness of their own culture and others', but also the willingness to find meaning in difference, to withhold judgment, remain curious, and ask, with genuine interest, not just why, but how and what, and be willing to create adaptive strategies.

Campinha-Bacote defines cultural competence as an ongoing process in which the provider is always becoming, never fully arriving. I wholeheartedly agree. I've seen this in my own development and in my professional work with students and clients. She writes, "Cultural competence is the ongoing process in which the healthcare professional continuously strives to achieve the ability and availability to effectively work within the cultural context of the client" (Campinha-Bacote 2002, 181).

Her model offers **five interconnected constructs**, each a step in the journey toward becoming culturally agile:

- **Cultural Awareness:** The inward look involves assessing your own biases, understanding how your training and background shape your worldview, and recognizing systemic discrimination within healthcare.
- **Cultural Knowledge**: Gaining insight into the worldviews of diverse cultural and ethnic groups, how they perceive health, illness, healing, and care.
- **Cultural Skill:** The ability to conduct meaningful cultural assessments, both physical and psychosocial, that respect the whole person.
- **Cultural Encounter**: Seeking out and engaging in direct interactions with people from different backgrounds, not to confirm assumptions, but to challenge and deconstruct them.
- **Cultural Desire**: The cornerstone. The internal motivation to want to engage, learn, and grow in these areas.

Campinha-Bacote warns that without cultural desire, the process will be fragmented, at best. Without it, we may go through the motions of thinking we are competent, but never embody its spirit. As Montenery et al. (2013) write, "Lack of cultural desire may impede the ability to meet the cultural needs of others" (52).

This also resonates far beyond healthcare. I believe that desire—our willingness to know, connect, and grow with one another—is at the heart of our collective ability to confront and overcome the challenges we face as human beings. Think of the early days of falling in love. When we truly care about someone, we listen in a different way. We offer space for them to be fully themselves. We lean in with curiosity and patience, eager to understand. That desire fuels deep connection. In contexts where differences could cause us to collide, we need something similar: a willingness to pause, to listen deeply, and to open ourselves to being changed by what we hear. We must be vulnerable so others can truly see us. This is how we begin to meet the biological need to connect.

If desire is the root of becoming culturally competent, how do we cultivate it in those who don't yet have the desire? How do leaders, those shaping institutions, policies, and futures, awaken their desire? How does their lack of desire inhibit their followers from becoming culturally competent?

This is the deeper work. It begins with self-reflection, humility, and a willingness to unlearn. And it continues with models like Campinha-Bacote's and Giger and Davidhizar's, not as checklists, but as living guides. Becoming culturally competent isn't about mastering a framework; it's about committing to a lifelong process of becoming more human, more open, more aware.

And that begins not with what we know, but with what we *desire* to know.

During a recent conversation, the safety director of an inner-city community shared that one of the most important lessons he wants his officers—whether in police, fire, or emergency medical services—to learn is that their greatest challenges will stem from poor communication, and their most effective solutions will come from becoming better communicators.

"People need us to be good at communication," he said with conviction. I agree with him and believe that the one thing that stands in the way of progress more than anything is not the lack of knowledge, skill, or even good intent; it's communication. Miscommunication has the power to derail even the most well-meaning efforts. It sits quietly at the root of misunderstanding, often unnoticed until the consequences are irreversible.

A powerful and tragic example is the story of Willie Ramirez. In 1980, a young Cuban American, Willie Ramirez, was admitted to a South Florida hospital in a coma. His family told caregivers that Willie was *intoxicado*, a term in Cuban Spanish that typically refers to someone being poisoned, perhaps by bad food or drink. But the hospital staff misunderstood, interpreting it as "intoxicated," and assumed Willie had overdosed on drugs. They treated him accordingly. In reality, he was suffering from an intracerebellar hemorrhage, an active brain bleed that, untreated, left him permanently quadriplegic. It's a haunting example of how cultural and linguistic assumptions can inflict lasting damage. Had someone paused to clarify, to ask rather than assume, Willie's life might have taken a different path.

This story isn't an anomaly. Communication, filtered through the lens of culture, is fraught with potential missteps. And the cultural lens isn't just something the patient wears, it's something the provider wears as well. The provider's culture, which is often invisible to the provider, can complicate interactions with patients. In the book *Black Man in a White Coat*, Dr. Damon Tweedy writes candidly about being mistaken for an orderly by patients, despite his white coat. But he also admits that under pressure, he, too, has made assumptions, especially when the hospital's fast pace tempts shortcuts. His honesty is a powerful reminder that cultural competence isn't a checkbox. It's a continual reckoning with our perceptions and habits.

As the medical field reckoned with health disparities, a natural next step was to address how we train future caregivers. Multiple studies have explored how to instill cultural competence in students. The focus tended to be on gaining cultural knowledge and seeking encounters with diverse patients (Allen 2010; Long 2012; Comer et al. 2013). These efforts have value, but often skip the crucial step of helping students understand their *own* cultural lenses first. Why do they hold certain expectations? Where do their assumptions come from?

The Institute of Medicine reported that disparities in health outcomes were partially rooted in provider bias, discrimination, and stereotyping. And while these findings were damning, they bring us right back to the question of what makes a person ready to change their biases?

Research by Altshuler et al. (2003) and Huckabee and Matkin

(2012) suggests that a provider's developmental level of intercultural sensitivity directly impacts their openness to growth. Those at monocultural stages, where cultural differences are ignored or minimized, were less responsive to training. In contrast, those at transitional or intercultural stages showed significantly more growth after interventions. This may seem intuitive, but it highlights again that before teaching cultural knowledge, we must nurture a mindset that values difference in the first place.

Long (2012) found that many nursing students were stuck in Minimization, a developmental stage where people emphasize similarities with no awareness or insight into the value of understanding differences. Often, believing that "we're all the same" is a progressive viewpoint. But this mindset can prevent healthcare providers from seeing the deep-rooted impact of culture on health and illness and how we present ourselves when we are sick. Helping students grow beyond Minimization requires intentional experiences with meaning-making activities that challenge preconceived notions.

Faculty development is also critical. Studies show that when educators commit to their own growth in cultural competence, their ability to guide students improves dramatically (Montenery et al. 2013; Wilson et al. 2010). Transformative teaching requires transformative teachers.

None of the major models, nor even the IDI, fully explains how to cultivate the desire to know others and better understand ourselves, which Campinha-Bacote's model is based on. They measure readiness and describe competence, but stop short of guiding us through awaking the will to change. Without developmental readiness in both teachers and students, knowledge becomes noise, and without desire, training becomes task work. True inclusion starts inside.

I first met Dr. Anita Rowe and Dr. Lee Gardenswartz in 1999 at the Society for Human Resource Management's Certification Course on Diversity and Inclusion. They were the facilitators that day, but the connection went far beyond the classroom. Anita and Lee are warm, grounded, and deeply passionate schoolteachers who have been doing the hard, transformative work of managing diversity since the early 1970s in the Los Angeles Unified School District. When school desegregation became the norm, the district felt it was important to equip educators and administrators. That task fell to Dr. Rowe and Dr. Gardenswartz. They later went from teaching others in the school district to founding a consulting firm grounded not just in philosophical approaches to managing diversity but in creating practical ways for any organization to implement the lessons.

I was immediately compelled by their approach. It wasn't just theoretical, it was practical, applicable, and rooted in real-world experience. They spoke the language of systems and people with equal fluency. When we began building the initiatives at Bryan Health, they were the first people I thought of. I invited them to lead a workshop for our senior leaders and the hospital's newly formed Council. Their work helped us prepare the ground for what they called the "seed of inclusion." It was a metaphor that stuck with me. They strongly believed in moving beyond training and surface-level celebrations, which is exactly the way I felt.

From that moment on, Anita and Lee became my mentors and trusted guides. They were the ones I turned to when the work felt heavy or when questions outnumbered answers. They listened with compassion, challenged without judgment, and offered direction with wisdom shaped by decades of experience.

In 2009, I received an unexpected email from them. They had been working on something new and wanted to share it with me. Together with their colleague and friend, Dr. Jorge Cherbosque, director of the Staff Counseling Center at UCLA, they had co-authored a book and designed a train-the-trainer program called *Emotional Intelligence for Managing Results in a Diverse World*. The title alone intrigued me.

I was already familiar with the concept of emotional intelligence (EQ), but I hadn't yet explored its application to cultural competence. As I listened to Anita and Lee describe their work, something clicked.

It made perfect sense. After all, as Dr. Richard Brislin wrote in *Culture's Influence on Behavior*,

 "We have our strongest emotional reactions when our cultural values are violated or ignored."

That single line echoed loudly in my mind.

Was emotional intelligence the missing link in our efforts to build environments as if people mattered? Could it help people not only understand human differences intellectually but *feel* their way through it, and respond to it with empathy rather than reactivity? As I began diving into the research, that question evolved into conviction. EQ wasn't just a helpful addition; it was a powerful link. It gave language to what so many of us were already sensing: that without emotional self-awareness, cultural awareness often stays at the surface. No matter how many models or frameworks we teach, lasting change only happens when people can regulate their emotional responses, recognize their biases, and practice empathy in the moment.

So, I began integrating EQ into the work I was already doing, alongside theories of mindset shifting, cultural agility, and leadership. Slowly, the pieces began to fit together in a way that felt holistic and human.

I also recognized a crucial distinction: Human emotions and human psychology are distinct. Emotion is primal. It rises quickly, often unconsciously. Psychology is the story we tell ourselves about what we feel, shaped by experiences, beliefs, and culture. To lead others through change and to help them grow into leaders who lead like people matter, we must address both. We must speak to the heart as well as the head. Emotional intelligence offers a way to do just that. But it wasn't the final piece of the puzzle, only the next one.

In the next chapter, we'll explore how EQ creates the conditions for real mindset shifts and why it may be the most underestimated tool in our pursuit of cultural competence.

About halfway through my PhD coursework, I enrolled in a class with Dr. Fred Luthans, a world-renowned organizational behaviorist. It was another turning point in my academic and professional journey. In that course, I encountered a body of research that illuminated something I had been wrestling with for years: *how a person's inner psychological state influences their desire for transformation.*

In Dr. Luthans' class, we dove deeper into the roots of organizational behavior. Beginning with the earliest theories of organizational behavior—Mary Parker Follett, the mother of modern management; Frederick Taylor, the father of industrial efficiency; and Abraham Maslow, whose hierarchy of needs still shapes modern psychology. These individuals sought to gain a better understanding of employee motivation, work performance, and job satisfaction, as well as the relationship between them. And then, we studied Luthans himself—his work alongside Carolyn Youssef and Bruce Avolio in pioneering the Psychological Capital (PsyCap) framework. PsyCap offered something new: *a measurable, developable psychological state* that could be cultivated in anyone.

PsyCap describes the set of internal strengths (level of resilience, hope, optimism, and self-efficacy) that help people thrive at work and in life. I was captivated. The idea that individuals could develop the mental and emotional stamina to change—not just survive but evolve—felt like the missing piece in understanding how people move from resistance to acceptance, from rigidity to growth.

The research around PsyCap focused on how a person achieves a state of psychological presence where it operates as a strength. A clue is found in the work of Mihaly Csikszentmihalyi, one of the fathers of positive psychology, who framed it this way:

"A positive psychological state is a capital that is developed through a pattern of investment of psychological resources that results in obtaining experiential rewards from the present moment while also increasing the likelihood of future benefit ... When you add up the components, experiences, and capital, it makes up the value (Luthans, Youssef, and Avolio 2007, 542).

In other words, PsyCap isn't a trait you are born with. It's a higher-order construct built intentionally over time through practice and reflection. It's composed of **four powerful psychological resources**: *self-efficacy, hope, optimism,* and *resilience*. Together, they become a kind of internal wealth—an emotional currency we can draw from when faced with the hard work of growth.

PsyCap isn't abstract. Each of its components has been grounded in decades of psychological research:

Self-efficacy, rooted in Albert Bandura's social cognitive theory (1994), is the belief in one's ability to execute tasks and reach goals. It's the conviction that, no matter the obstacle, I can and will figure it out.

Hope, according to Snyder's work, is more than wishful thinking. It's the ability to generate both the energy (agency) and the strategy (pathway) to pursue goals. Hope fuels forward movement even when the road isn't clear (Luthans, Youseff et. al. 2007).

Optimism is primarily founded in the work of Seligman and Csikszentmihalyi. It is defined as how we explain life events to ourselves. Do we believe setbacks are permanent and pervasive, or temporary and specific? This explanatory style shapes how we interpret and then act on challenges (Seligman 2002).

Resilience, as Coutu (2002) described, is "the capacity to rebound from adversity, not just bounce back, but bounce forward, emerging stronger and more focused after hardships and failure.

The magic happens in the combination. According to Luthans, there is a synergistic effect. When these four capacities are strong together, they don't merely add up; they multiply. Like calcium and magnesium, which work better in tandem, these qualities reinforce and amplify one another. Research has proven that people high in PsyCap are not only more productive, they're happier, more engaged, and more satisfied with life.

As I sat in Dr. Luthans' class, a question began to take shape that I couldn't let go of: If someone scores in the Monocultural Mindset (as measured by the IDI) but high in PsyCap, could it generate a greater desire to do the work of transformation, even if they don't yet know how? Would hope, efficacy, resilience, and optimism make them more willing to face their own limitations, preconceived notions of others, and risk vulnerability for the sake of development? If not, what would?

In 2010, when I had administered the IDI to the students, staff, and faculty at Bryan College, I hadn't measured their psychological state. PsyCap wasn't yet part of my toolkit. But after learning about it, I kept wondering, what if I had? Had those who progressed in their developmental level also been higher in PsyCap? Could their PsyCap have nudged them toward greater openness, empathy, and engagement with others who are different from themselves?

Fortunately, PsyCap comes with its own measurement tool, a validated questionnaire that assesses a person's levels of hope, efficacy, resilience, and optimism. The opportunity for a powerful quantitative analysis was there, but numbers would only tell part of the story. As a qualitative researcher at heart, I knew the real insight would come from the stories, the narratives of struggle, support, openness, risk, and humility. PsyCap might be measured in scores, but it's lived in moments. The courage to listen rather than defend. The humility to admit "I don't know." The decision to try again after failure.

If we want to understand how people shift from a monocultural to an intercultural mindset, we must ask them to tell us how it felt. What changed? What made them stay in the room when they wanted to walk out? That's where the heart of transformation lives, not in data points, but in lived experience.

Questions

1. How does the pace of your daily life shape the way you judge or interpret the actions of others? In what ways might the busyness of life limit openness to self-exploration and prevent deeper connection?
2. What are you truly willing to commit to grow in order to build your inner resilience, hope, optimism, and efficacy? What practices, support systems, or mindset shifts are you ready to embrace?
3. Recall a moment when someone's words or actions triggered a strong emotional response in you. What cultural value of yours (go back to the Brislin quote on page 168 may have been challenged or violated in that moment?
4. Which of the four PsyCap qualities (hope, efficacy, resilience, or optimism) feels most underdeveloped in your life right now? What would growth in that area look like, feel like, or make possible for you?
5. When have you chosen to step outside your comfort zone for the sake of growth?
6. What supported that choice? What did you learn about yourself?
7. How do you currently respond to failure or adversity? What would it take for you not just to bounce back, but bounce forward?
8. Do you believe you have the capacity to change deeply held mindsets or habits? If not, what is the story you're telling yourself, and is it time to rewrite it?
9. Who in your life models these qualities well? What can you learn from observing how they move through the world?

Chapter 10

The Inner Shift

The world is captured by your beauty and grace.
With unity you capture the world and space.
-S. M. Hafiz

When I was a little girl, my beloved Naneh, my father's blind mother, lived with us. She was kind, gentle, funny, and her presence wrapped around me like a warm blanket. I loved curling up beside her at night, pressed against her soft, warm body. With her, I felt utterly safe. The world made more sense in her company. I could sit for hours, mesmerized by the lilt of her voice as she spun stories from memory and imagination.

Whenever I got into trouble, I would scurry to her side and hide beneath the folds of her long, flowing dress. It was my sanctuary. In return, I helped her however I could—guiding her hand, fetching what she needed, offering the devotion that only a child in awe can give. My love for Naneh was beyond words, deep and sacred. Whenever I called to her, "Naneh," she would respond, "Naneh Joonam." In Farsi, it meant, I may be your Naneh, but you are what gives me life.

For that reason, I wanted to be a Nana for our grandkids whenever they would come. I knew deep in my heart that they would give me life, and I wanted to respond with Nana Joonam.

My father told me he chose the name Helen for me partly because of Helen Keller's courage, wisdom, tenacity, and drive. That may have been why I wanted to know what it felt like to be blind. It was more likely because of my deep love for my Naneh. I wondered what it felt like to live in her world. I wanted to understand her blindness, not from a place of pity, but out of reverence. On my way home from school, I began tying a handkerchief over my eyes, walking blindfolded down the familiar streets. I wanted to feel what she felt. I wanted to become her, if only for a moment.

One afternoon, as I wandered along the sidewalk in my self-imposed darkness, a drunk man on a motorcycle careened into me. I was thrown through the air and landed hard. A jagged piece of his fender tore into my leg. Had I been able to see him coming, I might have leapt out of harm's way. Bleeding and shaken, I hobbled home, and my parents rushed me to the hospital. I had no broken bones or any other injuries, but I did need stitches to close the gash in my right calf. After my return from the hospital, I told Naneh what had happened and why. Tears welled in her sightless eyes. She pulled me close, her arms trembling as she whispered, "No one has ever loved me like that."

I didn't understand the weight of her words then. Years later, I would come to see that this longing to feel what others feel, to walk in their shoes, even blindly, is a gift. Empathy, I later discovered, is one of my greatest strengths, as affirmed by the Clifton StrengthsFinder. It is also the heart of emotional intelligence. Empathy has always been with me, even as a little girl walking home with her eyes closed, trying to see the world through someone else's darkness.

Through my doctoral work, I continued to explore the possibility of helping leaders move from monoculture to intercultural mindsets.

First, I needed to quantify why and how people made that change. I believed this insight could illuminate both the harm and healing possible in intercultural interactions, but more importantly, I hoped it would offer a roadmap. A framework. Clues that could guide me, my students, my clients, and others toward a healthier, more accepting, and adaptable future. I turned to Bryan College, where in 2010 and again in 2013, faculty and staff had completed the IDI. To understand what may have driven changes in their IDI scores, I administered the Implicit PsyCap survey to those willing to participate.

Then came the data analysis. I examined who had grown in intercultural mindset and who had not, but numbers alone wouldn't tell the full story. So, I selected a group for in-depth interviews, including some who had experienced significant changes and others who had not. I wanted to know what happened in their lives, personally and professionally, during those three years. What had helped or hindered their mindset shift?

I learned that many participants had faced profound personal hardships, including the loss of loved ones, cancer diagnoses, marital strains, and children in crisis. Professionally, they had encountered shifting roles, institutional changes, and the uncertainty of guiding others in their academic endeavors. These struggles didn't show up in their IDI scores, but they poured out during our interviews, often through many tears.

This confirmed my belief in mixed-methods research as a more comprehensive approach to conducting research. The stories these individuals shared added soul to the data. Dr. John Creswell, who had written many books and articles on mixed-methods research and taught a few of the classes I took as part of my doctoral coursework, served on my committee. He not only equipped me with the knowledge but also held me accountable for the accurate application of the mixed-methods process in my study.

I had expected the greatest insights to come from each person's internal drive and efforts to learn and grow. What surprised me was how often participants attributed their growth not just to their own efforts, but to one leader in their professional life. Again and again, a single name came up, a leader with high PsyCap and a deeply intercultural mindset. Let's call them C.

For almost everyone I interviewed, C was a key teammate when they experienced hardships. C was the one person they turned to during crises. A source of hope. A steady presence in the storm. Although C had the highest PsyCap score in the study, their IDI score didn't significantly increase between 2010 and 2013. Yet nearly everyone who had grown cited C as a catalyst. C had also been a strong champion to improve cultural competence of all stakeholders at the college, especially students. They fought hard for accommodations for nontraditional and marginalized students, efforts that brought heavy resistance from their peers. It's possible that this opposition, combined with being immersed in a Minimization culture where differences are downplayed, stunted C's own development. But it did not prevent them from lifting others.

Through the lens of social exchange theory, it makes sense. We become, in part, who we are, based on whom we interact with and how. C's optimism, hope, and authenticity created an environment where others could stretch, grow, and thrive.

Another participant, X, showed the most dramatic increase in intercultural development, with a gain of more than forty points. X credited their growth to C, their immediate supervisor.

"When things come up," X said, "C is the person who helps me talk things through. They model what it means to live out our core value, 'know the way and show the way.'"

Research on authentic leadership and PsyCap supports what X was describing. Leaders with high PsyCap inspire trust and performance in others. Though my study didn't focus on leadership per se, the behaviors C embodied were deeply aligned with what defines authentic and transformational leaders.

Even those with low PsyCap showed growth in intercultural development if they had close interactions to a leader with high PsyCap. Participant P, for example, had the lowest PsyCap but one of the highest gains in IDI scores. Despite doubts and self-criticism, P was encouraged by a supportive colleague.

"A lot of people accompanied me on the journey," P told me. "Collaboration is the norm in our group."

Beyond personal stories, I wanted to know what structural changes had contributed to this mindset shift. The college's leadership had, by then, embedded cultural competence into strategic plans. One committed leader operationalized the initiative by forming both an internal council of students, faculty, and staff, as well as an external advisory board comprising community leaders with the expertise and passion for the cultural competence the college had committed to. Momentum began to build.

From the interviews, three key organizational changes emerged that had impacted outcomes:

1. Cultural competence training for all faculty, staff, and students.
2. The "One Book, One College" program created shared learning experiences across faculty, staff, and students.
3. Regular, accessible on-site learning opportunities, thoughtfully scheduled for maximum participation.

These policies reflected the values of an organization committed to transformation and aligned with existing research that links leader-driven initiatives to realizing lasting and sustainable impact.

To my knowledge, this was the first mixed-methods research study to combine PsyCap and IDI to assess developmental change in health sciences educators. The findings suggested that leaders with high PsyCap and even moderately high intercultural development levels can significantly influence the growth of others. And while the study didn't focus on how people reached their current developmental level, it left no doubt in my mind: We need leaders with high intercultural mindsets to guide the way.

The more deeply we understand those who are different from us, the better equipped we are to prevent tragedies, such as what happened to Willie Ramirez, Henrietta Lacks, participants in the Tuskegee study, and Lia Lee, and to co-create solutions for global crises like the COVID-19 pandemic. I believed then, and still believe, that we are in urgent need of leaders who not only value human differences but are equipped to bridge them because people matter.

After attending the train-the-trainer workshop on *Emotional Intelligence for Managing Results in a Diverse World* with Dr. Rowe and Dr. Gardenswartz, I was convinced that there is a profound connection between emotional intelligence (EQ) and the creation of culturally competent leaders, communities, and institutions. I returned home electrified by what I had learned and immediately shared what I'd learned with Dr. Matkin. EQ became the thread woven through my work.

Back at the University of Nebraska–Lincoln, I made the case to revise the Leadership and Diversity course that I had been teaching. I wanted to introduce a bold new objective: to explore how EQ could facilitate mindset development in students. I incorporated PsyCap into the way I taught, supported, and challenged students, so that no matter where life took them, they would have the internal capacity to manage differences with dignity, awareness, and skill. I also knew from what I was learning that transformation must hit a personal center for people to desire to do it. So, I began each semester with a question: *Whom would you be most afraid to bring home and introduce as your future spouse?* If the student is also a parent, the question shifted to *whom would you not want your child to bring home?* This question was the heartbeat of the course. It stripped away theory and dove straight into the soul. It invited discomfort, vulnerability, and the kind of honesty that sparked transformation. It's not just an intellectual exercise; it was intended to incite deep self-reflection.

I challenged students not to ask their parents directly, but to reflect on what they had seen and heard growing up that might reveal this belief. Most parents want what's best for their children, and, in that protective instinct, fears often surface that may help us discern the belief behind those fears. I know. I'm a mom.

I would explain to students that this exercise isn't about judging parents or grandparents, or going against religious or political beliefs.

 It's about understanding that **all of us carry unconscious beliefs that drive our decisions**, and the only way to mitigate their power is to bring them into the light.

When we shed light on the unconscious, we're less likely to be ruled by it and more likely to explore it.

We used the book *Emotional Intelligence for Managing Results in a Diverse World* by Dr. Lee Gardenswartz, Dr. Anita Rowe, and Dr. Jorge Cherbosque, to engage in self-reflection and conversation. Students participated in activities and small-group discussions that often led to profound personal revelations. One assignment asked them to reflect on how the media has shaped their perceptions of people who are different from them. We also watched the movie *Crash*, a powerful film that explores human complexity and how we metaphorically crash into each other with our unconscious beliefs. I asked students to notice their gut reactions when Sandra Bullock's character rails against the Latina locksmith, when a white officer molests a Black woman, when an Iranian store owner screams in anguish after his shop is vandalized, and to apply what they've been learning through emotional intelligence work to unpack those emotions.

As Chimamanda Ngozi Adichie poignantly stated in her TED Talk, "The Danger of a Single Story," "It's not that stereotypes aren't true; it's that they aren't the full picture." When our only exposure to a group comes from the media, we risk mistaking the part for the whole.

Students took the IDI assessment at the beginning and end of the semester. Throughout the first few weeks of the semester, I met with each student for a one-on-one conversation about their IDI results, and we explored the question I'd asked them on the first day of class. By then, they had time to wrestle with it through reflection, conversation, and assignments. To spur development, we wove the insights they gained about their starting IDI score and the EQ readings and activities into their coursework. By the end of the semester, they had completed an action project, which was a real-life service experience with the population they had identified in that question. This project often became a crucible learning experience for the students.

Some students pushed back, convinced they're nothing like their parents. But then the work began. By serving the very people they were once uncomfortable with, they uncovered buried beliefs based on faulty assumptions. Those who dove in and challenged the internal narratives experienced a kind of insight and growth that seldom comes from a single class.

In the decade of teaching the course, sometimes two sections a semester with twenty-five to thirty students in each section, I saw firsthand the power of this work in the students. I invited those who excelled, not in jumping through the hoops of assignments, but rather in the transformation the journey offered, to be teaching assistants (TAs) the following semester. They didn't earn money for doing this. They could earn some elective credits, but often those students didn't need the credits; they wanted the additional growth that comes with facilitating learning for others.

Katie took my class during the final semester of her undergraduate studies. Bright, compassionate, and globally minded, she dreamed of working overseas. When she answered the initial question, she named the homeless population. She loved her parents deeply and knew they had raised her to value education, hard work, and achievement. But she also sensed that if she brought home someone who was homeless, they would disapprove. That awareness revealed an internalized assumption she hadn't known she carried. Katie completed her project in a homeless shelter. The experience moved her in ways she hadn't expected. Later, she moved to Zambia. Four years later, when she returned home one Thanksgiving, her younger brother, Jake, who had taken my class and was serving as a TA, told her that his project had also been with the homeless. Neither had known the other's journey, yet both had unconsciously carried the same internalized assumption. That revelation was a turning point for Jake. It proved what researchers and neuroscience had revealed: *our internalized assumptions, even when unspoken, often begin at home.*

Gabe was a non-traditional student when he enrolled in the leadership class. He was a department manager at the university and decided to go back to school to get his bachelor's degree. I understood his needs because I was once in his shoes. Here's what Gabe shared about his experience in the class as a student and a teaching assistant:

"After a fulfilling career as an electrician, I unexpectedly found myself stepping into leadership roles. Initially, I viewed leadership through a narrow lens—delivering projects on time and within budget. However, as I advanced, I realized that this limited perspective would only take me so far. Without a college degree, my career growth began to stagnate. That's when I made the decision to return to school and enrolled at the University of Nebraska–Lincoln to pursue a degree in agricultural education, with a focus on leadership.

"Although I had taken several leadership courses before, returning to college as a non-traditional student in my forties was a uniquely different experience. I felt uncertain about what lay ahead. One of the first courses I enrolled was taught by Dr. Fagan. I walked into that classroom unsure of what to expect, but that class would become a pivotal moment in my life.

"The class transformed into more than just a class; it became a journey of self-discovery. We laughed, cried, danced, and shared deeply personal stories. We explored our identities and gained insight into the diverse experiences that shape the lives of others. These narratives shattered the distorted assumptions we often hold, replacing them with empathy and understanding. I was fortunate to serve as a teaching assistant for the class for the following two semesters. Alongside Dr. Fagan and several other students, this experience was invaluable. That ongoing engagement over three semesters allowed me to delve deeper into my identity and how I fit into the world. One of the assignments in the class required us to take fifteen minutes to share our identity stories, reflecting on the crucible moments in our lives that shaped who we are. During my two semesters as a teaching assistant, I had the opportunity to share my identity story with the students, and they reciprocated. Hearing so many more stories about unique individuals allows you to gain diverse perspectives and break down any biases.

"Dr. Fagan often reminded us that we are all 'works in progress.' That message resonated deeply with me. I completed the course as a transformed individual, with a broader perspective, a more open heart, and a deeper sense of purpose. I now take more time to reflect, to listen, and to empathize. I've learned not to rush to judgment, and most importantly, I've accepted that I will never be perfect, and that's okay. As I continue my journey, I know I will trip. But when I fall, I will fall toward progress."

Aleah is a former student and teaching assistant. She became Miss Nebraska 2015, married a US Navy pilot a few years after graduation, pursued a graduate degree in counseling, and is now a mom. Aleah shared some candid thoughts about her journey:

"Your class is the one class in college that changed everything for me. This material, the conversations, and the experiences in this class shifted my entire perspective. We started off by sharing our life stories with everyone. By doing so, we were able to understand why someone might value certain things based on their past experiences and how they grew up. We were able to get to know everyone in the class very quickly by knowing what shaped them into the person they are.

"I think everyone would like to believe they are accepting of people's differences and that there is no specific population they are uncomfortable with, including myself. So, when you suggested that I work with people in poverty, I was frustrated. I had no problem with homeless people, and I was almost offended when you suggested that

I should research this population. After learning more about this population, I uncovered some of my own unconscious judgments.

"Although I had volunteered at homeless shelters before and stopped to offer my leftovers to the homeless people on the street, I realized that I had never been denied an opportunity because I didn't have enough money. I found that I had some frustration with my father for making money such a huge priority. I realized that, growing up middle- to upper-class, I was angry with homeless people 'because they could be doing more to help themselves.' After volunteering at People's City Mission and interacting with some of these people, I had an internal conflict.

"I sat down with you, and you changed my entire perspective to help me see that although these people may look capable on the outside, their basic needs aren't being met. When a person is unsure of where their next meal is coming from, it is difficult to think about where they are going to apply for a job. I looked at the people going through the food line and kept questioning 'why aren't you doing more to get out of here?' and you challenged that thought and shifted my perspective by saying, 'You say why aren't you doing more to get out of here, when some of these people are saying look how far I have come, I made it here.'

"At that point, I was overwhelmed with empathy. I questioned how I got so lucky to be born into this family. For the first time, I saw that everyone's experiences shape their values and that not everyone's common sense is common. In just one semester, I went from Minimization to Adaptation on the IDI. My everyday interactions changed entirely. I am curious to know more about people. I want to learn what makes them who they are. I am so much more understanding and patient with others.

"I am so grateful for the opportunity to take this class, as it has taught me how to get to know people for who they are not what they look like on the outside. I think back to this class almost every single day and apply it to my everyday life."

Shannon, a woman I've known since she was very young, became a student and later a teaching assistant after returning from a year of study abroad. She is now married, a mom of two, and an attorney serving veterans. Shannon completed a master's in leadership education while she was in law school.

"I have aspired to leadership my entire life in order to gain the relevant skills to make the world a better place. In my quest to develop my efficacy and leadership capacity, I stumbled across a class taught by Dr. Fagan called 'Leadership and Diversity.' Although it was unexpected, my journey to becoming inclusive began right there, in an undergraduate class I needed to take to complete my minor. I learned many life-altering lessons from this class that I will always hold close to my heart. I learned about myself, about my hesitations, about my own biases. Because of one of the assignments, I took a step out of my comfort and toward the LGBTQA+ population. I learned firsthand that there was more to a person than a single, stereotypical narrative. The devout Christian who had just returned from international Bible college volunteered in my university's LGBTQA+ resource center ... and gained the gift of perspective. This was the first of several lessons I learned in Helen's class.

"That class was just the beginning of several years' worth of development. After the class, I became a teaching assistant for the class that had transformed my thinking. I learned that my painful racial experiences in life shaped how I perceived and embraced my blackness. In response, I understood that my painful experiences didn't have to evolve into life principles where I exclude, overinflate, or minimize my blackness, and that the actions of a few don't discount the value I intrinsically have as a Black woman today. Since then, I have explored my ethnic history, embracing my blackness and the ambiguity it requires, and developing a passion to remove barriers related to equity, access, and transparency for those in my culture.

"The next lesson I learned was that intercultural education is everyone's responsibility. Because I completed the assigned research project, I exposed myself to a new way of gathering information about someone's culture. To this day, I research cultures and gather information about cultures that I do not know much about from libraries, blogs, documentaries, and more. I have grown to believe that the members of a specific culture are not obligated to teach everyone about their customs, rituals, and beliefs. Through this practice, I have discovered that the background work we choose to do is much appreciated and is often considered a bridge when connecting with others.

"I learned that while most people have good intentions, many have wavering priorities when it comes to developing intercultural competence. Development requires intentionality, reflection, and continued exposure to differences. I currently work in the Honors Program, where I have developed workshops on emotional intelligence, leading with empathy, and teamwork that all stem from the lessons I learned when I began my journey. I even became a Qualified Administrator of the Intercultural Development Inventory, the same assessment we were required to take in the class. I train businesses, individuals, and students regularly to consider these principles ... and it all began in a classroom on UNL's East Campus.

"All of these lessons have not only supplemented my leadership, but they have also made me a better employee, friend, and person ... I couldn't be more grateful."

Julie, another former student and teaching assistant, went on to earn a graduate degree and is now an Extension Educator for the University of Nebraska-Lincoln in Colfax County, Nebraska. She is married and a mom. Julie explained how engaging with care and curiosity has become second nature to her:

"I learned so much during your leadership class as a student and Teaching Assistant, but the one thing that sticks out the most was how narrow my cultural view was before I took the class. I was able to expand my cultural viewpoint by volunteering as a student with the Hispanic community in Lincoln. Little did I know that I would end up working in a primarily Hispanic community, which also features community members from the Congo and Sudan. Without that class,

I don't feel I would have the comfort level to interact with our communities in Colfax County. The impact that it had on my inclusive thinking was huge.

"When I was a student, the class put inclusive thoughts in the forefront of my mind and made me rethink what my actions and words were. As a TA, inclusive thinking and language became more natural as I helped our students change their thought process on inclusiveness. Now, inclusiveness is second nature, and I question those who don't tend to think that way. The development of my inclusiveness serves me daily in my diverse communities by allowing me to make new connections and build our 4-H and Extension programs. That development serves as a strong foundation for my growth and capacity for development within my profession, community, and personal endeavors. I am forever grateful for both experiences I had in being your student and TA."

Since 2007, I've administered the IDI to more than 13,000 individuals, from CEOs to students, educators to first responders, across industries, generations, and continents. I've also taught more than 1,000 students using the IDI as both a pre- and post-course measure. Through this work, I've come to see something undeniable: There is hope for humanity because this mindset changes everything for the person.

These leaders cultivate specific attributes, including courage, curiosity, humility, and empathy that enable them to connect across lines of difference and wield their power to uplift others. When these attributes are paired with the right environment and a sincere desire to use power for good, something extraordinary happens. Innovation blooms, and these leaders become architects of spaces where human differences are seen as adding value.

In 1946, Albert Einstein gave a speech warning of the danger of nuclear proliferation. He said, "A new type of thinking is essential if mankind is to survive and move toward higher levels." The same is true today for human understanding. To survive and thrive in the twenty-first century, we need a new type of leader who is fluent in the language of inclusion and equipped with the developmental mindset to build bridges, not walls. But we have work to do. We can't delegate our individual growth to someone else.

As we've covered before, data from the IDI shows that approximately 60% of people are operating at the Minimization stage of development, the level at which differences are downplayed, and sameness is celebrated at the cost of true connection. This isn't a moral failing; it's a developmental reality. But it tells us how far we still have to go. The journey toward valuing human differences demands a new level of consciousness. It requires the courage to examine ourselves, our flaws, our assumptions, our inherited narratives, and the humility and courage to bring together people who are different from us in a spirit of respect and curiosity. Only then can we use our power to heal rather than to harm.

I've invited a few courageous individuals to share their experiences. These people have done the deep, often difficult inner work and emerged as leaders who inspire transformation in their communities.

Jeff is a former chief of police in Lincoln, Nebraska, a mid-sized city and the state's capital. I first met him when he was completing his master's degree. As part of his *Developing Coaching Leaders* capstone, he completed the IDI and explored the role of inclusion in effective leadership.

"While we discussed my upbringing, my educational background, and the lack of exposure to diversity, you provided a powerful message that resonates today: I need to be intentional about developing positive relationships with those whose life experiences differ from my own based on race, ethnicity, and culture.

"As those relationships developed and trust was gained, I could see, hear, and feel the influence of these differing perspectives in my personal and professional life. Using the tools you shared helped me to gain awareness and provided the opportunity for discussion, reflection, and change. Honestly, while getting my graduate degree and participating in the curriculum promoting inclusive leadership, I didn't see the full spectrum of how these lessons would impact my future.

"In 2016, when I received the appointment to serve as Lincoln's Police Chief, your voice and the awareness I gained became incorporated into every facet of my life. I was constantly searching for opportunities to build positive relationships in advance of tragedy. I needed to hear the voices of those we served from the marginalized members of our community. Your instruction provided a foundation that I continued to work to build upon. The day after George Floyd was murdered, you and I were scheduled for a Zoom call with a respected couple from our African American community. While we had scheduled this conversation weeks before, not knowing what we'd be facing the day of, the conversation we had and the way you facilitated that conversation helped me to stay humble and step into relationships that could have ended in misunderstanding. I believe the fact that you had encouraged me, and I encouraged our team to build relationships first, respect and appreciate others' differences, is what led to our community navigating that very difficult season with minimal negative impact.

"I was glad to be invited to the gathering you had for our faith community at the local church. While I wasn't sure how my presence and what I shared would help, I trusted you and the result was powerful in the connections we built with many leaders in the community that night."

Harry, a senior pastor, contacted me to help him navigate differences between members in the multinational church where he served. The congregation held three different weekly services in three different languages. Many Chinese and Burmese members wanted to hold a special church service for those who were learning English but weren't yet at a level of competency to comprehend regular services. Once a month, the three language churches held services together, and on the other weekends, they held church services in their own languages at different times. Three pastors worked together to make this happen.

Pastor Harry's wife, Deidra, along with other women in the church's book club, had read the book *The Help* and together watched the film adaptation. Their discussion sparked a realization: they may have been unintentionally excluding the Chinese and Burmese women in their church community. Deidra, who had known me from my work at Bryan College, introduced me to Harry. He invited me to help facilitate the development of their internal group, which was formed so that they could approach the work from an intercultural mindset. Here's what Harry had to say about insights he gained during that time:

"The concept of developmental mindset around cultural differences revolutionized my ability to understand myself and not feel guilty about letting others be who they are. As I grew in my developmental mindset to being more intercultural, I have been able to see this as a vital attribute of clergy leaders.

"I have sought to be a bridge builder, and the knowledge that I have gained has helped me to be more patient when there are divides created by differences. Dr. Fagan's ability to help me understand where I was in my journey, and seeking to take the next steps in a diverse context, is something that I had never experienced before. The internal work encouraged in me allowed me to be more open to understanding the thoughts and feelings brought on by my experiences, upbringing, and education, which then helped me to make more room in my life to accept others.

"The knowledge I gained by going through this process is giving me a new and more loving vision and version of the Gospel of Jesus and the Bible. And now I am in a position to avail other clergy leaders of this type of learning."

These stories are just two among many. They are proof that leading like people matter is not theoretical. It's personal. It's practical. And it's powerful. If we want a future marked by innovation, resilience, and peace, we must develop leaders who are both deeply self-aware and radically open to others. Leaders who see difference not as a threat, but as a resource.

We must become those leaders. And we must create spaces, homes, classrooms, congregations, boardrooms, where others can become them, too.

That accident with the motorcycle when I walked home blindfolded to understand what it was like to be Naneh left more than a scar on my leg. The pain was real, yes, but it was the pain in her heart that cut deepest. My sweet, blind grandmother was devastated to learn that my desire to walk in her world had nearly broken my body. Yet, even in her tears, I saw that she was profoundly moved that I would risk myself to feel what she felt. That I chose empathy over safety deepened our bond in a way that words will never capture.

Now, when I remember that moment, the screech of metal, the burn of the wound, the tremble in Naneh's embrace, I understand something more. Stepping into someone else's experience is not always safe. It may hurt. It may break us open. But empathy asks for courage, and courage invites transformation. If we want to understand, we must be willing to risk something—comfort, pride, even pain—because that's where the bridge to understanding is built. And that's where love deepens.

Questions

1. What intentional steps can you take to grow in your own intercultural sensitivity and cultural competence? In what ways can you create space and opportunities for others to grow alongside you?
2. What fears or internal barriers keep you from examining your developmental mindset around cultural differences? What would it take for you to move through those fears with honesty and courage?
3. Can you recall a time when you made an assumption about someone from a different culture or background? What did you learn from that experience, and how did it shape your perspective?
4. Who in your life has challenged your thinking around inclusion or cultural competence? How did their presence influence your growth?
5. What aspects of your upbringing, education, or environment might have shaped your unconscious biases? How are those messages still influencing you today—and what would it take to rewrite them?
6. How does your current environment (workplace, community, social circle) support or inhibit your intercultural development? What changes could you initiate or advocate for?
7. When was the last time you deeply listened to someone whose lived experience was radically different from your own? What impact did that conversation have on your understanding?
8. In what ways do you use your influence or leadership to create inclusive spaces? Where could you be doing more?

Chapter 11

Commit to Practice

> With the Seed of Wisdom did I sow,
> *And with my own hand labour'd it to grow:*
> *And this was all the Harvest that I reap'd–*
> *'I came like Water and like Wind I go.'*
> -Omar Khayyam

My doctoral research revealed two practical insights that led me to expand my research. These insights, although rooted in data, speak to something deeply human about how we grow, how we connect, and how we change.

First, leaders who are entrusted with any type of belonging and strategic engagement work must be developmentally ready themselves. That meant operating from Adaptation, as measured by the IDI. Without that foundational readiness, I believed that even the most well-intentioned strategies would fail. Without that inner transformation, leaders won't have the resilience required to challenge deeply rooted systems or the empathy needed to unite people across differences.

Developmental readiness is not just about where leaders are, but also how they bring others along. When paired with Psychological

Capital—the developable, state-like capacities of hope, efficacy, resilience, and optimism as defined by Luthans and colleagues (2007) —it becomes something akin to a superpower. Leaders equipped with both can navigate the chaos of change without losing themselves. They are whole. And they help others become whole as well.

In healthcare, this insight mirrored the work of Campinha-Bacote (2002), who identified cultural desire as the necessary first step toward achieving cultural competence. My research added another layer when it showed that before cultural desire can take root, developmental readiness must be in place. Without it, desire fades under pressure. But with it, transformation becomes possible.

A nurse manager, measured at Adaptation on the IDI, sat across from me in one of the most vulnerable conversations I've ever had. She was working in a community hospital while pursuing her master's degree in nursing. Part of her program required her to complete the IDI and debrief. At the end of our session, I asked her my usual questions. Then I added, "What do you think helped you grow to Adaptation?" Tears welled in her eyes. She began to tell me the story of a local farmer, a quiet, aging Czech man. When friends found him passed out in his home, they brought him to the emergency room.

"He had no heat. He had been drinking. He passed out. He was, in many ways, living on the edge. Hospital staff stabilized him, and we told him he had to quit drinking and smoking, and transferred him to the rehab unit. We never asked him what he wanted. Weeks later, he was released. One day, his friends brought him back with burns over 90% of his body. He went back to drinking and smoking after his release. He passed out with a lit cigarette. He didn't survive. I was devastated. He was such a nice man. We never once asked what he wanted. We assumed, because we are the medical staff, we knew what was best for him. And I can't help but wonder, if we had stopped and asked him—and then really listened to him—if he might still be here. We made him feel like his ideas and opinions didn't matter. We do that in healthcare a lot."

That moment was her turning point. It cracked something open and launched her into deep reflection about the kind of provider she wanted to be and also how she saw humanity. "We may be experts in medicine," she said, "but the patient is an expert in their own body. Their opinion matters. Their story matters. Their voice matters."

Second, my doctoral research revealed that even reaching the level of Adaptation doesn't guarantee permanence. Let's say it again: An intercultural mindset isn't a destination; it's a dynamic process. The world changes, cultures evolve, and we, too, continue to shift, which means that staying developmentally agile requires ongoing, intentional engagement with intercultural experiences. We can't rest on our progress. We must keep growing. And like a pendulum, our intercultural development can swing from Adaptation to Minimization or Polarization if we aren't actively training our minds.

Organizations that cultivate rhythms and rituals that challenge and expand perspective across all developmental levels on an ongoing basis offer a benefit to their employees that is far beyond paid time off. The benefit of ongoing learning enhances creativity and connection with colleagues. One of the most powerful examples I've encountered came from Bryan College. They had implemented a program called *One Book, One College*, a shared reading experience that became a catalyst for campus-wide dialogue.

In 2018, they selected *Small Great Things* by Jodi Picoult, a deeply provocative novel that explores race, bias, privilege, and the journey toward justice through the lens of fiction. Faculty, staff, and students were invited to read and then discuss the book, not only as literature, but as a mirror to their own lives. The college president and I were invited into a discussion about the book. As a leader whose doctoral work was in education and literature, he helped unpack the story's deep insights into our day-to-day actions. As a researcher and educator with expertise in intercultural mindset development, I helped the group see the shift in the developmental mindset of the attorney representing the nurse and the white supremacist woman who lost her child.

Through the program, the college created an opportunity for shared learning, connection, and a different way for students to engage with faculty and staff, and even for the staff and faculty to engage with each other. They used fiction to tap into a different part of the brain. We know from various research that fiction awakens our imagination and allows us to see through another's eyes. When done well, it can transform us.

Reading *To Kill a Mockingbird* shaped my understanding of justice and leadership as much as any lecture or leadership model ever did. Atticus Finch became more than a character; he became a compass. His quiet courage, his commitment to doing what was right even when it was hard, stayed with me. He reminded me of my father, and he reminded me of the leader I wanted to become.

When I completed my doctorate at the University of Nebraska-Lincoln, I stayed on as an adjunct faculty member, continuing to teach, research, and consult with organizations and leaders. I loved weaving real-world organizational needs into my classroom discussions and applying cutting-edge research to the companies I served. Invitations poured in. I facilitated in-services for departments across campus, partnered with interdisciplinary teams in engineering and science literacy programs, and spoke at extension programs statewide. Graduates of my classes invited me into their workplaces to teach what they had learned about valuing human differences. One former student's invitation to keynote at the Nebraska School Board Association blossomed into speaking engagements at multiple state and national conferences.

The research I began with my dissertation expanded organically. Initially, I sought to understand if we could teach someone the mindset of the chaplain in my early stories. But soon, new questions emerged: How does this mindset develop? And what is its ripple effect? As we uncovered powerful insights, colleagues urged me to publish. But I was busy teaching, coaching, and leading, caught between passion and bandwidth. Eventually, rather than submit peer-reviewed articles, I chose to write this book, weaving personal narrative, research, and the stories of others into something that felt urgent, needed, and alive.

In 2018, Chuck Schroeder and Dr. Connie Reimers-Hild from the Rural Futures Institute at the University of Nebraska, approached me to reimagine the Rural Internship program. While a brilliant idea to help drive economic development and a professional experience for young people in rural Nebraska communities, it was mainly a transactional internship experience for students. They wanted the program to offer more. They both knew about my teaching and the transformative experiences students reported in my courses, so they invited me to lead the program in an interim capacity that summer.

Part of the program involved a weeklong training that brought the students together, helped them get to know one another, and prepared them with knowledge about rural Nebraska communities. While many had experienced life in a rural community, most had never spent more than a day, if that, in one. Some thought rural communities had around 50,000 people. The communities these students would live and work in averaged 3,000 in population. Some were much smaller. The students had only met the community leaders during a short Zoom meeting.

That summer, I visited every community hosting our students. I observed. I asked questions and listened deeply to what was being said and what was not said, a skill I'd honed as an executive coach. I drew upon earlier experiences shadowing the best employees during my time in HR, believing that true understanding came not from job descriptions but from witnessing excellence firsthand.

The rural community experience was an intercultural experience for many of these students. Even if they grew up in a rural community, they were placed in a community very different from their hometown. I was surprised by the absence of team development between the community leaders and students. That felt like a big missing piece in the program. The other missing piece was acculturation for the students and the community leaders. Helping them understand and appreciate each other's cultural differences seemed critical to making the program effective. People and their stories matter. If you are being asked to move to a new town of 1000 people in rural Nebraska when you've grown up in the inner-city in another state, or another country, or near mountains or an ocean, adapting to life in a small, rural farming community can be quite isolating. And for those who came with personal baggage, it could be deeply frightening. I knew this from my own experience of moving to so many different places. I knew this from recruiting and helping acculturate nurses from the Philippines. I learned this from my experience with refugee resettlement in Lincoln and from working with international students at UNL.

This is not a backlash to the original program design. It is an acknowledgement that if you have not grown up in or experienced a rural community and no one on the program planning team has had those types of personal experiences, it is easy to overlook the psychological/social needs of the young people who are signing up for this program to earn money and gain professional experience. I reported my observations and suggested ways to enhance the opportunity for the students and the communities. We needed to do a better job of preparing students AND community leaders. We needed to be actively involved by coaching the whole team to create positive meaning from the many frustrations they would undoubtedly experience during their eight to ten weeks of working and living together. That would require each of them to go deeper, to look within, to be open to each other's differences, and see the differences as a gift to them because it will challenge them to grow, and to the whole community because it will help them come up with more innovative solutions. I knew that level of learning wouldn't happen without a deeper connection between the team members and our team with them. Thus, connecting them with one another early and often, and providing them the skills and tools on how to do it well, was essential. I took what I'd learned from my decades of professional experience, teaching, and research, and offered a process to elevate the program.

The feedback from students and community leaders about the intentional time I spent with each of them was overwhelmingly positive. I agreed to a long-term commitment on the condition that I'd also be allowed to continue teaching and doing research with the students and community leaders involved in the program. This would be a fellowship experience for not just students but for the leaders. Similar to fellowship experiences for physicians except in leadership instead of medicine. Thus was the birth of the Rural Fellowship program. I brought on two incredible graduate assistants, and we began to redesign the experience.

We introduced a bold new approach. First, we would pair international and domestic students whenever possible. Next, we would redesign the orientation to include students and community leaders. We adapted components of the previous orientation for students into an asynchronous online course, which participants would complete during the spring semester before the in-person orientation with the community leaders. The students were also required to meet with community leaders multiple times via Zoom to learn about the community and the specific project they were tasked with completing. We even encouraged the students to plan a visit to the community during the spring semester, if possible. We flipped the in-person orientation to an online format for cost-efficiency, but preserved deep, intentional engagement between students and community leaders. After the students moved to the community, they would do the orientation in person with the community leaders. The in-person orientation focused on team building. The two students and the two community leaders tasked with supervising them would work through specific activities that wove emotional intelligence and intercultural differences together to get them to connect at a far deeper level than the typical new employee orientation. We shipped them all the supplies in advance. We joined them to conduct the two-and-a-half-day orientation through Zoom or pre-recorded videos.

We collected qualitative and quantitative data. All participants took the IDI. We analyzed student journals, notes from individual interviews, team coaching sessions, program evaluations, and economic data to assess the impact of the student projects. The result I found most surprising was the resistance to doing the orientation. While resistance is inevitable, some, mainly community leaders, dismissed the team building, especially the components of emotional intelligence and intercultural differences, as unnecessary. But the data and the students' reflections proved otherwise. The students and community leaders who embraced the team development thrived. They had fewer overall issues getting along and often had greater gains in the economic impact of the work. And those who did the bare minimum during the orientation to say they did it floundered, and so did many of their projects. The community leaders who got it and really dove in saw a big difference even in the ways they connected with other community leaders after the students left. They took the lessons and activities and implemented them in their community. Many of those leaders recruited the students to their community. One example is a young man from Los Angeles who studied at UNL who has lived and owned a business in a rural Nebraska community for well over a decade.

True leaders, those who understood that leadership is about *people*, not just processes and tasks, recognized the value immediately. Before 2019, students had minimal preparation to work across differences or understand the deeper meaning of culture. After our redesign, students and community leaders spent the critical early days building authentic connections that would help them move from *forming* a team to *performing* as a team. The results were staggering.

In his study of highly effective teams, Tuckman found that teams that spent the time to do the forming stage well, moved through the storming stage (which all teams go through) in a way that enhanced their performance (the performing stage) so much better. However, teams that didn't invest time in the forming stage and instead rushed through the technical duties would get stuck in the storming stage. They would create norms that were often dysfunctional and would never really reach an enhanced level of performance. My decades of professional experience, teaching, and conducting research have proven that in our complex global environment, emotional intelligence and an intercultural mindset are essential to reach that performing stage. What we observed between the leaders who dove in and those who did the bare minimum led us to conduct a literature review to identify the key factors that made the difference.

During the COVID summer of 2020, while many programs shuttered, we adapted and persisted, proving once again that embracing diversity of thought and experience is a powerful survival strategy. That same summer, our team (Brooke Wells, Samantha Guenther, and I) conducted an extensive literature review. We called these leaders inclusive leaders because they exhibit a focus on people across differences that led to effective teams and better outcomes. In "The Path to Inclusion: Attributes and Impacts of Inclusive Leaders," we published our findings from more than 300 pieces of research. What we found confirmed that individual transformation must precede collective transformation. True leadership—the kind that is authentic, conscious, and inclusive—requires rewiring the default setting of the human brain. And as I've said before, transforming the leader's mindset is essential if the team is to be successful.

Brooke has a brilliant way of designing and conducting data analysis with the detail to ensure we are meeting the highest level of ethical standards in how we collect and use the data. I've learned that while my calling is in qualitative data analysis and my natural gifts are in translating our findings to the average person, none of it would be possible without having solid data. That is the gift Brooke offered and continues to offer our team. I invited Brooke to write this next section on how we designed our research.

Identifying the Attributes of Inclusive Leaders

Basically, a literature review is a summary of existing sources and scholarly work on a specific topic. Those who conduct literature reviews evaluate and synthesize the work of previous scholarly research to identify similarities and gaps, to inform future research on a topic. Our literature review built on foundational inclusive leadership scholarly work. We knew from early influential authors in the space, such as Drs. Ingrid Nembhard, Amy Edmondson, Avi Carmeli,

Roni Reiter-Palmon, and Enbal Ziv assert that inclusive leaders are individuals who foster inclusion through their words and actions by being open, available, and accessible to followers. In our work, we believed that an intercultural mindset and emotional intelligence were often at the heart of the inclusive leaders we experienced.

With the collaboration of Dr. Gina Matkin, we decided to explore how other scholars described inclusive leaders. The literature review answered three questions:

1. What are the attributes of an inclusive leader?
2. What are the impacts of an inclusive leader on followers?
3. How do the impacts of an inclusive leader on followers relate to Dr. Lynn Shore and colleagues' inclusion framework, which argues that inclusion is experienced when followers feel that they both belong and are valued for their uniqueness in groups?

We initially reviewed 330 academic articles. To be included in the analysis of the three research questions, each article had to meet two criteria. First, the article needed to focus on inclusive leadership, intercultural differences, diversity and leadership, or an inclusion framework or measurement. Second, the article needed to be theory- or research-based. These criteria were critical to helping us more efficiently answer our research questions. Ultimately, eighty-eight academic articles met our criteria, and we reviewed those in depth. By review, we mean we read, and re-read, highlighted, dissected, and used a thematic analysis process. We reviewed each of the eighty-eight pieces of literature for how the articles described the attributes and impacts of inclusive leaders. We've detailed our specific analysis process in our published article.

Our collaborative effort led us to identify seven attributes—the characteristics and actions—of an inclusive leader. While our literature review supported the way that early authors described inclusive leaders, we found that the majority of scholars writing about inclusive leaders had a more expanded view of what inclusive leaders do to make followers feel included.

Attributes of Inclusive Leaders:
  Authentic Leadership

- Balanced Processing
- Self-awareness
- Moral Perspective
- Relational Transparency

Ideals

- Empathy
- Humity
- Courage

Openness
Offers Follower Support
Collaboration
Commitment to Diversity and Cultural Competency
Being a Changemaker

One notable attribute for our team was the commitment to diversity and cultural competency. Throughout Dr. Fagan's life's work, understanding the backgrounds, lived experiences, and cultures of others has been crucial to her research and understanding of inclusion. While these undertones exist with the early scholarly work in this space, being able to highlight this commitment as an attribute affirms that for someone to feel included, a commitment to embracing and understanding human diversity and cultural competency cannot be overlooked.

We observed that the attributes are interactive and build upon each other. For one to develop as an inclusive leader, they cannot focus on only one of the identified attributes. Since conducting the literature review, our work with those interested in this approach to leadership has focused on actions and development across all seven attributes. The results of research questions two and three are detailed in our full literature review if you would like to explore them.

-Brooke Wells, PhD

The Rural Fellowship program was where we put what we were learning into practice. We began to apply our new knowledge in the way we intentionally trained and supported students and community leaders. I incorporated what I'd learned from the decade of teaching students at Bryan college, Doane university, and at UNL, using intercultural mindset development, activities to build emotional intelligence, leadership theory, and neuroscience, into the orientation. We carefully provided opportunities for self-reflection for students and leaders. We did the IDI assessment with each person, interviewed them, and reviewed their reflections, which were required as part of the program. The experience was powerful for so many people, even our team members. Samantha, who was from a farming community in Northeast Nebraska, and Brooke, who was from Topeka, Kansas, worked with me to redesign the orientation and facilitate it, along with the conversations with the community leaders and students. Samantha's role primarily involved working with students and community leaders. Brooke's role was to support Samantha and do our data collection and analysis. I've asked Sam and Brooke to share how the experience impacted them. We'll start with Sam.

"Serving on the Rural Fellowship team was a natural progression for me. Growing up on a farm in a rural community gave me the experience to relate to the rural community leaders and students newly experiencing those communities. Having pursued my degrees in leadership education and community economic development, I had the education, resources, and network necessary to bridge the gaps for the participants.

"I had gotten to know Helen while taking her leadership course the year prior, where she challenged me to grow from a Minimization mindset to reach Adaptation on the IDI. But there was also the opportunity to help her build a new kind of leadership development program. As a new graduate eager to be a leadership practitioner, I jumped at the opportunity.

"Over the next three years, our team coordinated dozens of students to support rural community leaders and projects. Our leadership development program leveraged a variety of learning methods, and we adapted often to accommodate in-person and virtual needs to support leaders across the entire state of Nebraska. Our team hosted a pre-training leadership academy and facilitated one-on-one and group conversations to foster team building, innovation, emotional intelligence, and intercultural competence. The goal was to set the teams up for success to drive meaningful change within their community. We measured leadership skills at the beginning and end to see how our work was impacting participants, and the continuous success each year made the end-of-summer celebration that much more significant. You can read more about the program specifics in a historical study from Brooke Wells and me, "The Development and History of the Rural Future Institute's Fellows Program" in the UNL Digital Commons.

"Any good teacher can tell you about the moments where they see their teaching truly hit home for their students, and it was such a valuable experience getting to drive that purposeful growth for our participants to take with them wherever they landed next."

Brooke details the challenges and learning she experienced below.

"A focus during my master's and doctoral programs was the concept of crucible moments. Crucibles, a concept driven by Warren G. Bennis and colleagues, are transformational moments that alter one's leadership journey and identity. I didn't know it at the time, but my assistantship with the Rural Fellowship program, which was initially financial relief, became one of my biggest crucibles. Knowing and working alongside Helen completely changed my trajectory and view of who I am as a leader.

"I focused on our research and program evaluation initiatives to learn more about the impact of the Fellowship Program both on the program effectiveness level and individual leadership development. While I developed a love for research and evaluation—my current career—during my time with the Fellowship Program, it was not without many learning moments. I learned about myself and worked on my intercultural competence. Helen, Sam, and I faced many challenges in a short amount of time, such as organizational disruption and restructuring, losing important Rural Futures Institute employees, and times of uncertainty for the program and our positions.

"Despite these challenges, I could constantly look to Helen for guidance and reassurance. She is an exemplar of inclusive leadership. She constantly worked to create a space where Sam and I felt valued and belonging. Our team was not only operating a fellowship program that used inclusive leadership as our framework, but we also lived through that framework every single day. I am a better person because of the immersive development I experienced through my assistantship. From Helen's coaching, the IDI, collaboration with our small team, research, and the opportunity to assist in Helen's leadership class, I experienced an incredible crucible moment. Who I wanted to be as a leader drastically changed. I wanted to be more like Helen; I wanted to become inclusive. I don't always get it right. But I am often drawn back to my time with the Fellowship Program and the lessons it taught me."

After Sam graduated with her master's degree and could no longer serve as a graduate assistant with the Rural Fellowship program, I interviewed and hired Jennifer Okoliko from Nigeria to do what Sam had done. Jenny, a nonprofit leader who had been part of the Mandela Leadership program, had spent time in Nebraska and was excited to return and pursue her graduate degree. As a wife and mom of two young girls whose husband and daughters would be arriving with her, I drew on my experiences as an international student and from working with the Filipino nurses we hired at Bryan to help ensure Jenny succeeded in her academic life and professional growth, as well as being a mom and wife in a new country.

Jenny is an infectious communicator who loves life and fills up the room with her boundless energy and gracious ways of engaging others. She was a natural fit to support the students and to co-facilitate the orientation with me.

Jenny shares her experience of arriving in the United States and learning to navigate life as a graduate student and a graduate assistant with the Rural Fellowship program.

"When I first arrived in the United States as an international student, I thought I was ready. I had the academic background, the drive, and what I believed was a strong sense of who I was. But it didn't take long to realize that thriving in a new culture takes more than that. I needed more self-awareness, and nothing prepared me for the discomfort that real growth and success would require.

"One of my first eye-opening moments came when Dr. Helen Fagan handed me a copy of *The American Ways*. That book gave me more understanding of American culture beyond what I'd seen in movies or heard from friends. It helped me see things I hadn't noticed and gave language to the unfamiliar practices around me. Surprisingly, it made me realize that to really navigate this new environment, I needed to understand not just American culture, but my own, and that awareness changed a lot for me.

"The next experience was with the IDI. I remember being stunned by my initial result when I landed in the Denial stage. I honestly thought the assessment was faulty because I believed in treating everyone the same and often said things like, 'I don't see culture; I just see people as human beings.' But I came to understand that this well-meaning mindset was part of the problem. If we ignore cultural differences, we miss the chance to connect more deeply and genuinely, and that was another pivotal moment of change for me.

"Helping Dr. Fagan teach the leadership class was a real turning point, as I wasn't just supporting undergrads in their learning, but I was doing my own learning, unlearning, and relearning in the process. Planning classes, leading and listening to discussions, and reading books helped me grow more aware of the cultural lenses we all bring to our work and relationships. I started to see cultural differences not as things to smooth over but as opportunities to connect and learn. One of my favorite memories was an activity in the class that drove home the point that to learn and grow, we must become comfortable with the uncomfortable. Those experiences have changed how I teach and relate to people. I have become more thoughtful about helping my students, my children, and everyone around me adjust and feel confident in their own identities, and to make space for others.

"Also, working in small Nebraska towns through the Rural Fellowship program showed me another layer of differences that wasn't about nationality or race, but geography, income, age, and lived experience. Sitting in community meetings, listening to people's stories, and supporting students on their projects broadened my view and provided focus for my research. I became interested in intergroup relations. I eventually started a peer group on intergroup humility and led workshops exploring different models to help improve this skill in myself and others.

"Looking back, I can't imagine what tangent my experience would have taken if I didn't have the mentorship and exposure I received early on in my journey. This has not only impacted me as an individual but also my kids who are growing up as Third Culture Kids who won't have to struggle with that identity because I can guide them through the chaos. It's also impacted the students I teach every semester, who will go out into the world and continue to do this work. It makes me recognize and appreciate the potential resources like these have to change the world one person at a time."

After Sam's departure and Jenny's arrival, it became evident that we needed to hire a university employee to create continuity in our connection with community leaders. We hired Darrell King, Jr., a young man from Chicago, whose role as our community engagement coordinator for the Rural Fellowship program was part of his duties as an employee of our college's extension and outreach.

I was intentional about how we onboarded Darrell, mostly because of my preconceived notions. I wanted Darrell to have a positive experience as a young Black man originally from Chicago working in a predominantly white university and serving leaders in rural communities that had minimal, if any, racial diversity in their community. Knowing what I knew about the brain and the experiences of young Black men in America, I was hypervigilant in protecting Darrell. I wasn't as hypervigilant with Jenny or even our other graduate assistant from Ethiopia, Fikadu, who later joined us, mostly because when they spoke, you could immediately tell they were international students. While I acknowledge this may be a bias on my part, my experience has been that some community leaders would receive international students, even if they are Black, differently than an American-born Black male.

Darrell is an energetic, fun-loving, never-met-a-stranger, always laughing and enjoying life kind of guy who wins people over during their first encounter with him. He exudes positivity, and you can't help but like him. All my worries were for not, because the community leaders welcomed him with open arms and engaged with him in the best possible ways. I commend Darrell and them for this. This is his story.

"My time as the community engagement coordinator for the Rural Fellowship program was a period of significant personal growth, understanding, and realization of impact. The effects of the program were far-reaching. Many people identified the projects and the students' stipends as the primary benefits. Indeed, projects such as building houses, working on community initiatives, and volunteering at various events were important. Students frequently mentioned the $5,000 they earned during the program. However, for me, the most profound impact was the connections formed within the communities and in the students themselves. The significance of the projects, combined with the relationships we built with community leaders, fostered bonds that contributed to mutual growth and understanding.

"During the last year of Dr. Fagan leading the program, we added a mentoring component. High school students on track to go to college partnered with the college students we'd placed in their community. This next layer of development allowed the high school students to serve in their own community and connect with college students; it expanded their perspective of the world. Since many of the students in the fellowship program were from different parts of the country and even the world, this enabled all of them to learn from one another, fostering growth even across generations.

"As a native Chicagoan, this was an eye-opening experience for me. One key takeaway from my time with the Rural Fellowship program was that agriculture is always present, whether in a rural town like Gibbon, a larger city like Lincoln, or a metropolis like Chicago. This understanding has deepened my connection with nature and helped me recognize my role within it. It has also contributed to my health by allowing me to connect more meaningfully with my food.

"Finally, one of my favorite parts of the program was working with our amazing team. None of us was originally from Nebraska. In fact, only two of our five team members were born in the United States. Yet we all converged in this beautiful state with the shared purpose of assisting in the growth of communities and their leaders and providing students with experiences that would help lay a strong foundation for their future. I believe we were all changed because of the way we worked together and the work we were doing."

Later, when Brooke transitioned to become a graduate teaching assistant, we hired Fikadu Alemayehu from Ethiopia. Fikadu joined our team to collect data that we would use in our research. Fikadu, who had been a professor in his home country of Ethiopia and a nonprofit founder and leader supporting youth education, training, and successful transition to work, was fascinated by our program. Fikadu, had left his wife and daughters in Ethiopia to get settled here first. It was tough to watch the impact of that decision on him and his daughters. Since, I'd experienced separation from my own father, I could relate to his daughters' needs to connect with him often. And the joy I saw on his face when he'd walk into the office while on FaceTime with them was delightful and warmed those deep recesses of my own heart and mind. Here are some thoughts from Fikadu:

"Working with Dr. Fagan as a graduate teaching assistant for the leadership class she taught and as a graduate research assistant on the Rural Fellowship Program at the University of Nebraska-Lincoln has been one of the most transformative and impactful experiences of my academic and professional journey.

"What made this experience uniquely meaningful began even before I set foot in the United States. I first met Dr. Helen through a virtual interview while I was still in Ethiopia, preparing to begin my PhD in leadership studies. Her interview was not just a formal screening; it was a welcoming conversation that acknowledged my background, values, and career vision. She asked thoughtful questions and gave space for my story to be heard. She recognized the path I had taken through education, nonprofit work, and youth development, and understood how my goal of studying in the US was not simply a personal aspiration, but a way to amplify my service to others.

"Upon my arrival in Nebraska, I was honored to begin working with Dr. Helen on the Rural Fellowship Program, a visionary initiative aimed at revitalizing rural Nebraska by connecting university students with real-life, community-driven development projects. The model was both practical and inspiring: students were given the opportunity to live in rural communities, receive mentorship, housing, and a $5,000 stipend, and contribute meaningfully through carefully selected projects that aligned with their skills and the needs of local leaders.

"Our team, including Dr. Helen, Darrell King, and Jenifer Okoliko, functioned with trust, purpose, and synergy. Together, we recruited students, designed placement strategies, conducted orientation and training, and supported students throughout their engagement in the field. I had the opportunity to travel across ten rural communities in Nebraska—from Scottsbluff and Sidney to Chadron, Gibbon, Grand Island, North Platte, and David City—visiting the students, listening to their progress, and building connections with local leaders. These visits were deeply insightful, offering not just data or outcomes but human stories of growth, challenge, and impact.

"The Rural Fellowship experience also shaped my understanding of community-based leadership, especially in rural American contexts. Coming from Ethiopia, it gave me new perspectives on how community values, civic participation, and student engagement can intersect to drive meaningful change. I witnessed students develop not only professionally but also personally, discovering new strengths, building relationships, and gaining clarity about their purpose.

"In parallel, my role as a teaching assistant for the leadership class gave me a front-row seat to Dr. Helen's educational approach, which blends intellectual rigor with emotional intelligence. Her leadership course was more than academic content—it was a space for deep personal reflection, growth, and healing. I saw students move from fear and confusion to confidence and clarity. Many shared personal stories, some involving trauma or self-doubt. Through structured reflection, inclusive dialogue, and meaningful assignments, they began to see themselves as capable leaders in an expansive and complex world.

"Looking back, working with Dr. Helen has shaped me in profound ways. I've gained not only technical skills in program management, leadership development, and intercultural communication, but also a deeper perspective, resilience, and purpose. It has shown me the power of servant leadership, the importance of listening deeply, and the lasting value of investing in people's growth.

"I will carry these lessons forward in all that I do—in Ethiopia, in Africa, and wherever life takes me."

My time teaching at UNL and leading the Rural Fellowship

program confirmed what I had long observed in both research and practice: the more diverse the group, the more intentional the leader must be. When people bring different lived experiences, identities, and worldviews to the table, leadership cannot be passive or routine—it must be deeply human. Leading like people matter isn't just a strategy; it's a commitment, and it starts with an honest, unflinching look within.

At the heart of effective leadership is a desire to create spaces where individuals can bring their whole selves, using their unique gifts, talents, and passions to pursue something greater than themselves. When leaders lead with that kind of purpose, people don't just follow—they thrive. And when people thrive, so does the vision.

Questions

1. What experiences or turning points in your life have challenged your assumptions about others and shifted how you relate across cultural differences? Think about a moment that invited you to see the world through someone else's lens. What changed in you?
2. Are you developmentally ready to lead inclusive change? Reflect on where you might fall on the IDI continuum. What would it take for you to move toward Adaptation, or to stay there?
3. How do you currently develop Psychological Capital (hope, efficacy, resilience, and optimism) within yourself and in those you lead? Consider which components come naturally and which require more attention.
4. In what ways are your current leadership practices shaped more by strategy than by human connection? How might integrating stories, emotional intelligence, or shared learning (like book dialogues) create deeper impact?
5. What systems, rituals, or routines in your organization support or hinder developmental growth across differences? What might it look like to embed continuous intercultural learning into your daily team culture?

Chapter 12

Healing and Belonging

*Flowers every night
Blossom in the sky;
Peace in the Infinite;
At peace am I.*
- Rumi

My beloved Agha, my father, once told me that grandchildren are God's reward to parents for surviving raising their own children. I didn't understand the depth of that sentiment until much later. But now, with the soft weight of my grandson's head nestled against my shoulder, I finally do.

When I think back to the delight on my father's face as he watched our sons play, even after all the heartbreak, exhaustion, and trials he and our mother endured raising me and my siblings, I see what he meant. He had precious little time with Alan and Jonathan before he passed, just one month during his visit to Virginia. But even in that sliver of time, I saw how deep his love must have run. That glimpse into his heart, seen now through the lens of my grandmotherhood, soothes a long-aching place in mine.

Beckett Alan Fagan, God's first wonderful gift to our family, was born on October 12, 2017. He arrived like a sunrise, a breathtaking gift from heaven. We had waited for him with such joyful expectation, our hearts stretched wide open.

Months earlier, on February 17th, the ordinary rhythm of life had quietly shifted. Scott was flying home from a business trip when Alan and Kacy stopped by our house. "What are you doing for dinner?" they asked casually. We decided to eat out, and I called Scott to meet us at the restaurant. Just as I hung up with Scott, my niece, Lindsay, called and told me she was pregnant. My heart leapt with joy. Lindsay and Alan are just four months apart in age. She and her husband, Steven, had gotten engaged the same day as Alan and Kacy, and their weddings were only weeks apart. The two young men had even made a playful bet: whoever had a baby first owed the other $100. Clearly, the women were ready for motherhood; the men, less so.

When Scott arrived at the restaurant, I greeted him with a grin. "Guess who's pregnant?" I teased. He looked at Alan and Kacy, his eyebrows raised. "You two?"

I laughed. "No, it's Lindsay." We all chuckled and spent the evening dreaming of baby shoes and family gatherings and congratulating Alan on winning the bet. But the real surprise was waiting at home.

Back at the house, Alan and Kacy handed us a small envelope. "A Valentine's gift," they said. I opened the letter. Alan had written from his heart about the lessons we had taught him, the strength he found in our love, and the courage born of being raised by an immigrant mother and a disabled veteran father. Then, in the final lines, came the reveal: the greatest way he could ever thank us was by making us grandparents.

The tears came fast, then the screams, the laughter, the jumping up and down. We framed that letter, a sacred artifact hanging in our bedroom, marking the moment we learned that Beckett was on his way. In one of life's beautiful synchronicities, Lindsay and Kacy gave birth within minutes of each other.

That same year, we welcomed another radiant light into our family, Liz, our second daughter-in-love. Jonathan married the love of his life on June 1st in a quiet ceremony at the Beverly Hills courthouse. It wasn't their original plan. In fact, it was their third. Tragedy rewrote their story. Liz's mother, the graceful and kind Esperanza, an immigrant from El Salvador, passed away unexpectedly on March 21st, just four days before the wedding they had so carefully planned. It was a time steeped in sorrow and loss that carved deep canyons in our hearts.

I'll never forget meeting Esperanza and her husband Victor over FaceTime. Liz translated as they told us not to worry about our son living so far away in Los Angeles, because he had found a home in their hearts. Esperanza cooked for Jonathan with joy, and he devoured her Salvadorian dishes like a son born to her table.

Months earlier, during a time of quiet prayer and reflection, I had a feeling—an unshakable knowing—that Jonathan would find love in Los Angeles. And when we met Liz and her parents and felt their warmth and embrace, I knew. He was home.

After Esperanza's funeral, Jonathan and Liz set a new wedding date for May 27th. But life had other plans again. On May 22nd, our dear friend Randy, more like a brother to Scott and me and a second father to our sons, was killed in a tragic car accident. The grief of those weeks was overwhelming. Jonathan and Liz postponed the wedding once more and flew to Nebraska for the funeral.

When it came time to decide what to do next, they chose simplicity over ceremony. On June 1st, they were married at the Beverly Hills courthouse with Liz's father and extended family by their side. We watched the vows from afar, grateful to be included by the grace of technology. A few months later, we held a joyful Nebraska celebration for them. Just weeks later, Beckett arrived.

That year was a mosaic of joy and heartbreak, laughter and loss. Through it all, we held fast to one another. And when I looked at Beckett, his smile, his tiny hands wrapped around mine, I knew the circle of love continues, wider and deeper than we could have ever imagined.

Becoming Nana and Papa for the first time when Beckett Alan Fagan entered the world opened a new chapter in our lives. But we had no idea then that just three years later, another chapter, one even more layered and deeply transformative, would be written with the arrival of our second grandson. Kash Steven Fagan was born on October 15, 2020, in Los Angeles, during the height of the pandemic. The world was shut down, hospitals were locked tight, and families met newborns through glass or glowing screens. But love finds a way. Within minutes of his birth, Scott and I were there, although not physically, through the miracle of FaceTime. We saw our grandson's tiny face as he was cradled in his mother's arms, brand new to the world. One photograph from those sacred first moments remains etched in my heart: Kash lying on his back, gripping Jonathan's index finger tightly, his eyes locked onto his father's as the nurses gently bathed him for the first time.

Because of COVID restrictions and the shift to remote work, Scott and I decided to live in Los Angeles for two months. We worked by day and held Kash in the evenings, letting the rhythm of bottle feedings, lullabies, and bedtime stories soften the noise of the world outside. It was a gift we hadn't expected, to fall into the ordinary, holy rituals of new parenthood side by side with our son and daughter-in-love.

Early on, Kash showed us he was unique. He learned words in three languages: English from his father, Spanish from his mother, and bits of Farsi from his Nana. His mind moved in brilliant, mysterious ways. And yet, by the time he was two years old, we began to sense that his needs might extend beyond multilingual milestones. Something wasn't quite connecting, and our hearts told us what tests would later confirm: Kash is on the autism spectrum.

It took two more years, until he was four, for Kash to be fully diagnosed and begin to receive the support he needed. The medical and special education systems in Los Angeles, like those in so many parts of the country, are overwhelmed. Waiting lists stretch for miles. Diagnoses are delayed. Services are hard-won. And for children of color like Kash, the wait is longer, the road steeper, and the system far more unforgiving. We've come to see Kash not only as our grandson, but also as a mirror reflecting a heartbreaking truth about America: the very children who most need protection are often the ones who are most overlooked.

Research shows that children of color with disabilities face significant disparities in how they are diagnosed, supported, and educated. They are more likely to be misidentified, less likely to receive early intervention, and far more likely to be placed in restrictive or punitive educational environments. In fact, Black and Latino children with special needs are disproportionately disciplined, suspended, and pushed out of the schools that should be nurturing their unique brains, not punishing their differences (Skiba et al. 2016; US Department of Education 2016).

For the sake of our children and grandchildren, we must do better. We must train teachers and healthcare professionals in ways that elevate their mindset and equip them to find creative solutions to complex needs. We must fund and expand programs that serve all children, especially those who, like Kash, speak with their eyes, their hands, and their hearts before their words catch up. Our love for Kash is boundless, and so is our commitment to the world he will grow up in. He has taught us that the most meaningful acts of love often come not in grand gestures, but in fierce advocacy, in refusing to let any child be invisible.

Wyatt Carl Wayne Fagan arrived on September 16, 2021, the third brilliant star in the constellation of our growing family. From the very beginning, he showed the same spark, the same mischievous grin, and fiery spirit as his big brother Beckett. But in one glance, you'd know, Wyatt is his father's twin through and through. He is Alan's mirror image with the same eyes, the same determined chin, the same way of filling a room with life.

Whenever all three boys are together, Beckett, Kash, and Wyatt, my heart stretches wider than I thought possible. In their laughter, in their sibling squabbles, and in their sticky hugs, I find a love so profound that it renews my sense of purpose. If there was ever a time I wanted to change the world, it's now, because of them. For them.

From the moment I learned each of our daughters-in-love was pregnant, I began whispering Farsi to their bellies, placing my hands over the curves of new life and vowing something sacred: I will teach them the language of my soul—the language I once buried.

I hadn't taught my sons Farsi. I wish I had, but shame, fear, and survival kept me quiet for too long. But with our grandchildren, both the biological ones and those who have adopted us as their Nana and Papa, I chose something different. I chose visibility. Connection. Legacy. So, from their first weeks, Nana spoke differently from everyone else. They learned quickly that when I ask for a *boos*, I want a kiss. That when I call them *Azizam* or *Joonam*, I'm wrapping them in love the way my parents wrapped me in their arms with those same words. My endearments are bridges, connecting them to the lineage and language of their Iranian American Nana.

They don't look like the grandsons of an Iranian immigrant, not by the world's narrow expectations, yet they are mine and I am theirs. We are stitching together something beautiful, something profoundly American and unapologetically Iranian. Nana and Papa are doing our best to raise them in a world that teaches them every human being matters and that the world is a rich mosaic, not a mirror. I want them to know the stories my parents and grandparents told me under the fruit trees in Iran. I want them to understand singing Happy Birthday in Farsi, and tasting the saffron-laced rice and *Ghormeh Sabzi* that once simmered in my grandmother's kitchen. I want them to know that their heritage isn't just something in the past; it's alive in our celebrations, in our recipes, in their roots.

In many ways, with each grandson's birth, I've been born again, too. The fifteen-year-old me, the one who arrived alone in a strange country, clutching trauma tighter than luggage, would never have dared speak Farsi in public, and worked hard to speak English without the faintest accent. Even the thirty-five-year-old me remained vigilant as a parent and avoided being "too Iranian."

But now, I speak Farsi phrases to our grandkids in grocery store aisles and at the park. I see the stares. I hear the questions in people's eyes. How does she speak Farsi and then turn around and sound so ...

American? And I smile. Sometimes, I even laugh to myself because I can. Because I do. Because I finally want to. Maybe it's age. Maybe it's becoming a US citizen. Maybe it's the moment Beckett first smiled up at me, and something inside whispered, *You belong now. Truly.* Maybe it's all of it—the letting go of fear, the claiming of joy, the choice to embrace every part of my story, even the painful ones.

Yes, the pain still lingers. The echoes of hate still reach me, even as recently as a few months ago, reminding me of every time someone told me, "Go back where you came from." Those moments no longer define me. They are chapters, not conclusions. And when I look at Beckett, Kash, and Wyatt, and the dozen other kiddos who call us Nana and Papa, each uniquely beautiful, loved, and whole, I know why I've held on all these years. Because I love who I am, and I love who I'm becoming through them.

In more than three decades of guiding leaders toward transformation, I've learned that true growth requires three essentials: patience, grace, and humility, not just with others, but with ourselves. For years, I yearned for this type of leadership development to be simple, linear, and even easy. I thought, as many do, that if I could just gather enough knowledge or find the right checklist, everything would fall into place. But then I began to understand how deeply culture shapes human behavior. Our brains' neurocircuitry requires ongoing training to reset its default from self-protection to the beautiful curiosity that comes from expanding our minds. That realization unraveled my assumptions and forever reshaped my approach.

People often come to me eager for a shortcut. "Just tell me everything I need to know about _____ group of people," they'll say. I now recognize that request for what it is: a well-intentioned but shallow attempt at mastery. Those who say it often sit at the stages of Minimization or Acceptance, good-hearted people who believe in fairness, but haven't yet dug deeply enough to see how their own story fits into the broader human narrative. I usually answer their question with another question: "Who are you as a cultural being?"

Most pause. Some stare blankly. Many respond with a shrug or a joke: "I'm a mutt" or "I don't have a culture." Others describe where they've lived, people they've known, or the languages they've picked up along the way. These responses are not wrong, but they're incomplete.

We live in a world that hasn't taught us to think of culture as something intrinsic, something rooted deeply in the soil of our identities. Instead, we're conditioned to see culture as a set of external markers: race, ethnicity, nationality, religion, age, and gender. We rarely reflect on how culture shapes our values, our beliefs, and our behaviors, or how it filters the way we see the world and the way the world sees us.

A compelling body of research in language acquisition shows that individuals who are illiterate in their own language struggle exponentially more when trying to learn a new one. The same holds true for culture: those who lack awareness of their own cultural identity are far less likely to empathize with or understand someone else's. Without cultural self-literacy, the journey toward cultural competence often ends before it begins.

This insight was one of many that led me to pursue a PhD. I needed answers to questions I could no longer ignore that lived at the intersection of personal experience, academic inquiry, and societal urgency. During my doctoral research, I interviewed people who had demonstrated a significant shift in mindset toward greater empathy, openness, and intercultural competence. I wanted to know what created that shift and what helped them grow. The answer surprised me in its simplicity and its humanity. They had faced difficult challenges that redefined their identity, and they had someone who stood beside them. Support was the catalyst. Support turned hardship into transformation.

When I first began interviewing participants, many of whom I had known for more than a decade, I worried that they might hold back.

Would they be real with me? Would they share the truth of their struggles? What I received was raw honesty, vulnerability, and a willingness to go there. Their stories changed me. I was no longer the same person who had started that research. What they gave me wasn't just data, but insight into the resilience of the human spirit. It deepened my passion to draw out potential in others and to help leaders, educators, and healers become more than they thought they could be. To become, in the words of my mentor, Dr. Fred Luthans, a bridge between scholarship and practice. He once told me, "If you're going to teach or consult, ground it in research. Help close the gap." That's what I've committed my life to doing.

This book is the embodiment of that commitment. It's not just theory, it's a guide, a challenge, an invitation. If you apply the principles to your school, your company, your place of worship, your community, or even just your family, I ask you to remember that **you must begin with yourself.**

You cannot expand your team's capacity without expanding your own. You cannot lead others to a mindset you've not reached. You can hire new people for your team, individuals who don't look, think, believe, or behave like you. If, however, you haven't examined your own lens, your own story, and your own unconscious behaviors, those innovative solutions you desire to achieve will remain out of reach. At best, you'll get along with your team and work together without the groundbreaking innovation you hope to bring into the world. At worst, you'll experience numerous challenges as a leader and an organization, without recognizing that the real solution lies within you, not outside of you.

In our increasingly interconnected world, I believe the most essential leadership quality isn't strategy or charisma or even intelligence. It's a mindset that's curious, humble, adaptive, and grounded in empathy. These are the qualities we need to solve the global challenges facing us today: food, water, health, education, and the environment.

To develop this mindset, we must be willing to look inward and ask ourselves uncomfortable questions. We must explore how our upbringing, beliefs, fears, and assumptions shape how we treat others, especially those who are different from us. Again, this kind of transformation takes courage. It requires vulnerability. It requires you to sit with questions such as "Whom would I not want my child to marry, and how does that influence my decisions as a leader?" Then you must bravely explore why. Until we make leadership development personal, nothing will truly change.

I believe to my core that human beings are designed for connection. I've seen it firsthand in healthcare, the field that drew me into this work. Healing, at its essence, is relational. A practitioner must connect to heal. A patient must feel seen to trust. An employee must feel valued to contribute. This type of leadership development involves connection and healing—connecting with the person within and healing the places where there is brokenness. When we heal ourselves, we are less likely to hurt others.

As a researcher, an educator, and a practitioner, my purpose is to help strengthen the connective tissue between people, starting with those who teach and those who heal. If I can help them connect more authentically with themselves, they'll be better equipped to connect with others from all walks of life.

Ultimately, that's what I want:

To help humans genuinely connect.

To move past the divisions that keep wounding us.

To walk toward one another with empathy, truth, and the hope that we can still change the world.

One heart.

One mind.

One story at a time.

In the thousands of conversations I've had over the past three decades, whether in classrooms, coaching sessions, or IDI debriefs, I've come to understand that this work is deeply personal. For most people, it isn't just a theory, a checklist, or a corporate policy; It's a feeling. A sensation in the gut that says, I belong here. I matter here.

Words like *belonging* and *mattering* continue to surface both in research and in lived experience. Rowe, Gardenswartz, and Cherbosque addressed this in their 2010 book, observing that leaders must meet two fundamental human needs, **ego** and **affiliation**, if they want to create environments where diverse individuals feel genuinely included. In other words, building a diverse workplace is not enough. To truly foster inclusion, we must build environments where people feel seen, valued, and connected.

Over a decade, asking two simple but profound questions has shaped my understanding of how people experience inclusion:

1. Think of a time you worked in an inclusive environment. How would you describe it?
2. Think of a time you worked in a place that wasn't inclusive. How would you describe that?

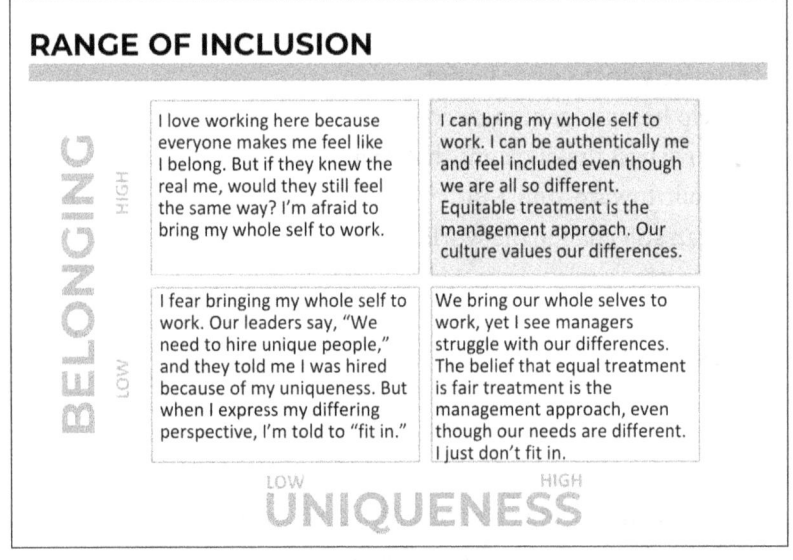

© 2018 by Helen Fagan.

The responses, always heartfelt, often tearful, have been a gift. The privilege of hearing these stories reminds me that inclusion is a human need.

When I administer the IDI, each person sits with me, sometimes nervously, sometimes eagerly, as we walk through their profile together. Some are stunned by what they learn. Others exhale, finally understanding parts of themselves they hadn't been able to name. But nearly all of them say something like I wish I had known this sooner. They tell me how it's going to change how they relate to their children, their coworkers, and even their in-laws, because creating belonging begins at home.

For me, this work is deeply personal. It's one of the most important values I want to pass on to my grandsons, Beckett, Kash, and Wyatt. I'm not their mother or father, but I'm their Nana, and when they spend time with me, we don't just have fun. They learn that they are valuable, and so is every other human being they will encounter in their lives, whether they look like them, behave like them, believe like them, or not. That is the greatest gift I can offer my grandchildren. It's the greatest gift I can offer my students, my clients, and anyone who walks through my life.

I've said it before, but this work is hard. Sometimes it downright sucks, but I've learned to embrace the suck, because I've seen what's on the other side. I encourage anyone walking this road to do the same. Growth doesn't come without discomfort. Transformation requires tension. If it doesn't challenge you, it won't change you.

Rewiring the default setting in our human brains to being open to differences isn't a weekend workshop or a checkbox but a lifelong endeavor. As our world shifts and as we evolve, we'll constantly encounter the unfamiliar. We're biologically conditioned to reject the unfamiliar, unless we learn to rewire the default (the innate impulse to be with the comfortable and the familiar) with curiosity, humility, and a desire to understand. As leaders, educators, healthcare workers, parents, and community members, we must engage in this work with the intensity of Olympians. We must lean into the discomfort and not shrink back. This isn't a sprint, it's a marathon. It's a lifelong athletic event for the heart and mind.

But here's the good news: there is gold at the end. Not the kind you hang around your neck, but the kind that radiates from your relationships. The gold is found in the richness of connection with people who once felt distant, foreign, or even opposed to you. The prize is the ability to hold space for conversations that once might have turned combative, and walk away with mutual respect, feeling heard and understood. I know, I know, it sounds like a dream, maybe even an unattainable one. But I urge you not to let the fear of imperfection stop you from reaching for it. Utopia may not exist, but striving for it will carry us farther than cynicism ever will. Margaret Mead captured this truth when she said, "Never doubt that a small group of thoughtful, committed citizens can change the world; indeed, it's the only thing that ever has."

So, for Beckett.

For Kash.

For Wyatt.

And for every soul who will come after us, let us strive. Let us stretch. Let us commit to the hard work, not because it's painless, but because humanity is worth it.

The Fagan Family 2024.

Since 2015, when Donald Trump first launched his campaign for the presidency, and again in 2024 and today, old memories have resurfaced, pulling me back to the anxious days of applying for US citizenship. I remember the gnawing pressure to ensure I was behaving, to leave no room for doubt that I belonged.

Between 2015 and 2019, I was invited to teach in Qatar by Dr. Janet Bennett, the founder of the Qatar Institute for Intercultural Communication (QIIC). In the late 1990s and early 2000s, the Qatar Foundation invited six prestigious US universities—Weill Cornell Medical College, Georgetown University, Carnegie Mellon University, Northwestern University, Texas A&M University, and Virginia Commonwealth University—to establish campuses in Doha. While many faculty and administrators were American, the student body and staff were a mosaic of nationalities from every corner of the globe. Teaching and connecting with people from over thirty countries was a profound privilege.

While I was honored to be among the handful of faculty members entrusted with intercultural training, a quiet sadness lingered beneath the surface. I grieved for what US campuses had lost by not having these brilliant international students learning alongside American peers. I grieved for a world that once was, when my father proudly welcomed engineers from across the globe to Iran, working side by side to discover and export oil. I longed for that time before Iran and America became adversaries. Throughout my life in America, that hostility has been a heavy cloak I could never quite take off. Nearly fifty years later, it still presses against my shoulders.

The weight of it nearly crushed me in 2018. After returning from Qatar, I landed at JFK Airport. As I stepped into the customs line reserved for US citizens, an officer glanced at my passport and waved me to a different line without explanation. My heart raced. My stomach turned. The panic I felt was primal, physical, an eruption of PTSD symptoms I hadn't anticipated.

"Why were you in Qatar?" the officer asked.

I explained that I taught leadership, emotional intelligence, and intercultural communication. I detailed how I had been traveling there yearly since 2015 at the Qatar Foundation's invitation.

He pressed further. "Did you visit Iran while you were there?"

"No," I answered. "I was busy teaching."

"When was the last time you visited Iran?"

"1978." I said.

"Do you have family there?"

"Yes. My mother, grandmother, aunts, uncles, cousins ..."

He left his booth, leaving me standing there in my fear. When he returned, he said, "Welcome home," and waved me through.

But my body had already absorbed the trauma. Physical pain replaced fear. I collapsed into a cab, checked into a hotel instead of my sister's house, and called her sobbing. She brought food and reassurances. By morning, the symptoms had vanished, confirming that the sickness had been born not of a virus, but of fear.

Since then—and especially since January 2025—I have lived in a state of near-constant turmoil. I believe in the promise of America, a nation expansive enough to hold multitudes. And yet, it is deeply painful to witness the actions and policies of those who believe that people like me do not belong. I want to speak up, but fear holds my tongue. I want to decry what I see happening in America, but the complicity of loved ones stings too deeply. Strangers embracing exclusionary policies is one thing; hearing the same from family, from friends, from those who tell me they love me but vote to sustain leaders who vilify me is another wound altogether. How does one reconcile this incongruence? That question has haunted my thoughts and conversations for years.

Through reflection, research, and countless sleepless nights, I've realized the answer lies in intentionally tuning into what's happening in my brain that is driving my reactions and thoughts. When threatened or frightened, System 1, my reactive brain, takes over. My System 2, the logical, reflective mind, is not accessible to me in the immediate moment. Knowing this, I quickly acknowledge it and give myself space. On some days, space is about taking a walk. Some days it is turning everything off and connecting with my grandkids. Some days, it is a combination of prayer, journaling, and meditation.

Economic insecurity, rapid change, and cultural shifts can trigger our self-protective, emotional responses that constrict our ability to reason and empathize. Friends sometimes confide their resentment.

"I only get into car accidents with illegals who don't have insurance."
"Mexican laborers underbid us because they don't pay taxes."
"My child lost scholarships because of affirmative action."

And while evidence shows otherwise—that immigrants pay taxes, that uninsured drivers span all backgrounds, that Black students still face immense barriers—fear keeps System 2 offline. Logic drowns under the weight of emotion. And so, the cycle of division continues.

In a recent Forbes article, *Outsourcing Emotional Intelligence*, the author reflects on how artificial intelligence is increasingly replacing authentic human interactions, particularly in the workplace. A poignant example of a long-time employee receiving an AI-generated anniversary email from her boss highlights a broader issue: emotional intelligence is being outsourced, and people feel the loss. Emotional recognition, unlike appreciation, lacks sincerity when it isn't rooted in genuine emotion. This growing trend is explored through an in-depth conversation with Joshua Freedman, CEO of Six Seconds. Freedman argues that each technological advancement alters our emotional and social dynamics, and we are now in what he calls a "global emotional recession." In their research during the previous five years, global emotional intelligence has declined by 8.6%. Evidence of this is present in the rising anxiety, burnout, and a marked decline in empathy and optimism, particularly among younger generations.

As leaders, we hold a significant responsibility not only in decision-making but also in shaping the culture of the environments we lead; environments that respect and value the differences our people bring into the workplace. As machine learning advances, if our ability to remain connected emotionally doesn't evolve, our brain's wiring and social programming will influence our judgments and actions, often without our awareness. However, by combining our understanding of the brain's wiring, developing emotional intelligence and cultivating an intercultural mindset, we can take the critical step in effectively managing our thoughts and immediate reactions, while also guiding those around us, whether peers or family members. This is what we call leading like people matter.

Questions

1. In what ways has becoming a parent or grandparent—or witnessing intergenerational love—shifted your sense of identity or purpose? How has this shaped the legacy you hope to leave?
2. What family or cultural traditions have you reclaimed or redefined as part of your healing or transformation? What role do these traditions play in how you express love or create belonging?
3. Have there been moments when your cultural identity felt like something to hide? What allowed you—or could allow you—to begin embracing that identity more fully and visibly?
4. How do personal stories of loss, resilience, and advocacy (like Kash's diagnosis and journey) invite you to examine the systems around you? What responsibility do you feel, as a leader or community member, to challenge those systems?
5. This chapter suggests that transformation requires both personal and systemic change. Where are you being invited to grow personally right now—and how might that growth ripple outward to your family, workplace, or community?

Chapter 13

Legacy

*This place where you are right now,
God circled on a map for you.*
-S. M. Hafiz

"Mom, Nipsey's been shot. Please pray." March 31, 2019. We were sitting down to dinner in Nebraska, gathered with our youngest son Alan and his family, when our oldest, Jonathan, called from California. His voice cracked across the line, trembling and urgent. My heart clenched. I knew who Nipsey was, not just a rising star in music, but a man who had become family to my son. This wasn't just news. This was personal.

Jonathan fell in love with rap music around age ten. He knew we wouldn't approve, so he listened in secret. When I discovered it two years later, I confiscated every album and declared it off-limits. I saw rap as noise, a bad influence, a culture I didn't want to shape my son.

Jonathan, even then, had the mind of a philosopher and the heart of a rebel.

"Why can't I listen to it?" he asked, his tone adamant and firm. "I like the beat. I don't even pay attention to the words."

I launched into my best educator's explanation about neuroplasticity, impressionable minds, and the dangers of absorbing destructive narratives. He listened quietly, then said something that stayed with me for years:

"Mom, just because something doesn't make sense to you doesn't mean it's bad for me."

I carried his CDs away in a box. But I carried his words even deeper.

As a leader, executive coach, and an educator, I had taught people to lean into ambiguity (the things that don't make sense), and to embrace the discomfort of not knowing as the doorway to growth. But it's a whole different challenge when the ambiguity and discomfort come from your child asking you to trust and explore with him. In hindsight, that moment marked a turning point for both Jonathan and me.

Jonathan's teenage years were difficult for both of us. He was brilliant, creative, and headstrong. His senior year nearly broke us both. My only goal was to keep him alive and out of jail long enough to make it to college. One March morning, after yet another suspension, I was in tears.

"I love you," I said, "but I'm not enjoying this season of life with you." Silence. Then I asked, "What do you want to do with your life?"

More silence.

"Okay," I said. "If someone invited you to something—something so meaningful you wouldn't be late, wouldn't miss it—what would it be?"

He looked up. "Music," he said. "Or basketball."

"Then find a way to make that your career."

A week later, he handed me a book from the school library, bookmarked to pages about audio engineering and music production. "This," he said, "is what I want to do."

He found Full Sail University in Florida. He enrolled in October 2004 and never looked back. By 2012, he earned two degrees: a bachelor's degree in Audio Engineering and a master's degree in Entertainment Business and Marketing. That same year, we helped him move to Los Angeles.

He started at Foot Locker. Eventually, he left the security of a paycheck to intern at music studios, chasing a dream. It paid off. He began working full-time with Nipsey Hussle. I won't lie; I was scared. He worked every day in "the hood," as Nipsey called it. But I was also proud. Jonathan had found a kindred spirit in Nipsey, a man determined to transform his community from the inside out. They were inseparable for more than three years. In the studio. On tour. At home.

They weren't just collaborators. They were brothers born to different mothers. Nipsey once said, "Moms, I was educated in the streets. Jonathan was educated in school." Their bond was forged in curiosity. They debated philosophy, spirituality, health, music. They dreamed wide and wild. Both were children of immigrants. Jonathan and Alan were raised in Nebraska, while Nipsey and his brother Sam hustled on the streets of L.A. It was a study in contrasts. And yet, they found common ground.

I remember visiting Jonathan in L.A. and sitting with Sam. I thought about the journeys that had shaped these young men. While I was driving Jonathan to basketball practice and Alan to flag football, Sam and Nipsey were selling T-shirts at the corner of Crenshaw and Slauson—now named Nipsey Hussle Square. Same country. Same generation. Different realities. But somehow, they all became family.

Jonathan and Nipsey devoured books together. Sometimes Jonathan would FaceTime me while he waited at Nipsey's house. Occasionally, I'd get to chat with Nipsey, sometimes even pray with him. He called me Moms. He told me how much he respected Jonathan. I told him the feeling was mutual.

Never in my life did I think a rapper would be my teacher. But Nipsey taught me that leadership doesn't require credentials. It requires commitment. I used to think leadership development would mostly come from formal education first, then experiential learning at work. But sitting in a studio in September 2018, watching as they filmed a documentary about Nipsey, I realized how wrong I was. I always knew education doesn't just happen in the classroom, and college doesn't guarantee wisdom. In fact, it can breed a quiet arrogance toward those who learned in different ways. Listening to Nipsey's collaborators describe his leadership, I heard the phrases I would use to describe exemplary leaders: courage, humility, openness to others, and a commitment to ongoing learning and growth.

After his death, more stories surfaced. Quiet acts of service. Scholarships. Community investment. A transformational servant leader. And I was reminded that I'm just as much influenced by the incomplete stories about groups as any other human. It's a daily decision not to fall into the trap of my System 1 brain.

Nipsey Hussle with Jonathan Fagan.

As leaders, we wield considerable influence, not just in our organizations but also within our families and communities. By integrating emotional intelligence, neuroscience-based strategies, and an intercultural mindset, we enhance our leadership effectiveness and actively build more inclusive and empathetic societies. This is a high bar, and this won't happen by reading a book, attending a workshop, or even a one-off retreat or conference. Managing bias is an ongoing journey that requires deliberate practice, emotional insight, and openness to learning. By committing to the work, we guide ourselves and others toward growth, empathy, and what we call intercultural maturation.

Let's consider how we develop bias and reflect on what we model for our children. We know that if those who have the most important influence on an adolescent's view of differences see them as a value-add, instead of a negative, the adolescent will begin to be curious about differences while appreciating similarities. Fostering open discussions about the appreciation of all the differences and similarities that make us human and consistently modeling empathy and kindness, shows a young person that there is value both in fitting in *and* standing out.

The key is in the *AND*. For instance, we celebrate the Christmas holiday with our family, *and* we attend our neighbor's Kwanza celebration. We aren't insulted when our Jewish colleague says, "Happy Holidays" when we run into them at the grocery store and our adolescent children are with us, because we realize the holidays they are celebrating are different than ours. We create space for our children to see us being curious and kind, instead of walking away and expressing under our breath how insulting it is that "Merry Christmas has been hijacked by those people." We live with a curious sense of wanting to understand and make our colleague feel valued for the things that are important to them, while we are perfectly okay with saying, "Merry Christmas" to a friend who also celebrates Christmas.

The ability to live in this space begins in our early teen years. The neuropathways we create during that season become the neuro-highways that will help us regulate our emotions with curiosity when our neighbor puts out the flag of a political party we don't align with, instead of being outraged that they could "support someone like that person." Research shows that children who grow up with siblings or family members who have a disability tend to be more empathetic and potentially mature more quickly. For them, individuals with disabilities have value and deserve the love and kindness of others. The exposure results in their brains not seeing disabilities as a threat.

Neuroscience research underscores the pivotal role of the amygdala, a brain structure deeply involved in emotion, threat detection, and unconscious social conditioning. Studies suggest that the amygdala does not inherently categorize individuals into ingroups and outgroups. Instead, it reacts to group-learned associations that we unconsciously internalize. For instance, heightened amygdala responses to individuals from racial outgroups primarily occur due to perceived threats that have been socially learned, not because of intrinsic differences (Hart 2000).

Crucially, research highlights that bias-related amygdala activity isn't something we are born with, but rather develops significantly during adolescence, influenced by social cues, environmental exposure, and socially ingrained assumptions about those who are different from us. It is during these formative years that young people begin to internalize biases deeply. During adolescence, there is a strong desire to fit in, and development of an identity separate from family members begins to form. The combination of these factors, along with the critical role family members and friends play in the person's life, can either increase or decrease the development of bias. Actively exposing adolescents to people whose lives are different from their own, while creating space for being heard and processing the big emotions that come with that age, can vastly impact the adolescents' perception of differences and their brain's development of bias (Telzer 2013).

But what if we didn't have such exposure or models of intercultural grace when we were young? Or what if we are unaware of our unconscious biases that affect the way we work and lead? We can work to develop our emotional intelligence, which is the ability to recognize, understand, and manage emotions, and is a powerful tool in bias reduction. Leaders with high emotional intelligence demonstrate greater self-awareness, allowing them to recognize their unconscious biases, their automatic learned responses, and their emotional reactions more effectively. This awareness enables leaders to govern their emotions, respond thoughtfully rather than reactively, and cultivate empathy toward those whose perspectives differ from their own.

An intercultural mindset, as defined by the Intercultural Development Inventory, involves the capability to deeply understand and appreciate cultural differences, transitioning from denial of difference to learning to adapt to differences effectively. Leaders with this mindset actively seek to gain cultural self-awareness and cultural differences in others' experiences, perceptions, and approaches without premature evaluation or judgment. This mindset fosters genuine curiosity, enabling leaders and their teams to engage authentically across cultural boundaries, further reducing the impact of the automatic, learned responses while fostering a team culture that appreciates the differences of everyone.

Practically, awareness is crucial. Recognizing that our brains are wired for bias and that biases are largely unconscious and socially learned allows us to approach bias with curiosity rather than defensiveness. This level of curiosity is important when reflecting on our own thoughts and actions, as well as those of others. Leaders who regularly engage in self-reflection and seek feedback to identify potential biases in decision-making processes are rewiring their default setting to be curious and inclusive.

Emotionally intelligent leaders who foster an atmosphere of openness and vulnerability, facilitating candid conversations with authenticity, do so because they regularly engage in self-reflection and seek feedback. They intuitively recognize that intention is not the same as impact. As humans, we often judge ourselves based on our intentions, while judging others based on their impact. Since humility plays a crucial role in bridging this gap, leaders who combine self-reflection with seeking feedback, emotional intelligence, and humility are often the ones who recognize that even when their intentions were positive, the actual impact on others may not align with those intentions. Instead of becoming defensive, they acknowledge the unintended consequences of their actions and take responsibility.

> By owning the impact, regardless of intent, they build deeper trust, model accountability, and create psychological safety within their teams.

Secondly, leaders must foster environments rich in diversity and inclusive interactions. Exposure to diverse groups and perspectives can reduce amygdala-driven biases over time. By deliberately creating opportunities for meaningful cross-group interactions within teams and families, leaders significantly mitigate unconscious bias. They encourage family members and colleagues to actively seek experiences and relationships beyond their immediate circles, utilizing empathy and social skills—core elements of emotional intelligence.

Thirdly, cognitive control strategies, such as mindfulness and deliberate perspective-taking, activate the brain's regulatory mechanisms (such as the prefrontal cortex), moderating the automatic responses of the amygdala. Emotionally intelligent leaders leverage mindfulness practices to enhance emotional regulation, allowing space for thoughtful consideration of biases and alternative viewpoints.

Lastly, emphasizing individual identity over group identity in your interactions can weaken stereotypical associations. Celebrate individual achievements and distinct qualities rather than defaulting to generalized group attributes. This personalizes interactions, disrupts automatic bias triggers, and aligns with emotionally intelligent leadership that values authenticity and individuality.

Even as university funding cuts and political backlash threatened our work, the seeds had been planted. In 2024, after years of quiet soul-searching, I decided to leave the University of Nebraska-Lincoln and pour myself fully into the vision I had been building all along. Helen Fagan & Associates was born. Samantha Guenther reached out to see if she could return and work with me part-time. Brooke Wells did the same thing. Since they had both been trained in the IDI assessment and could see its value in the numerous places they had now worked, lived, and experienced, they were glad to continue to use that knowledge and skill as part of our team. Cindy Conger and a handful of brilliant former students joined forces to ensure we could change our world by developing one leader at a time.

Together, we developed something revolutionary: a twelve-month guided leadership journey rooted in neuroscience, emotional intelligence, intercultural competence, and inclusive leadership theory. What made it revolutionary wasn't the time but how we designed it to be delivered and facilitated. Instead of a single workbook, we created monthly guidebooks, monthly reflections, and monthly actions. We combined this with individual and group coaching. This work is a marathon, not a sprint.

Our guided journey was born out of a desire to offer a self-paced, transformative experience that goes beyond a traditional development program. Through our years of working with clients, we observed that leaders rarely have time to enroll in traditional advanced learning programs, or the requirements of such programs do not align with their mental capacity to participate. However, we know that leadership mindset shifts require intentional and consistent time investment, so we wanted to meet people where they are and provide them with options to work on their development when they're able to make time. This solution enables individuals to receive new information, activities, and resources each month for one year, which they can use to continue their development at their own pace.

To create that solution, we tapped into the expertise of others in our network who were doing similar work. We invited several individuals to participate in writing activities, reflection questions, and resources. Over several months, we finally had a draft of our Twelve-Month Guided Journey—a journey that teaches and supports the development of the attributes of inclusive leaders, as well as the components of emotional intelligence for managing differences. Our initial participants reported how these activities have challenged them to think in new ways and encouraged them to reflect on how their personal experiences have shaped them.

For those who want to dive into the hard work, we also offer individual coaching to deepen reflection and accountability, as well as group coaching to support teams or groups working toward their collective strategic goals. In these instances, we implement measurement tools to test the effectiveness of the journey in growing transformative leaders.

From our research with groups from a variety of sectors and

leaders at all levels, we know that those who have developed to the level of intercultural grace have done so intentionally and through consistent effort. Through our year-long program, we have collected and analyzed data that shows developing intercultural grace is not only possible but has a powerful impact on individual leaders, their teams, and their organizations. We've been able to assess, coach, challenge, and support the growth and development of a few hundred over the last few years, and that number is expanding.

We launched our first cohort of twenty-one leaders across three organizations with individual coaching, group sessions, monthly packets—the full experience. The results were astonishing: statistically significant improvements on the IDI assessments, and an average 116% increase in goal attainment. A second cohort, without the individual coaching touchpoints, struggled to sustain momentum, a lesson we swiftly integrated into future designs. Through it all, one truth became undeniably clear: **Transformation requires connection.** Monthly engagement is essential. One leader recently said, "I came into this skeptical as a white male leader. But the readings, the reflections, the coaching—they made me a better human. I wish I'd known this at the start of my career. I would have been a better leader. A better father. Now, I can be a better grandfather."

Another shared, "The impact on me and my organization has been powerful. The reflections and activities are directly relevant to the work we do every day."

Leaders, we ask you to consider what talent, what growth, what innovation, or opportunity you are leaving on the table because you don't recognize the unconscious biases that are limiting you and your organization. What is it worth to you to change not just your team but your community and the world? We need leaders who tap into the power of difference rather than reject it out of fear. People matter too much for us to do any less.

Because people matter.

That is our vision: to change the world—one leader, one heart, one mind—at a time.

Questions

1. Have you ever dismissed or misunderstood something important to someone you love—like music, culture, or belief—because it didn't make sense to you? What would it look like to revisit that experience with openness and curiosity?

2. In what ways has someone unexpected—like Nipsey was to me—become a teacher in your life? How did that person challenge or expand your understanding of leadership, wisdom, or community?

3. The chapter emphasizes how bias is learned and can be unlearned through intentional exposure and empathy. What early messages shaped your own unconscious biases? How are you actively working to rewire those narratives today?

4. When have you experienced a disconnect between your intention and the impact of your actions as a leader, parent, or community member? How did you respond, and what did you learn about emotional intelligence in the process?

5. I write about the creation of a leadership journey grounded in neuroscience, intercultural maturation, and emotional intelligence. What kind of legacy are you building through your leadership? How will you ensure that people—especially those different from you—feel like they matter?

Epilogue

October 24, 2022

We were getting ready for bed when the phone rang. Scott answered, and I could tell by the way he froze that something was wrong. His younger brother, Steve, was on the other end. Steve's voice was shaky. They'd been playing pool in their weekly billiards league when our son, Alan, suddenly hit the floor hard. A seizure. A bad one.

The ambulance was already on its way. Steve had already called Alan's wife, Kacy, to tell her what was going on. Since it was late and the boys were asleep, we knew someone needed to be at their house so she could go to the emergency room. Scott and I acted quickly without words. He dropped me off at their house and drove Kacy to the hospital.

I wish I could say Alan was treated with urgency and compassion. He wasn't. The ER doctor barely looked at him before making assumptions. He saw a man with tattoos, coming from a pool hall, and immediately zeroed in on the idea of substance abuse. The questions weren't about symptoms or possible head trauma. They were laced with judgment: Did he drink? Was he high? Had this happened before? They conducted very minimal tests. No scans. Just a dismissal and a referral to a neurologist. And then he sent Alan home.

But here's the truth about Alan: he was an athlete in high school and college. Rarely sick. Introverted, soft-spoken, deeply loyal. He still hangs out with the same handful of friends he grew up with. He loves his wife, adores his boys, and finds joy in doing anything with his hands. He'd made his own backyard smoker and loves smoking meat. Drugs and alcohol abuse have never been part of his story. But tattoos and assumptions apparently were enough for a doctor to miss that.

Getting in to see a neurologist in Lincoln isn't easy. And before he was able to be seen again, it happened again.

A few weeks later, while we were gathered as a family in our home watching a Nebraska football game, Alan had another tonic-clonic seizure. One moment he was sitting next to us, the next he was convulsing. I screamed; a guttural, panicked sound that came from a place I didn't know existed in me. He was biting his tongue and had blood in his mouth. I wedged my fingers between his jaws to stop him from biting through it. The force of his bite was so strong that I bruised my thumb and index finger. I didn't care. My only thought was to keep him safe. Protect him.

Kacy followed the ambulance to the hospital. We waited for Kacy's parents to come and get the boys, then Scott and I both went to the hospital. I didn't ask, I told the ER team that we weren't leaving until they ran proper tests. The doctor glared, but I didn't blink. I've learned how to stand my ground. They admitted Alan and ran the tests. And yet—nothing. No growths. No lesions. No stroke. No known cause. They again recommended he follow up with a neurologist. We explained we were trying. In the meantime, they prescribed Keppra, a common anti-seizure medication. But it hit Alan hard. He became foggy, slow, detached. Not himself.

Eventually, through the help of physician friends and referrals by the right people, Alan got into the Mayo Clinic. It took time, persistence, and a whole lot of effort. That's where they finally got some answers. Alan has late-onset epilepsy disorder—no known origin. No trauma, no metabolic issues. Just life, handing him this unexplainable thing.

Under Nebraska law, you must be seizure-free for ninety days to drive. For nearly a year, Alan would make it to day eighty-nine, ninety, ninety-one, and then seize. The cycle repeated. So, Chanse, a bonus son to us, Scott and I, and other family members became his drivers. To work. From work. To appointments. It took a village. We were all grateful for our village, which included Kacy's amazing parents.

One day, Alan said quietly, "I hate this. I never imagined being in my thirties and having my parents drive me around." I could hear the grief in his voice. "This is what family does," I reminded him. "I'd drive you for the rest of your life if you needed me."

Alan had finally gone well beyond the ninety-day requirement. He was driving again and slowly reclaiming his freedom. Around that time, I found a golf cart for sale in a nearby town. I wanted to surprise Scott for Father's Day. We keep a camper near a lake where the family gathers, and the golf cart would be perfect for those slow summer weekends.

Alan offered to go with me to pick it up. We loaded the trailer and hit the highway. It was a beautiful day: light conversation, music humming beneath our voices. Then, in the span of seconds, everything changed. Out of the corner of my eye, I saw his body tense. The seizure began. His foot slammed the gas pedal, and we shot forward. We sped up way past the seventy miles per hour speed limit. The truck swerved. I grabbed the wheel with one hand, his collar with the other, trying to steady his flailing head as it slammed against the truck's metal frame. My body was in fight-or-flight, but somewhere deep inside me, the tools I'd learned in my Mindfulness-Based Stress Reduction (MBSR) training kicked in. I took a deep breath and focused on the present moment.

I let go of Alan long enough to shift the truck into park, kill the ignition, and guide us safely off the road. We drove down the grass on the side of the road for what seemed like forever, but likely four or five minutes. The truck finally came to a rolling stop. I called 911 as a sheriff's car was already pulling up behind us. I'm guessing someone had seen us swerving and called 911.

I jumped out of the truck while talking to the 911 operator, ran to the driver's side, and opened Alan's door. I wanted to make sure his tongue wasn't blocking his airway. I told the sheriff what was happening. Alan was unconscious, slowly coming to. I hung up with the 911 operator and quickly called Scott. The paramedics arrived and took over. Since we were only ten minutes from home, Kacy and Scott got there very quickly.

The sheriff looked me in the eye and said, "You're our hero of the day." I shook my head. "No. I'm just a mom trying to keep her son alive."

That seizure triggered another visit to Mayo and a new plan. Alan would need a dental appliance to keep his airway open at night. He needs the dental device to pull his lower jaw forward to improve oxygen to his brain.

As of this writing, Alan has been seizure-free for more than seventeen months. He still takes anti-seizure meds twice a day. He doesn't drink alcohol and hasn't since the first seizure. He's learned how to live with this disorder instead of fighting against it. What's been most joyful is watching his personality come back. Early on, there were changes that scared us: fogginess, memory lapses, and a short fuse. We now know it was partly the seizures, partly the meds. But today, his laughter has returned. His wit. His mischievous ways.

When this all began, I had to wrestle with old wounds. Watching Alan dismissed by healthcare professionals brought back painful memories of my father's mistreatment. The same helplessness. The same rage. But this time, I journaled. I talked with my therapist. We talked as a family. I processed. Instead of blowing up at the doctor the way I had the nurse, I remained calm and firm. I held my ground and I called them out on the stereotyping with the persistence and resolve that has driven me in this work for three decades.

"Alan is lucky to have you," a dear friend said. "You know how the healthcare system works. You know how to fight for him. Can you imagine how many people around the country experience the same thing and have no one to advocate for them, and don't know what they can do in situations like these?"

I do, actually, and that's why I keep doing the work. While I can respect that healthcare providers are being pulled in many directions and resources are being removed for the average person, I also firmly believe there is something we can do about it, that we *must* do about it. Because people matter.

Friday, June 13, 2025

The day had been full, and I was going from one thing to another. By that night, I was exhausted and sat down to catch my breath. I thought I'd see what was going on in the rest of the world. Never in my wildest dreams did I expect what I saw.

"Isreal Launches Attack on Iran, Stoking Fears of All-Out War," the headline read.

My heart stopped.

Tehran.

My mother lives there. So do my brother and his family. Most of my extended family. I grabbed my phone. It took two tries, but I reached my mom on FaceTime. She'd just woken up. It was early Saturday morning there. They were okay. Shaken. But okay.

Then the lines went dead.

For more than ten days, we couldn't get through. I tried. Everyone tried. My uncle in England. Siblings in the US. The internet was down in Iran. I was spiraling. Sunday, June 22, was my mom's eightieth birthday, and I couldn't even hear her voice. We celebrated anyway. I cooked Iranian spaghetti the way she taught me. We bought a cake. We sang "Happy Birthday" in English and Farsi. We filmed it and promised ourselves we'd send it once the internet was back.

That same night, the US bombed Iran.

It felt like three world leaders, all old men, had decided to have a cockfight, and innocent people were paying the price. That's what I wrote in my journal.

I've learned that if I can get the chaos out of my head and onto paper, it stops holding me hostage. To get through the twelve days that felt like twelve weeks, I gave myself permission to grieve a few minutes each day. Then I got up and kept going.

My MBSR training taught me that pain is inevitable, but suffering is optional. Pain is what happens to us. Suffering is what we perpetuate when we relive it over and over. So, I chose to anchor myself in the present. I still get hijacked by emotion, but now I recognize the hijack when it happens. I pause. I breathe. I remember who I want to be.

I may have a PhD and decades of experience, but I am still learning every single day how to show up with intention. How to pause before reacting. How to quiet the primal, protective instincts of my unconscious, emotionally charged System 1 brain, and instead invite in the slower, wiser voice of System 2. This is the lifelong practice: choosing being present with, and wanting to protect, ourselves and our loved ones, reflection and empathy guiding our reaction, discomfort of pushing myself to grow alongside what is comfortable.

This is the work I'm inviting you into.

It is not easy work. It will stretch you. It will require courage, persistence, and a willingness to turn inward again and again. But it is necessary—because without it, we risk becoming numb. We risk outsourcing our empathy to algorithms, hardwiring ourselves to stereotype, to lash out, to shut down. And in doing so, we strengthen the primitive parts of our brains while starving the parts capable of compassion, connection, and higher reasoning.

If we want a different world, one marked by understanding instead of division, we must begin by transforming ourselves. As my mother always says, "As long as I have breath, I need to keep learning because I am a work in progress."

So am I.

So are you.

Let us do this work, not just for ourselves, but for the people we love. For the future we hope to build. For the kind of humanity that remembers we are wired to protect, yes, but also to connect and love.

So today, lead like people matter. Do your best. Then wake up and do it again tomorrow.

Walking with my grandmother in Hyde Park, London.

Bibliography

Acheson, Kris, and Schneider-Bean, S. 2018 "Representing the Intercultural Development Continuum as a Pendulum: Addressing the Lived Experiences of Intercultural Competence Development and Maintenance." *European Journal of Cross-Cultural Competence and Management*. **https://hubicl.org/publications/3/1**

Agency for Healthcare Research and Quality. 2004. *Setting the Agenda for Research on Cultural Competence in Health Care: Introduction and Key Findings*. http://www.ahrq.gov/research/findings/factsheets/literacy/cultural/index.html

Agency for Healthcare Research and Quality. 2016. *2015 National Healthcare Quality and Disparities Report and 5th Anniversary Update on the National Quality Strategy. Agency for Healthcare Research and Quality*. https://www.ahrq.gov/sites/default/files/wysiwyg/research/findings/nhqrdr/nhqdr15/2015/index.html

Al-Amin, Mona, et al. 2022. "Is There an Association Between Hospital Staffing Levels and Inpatient COVID-19 Mortality Rates?" *PLOS ONE*, 17 (10): 2022, e0275500. https://doi.org/10.1371/journal.pone.0275500.

Allen, Jacqui. 2010. "Improving Cross-cultural Care and Antiracism in Nursing Education: A Literature Review." *Nurse Education Today*, 30: 314-320.

Altshuler, L., Sussman, N. M., and Kachur, E. 2003. "Assessing Changes in Intercultural Sensitivity Among Physician Trainees Using the Intercultural Development Inventory." *International Journal of Intercultural Relations*, 27: 387-401.

"Atomic Education Urged by Einstein: Scientists in Plea for $200,000 to Promote New Type of Essential Thinking." 1946. *The New York Times*, May 25.

Avey, James B., Reichard, Rebecca J., Luthans, Fred, and Mhatre, Ketan H. 2011. "Meta-analysis of the Impact of Positive Psychological Capital on Employee Attitudes, Behaviors, and Performance." *Human Resource Development Quarterly*, 22: 127-152.

Ayas, H. M. (2006). "Assessing Intercultural Sensitivity of Third-year Medical Students at The George Washington University." PhD diss. Dissertation Abstracts International, 67 (10) (UMI No. 3237032).

Bandura, Albert. 1994. *Self-Efficacy: The Exercise of Control*. Academic Press: 36.

Bass, Bernard M., and Avolio, Bruce. J., eds. 1994. *Improving organizational effectiveness through transformational leadership*. Sage Publications.

Bass, Bernard M., and Riggio, Ronald E. 2005. *Transformational leadership* (2nd ed.). Lawrence Erlbaum Associates.

Batalova, Jeanne. 2025. *Frequently Requested Statistics on Immigrants and Immigration in the United States*. Migration Policy Institute. https://www.migrationpolicy.org/article/frequently-requested-statistics-immigrants-and-immigration-united-states

Bednarz, Hedi, Schim, Stephanie, and Doorenhos, Ardith. 2010. "Cultural diversity in nursing education: Perils, pitfalls, and Pearls." *Journal of Nursing Education*, 49 (5): 253-260.

Bennett, Milton J. 1986. "A Developmental Approach to Training for Intercultural Sensitivity." *International Journal of Intercultural Relations*, 10: 179-196.

Bennett, Milton J. 1993. "Towards Ethnorelativism: A Developmental Model of Intercultural Sensitivity." *Education for the Intercultural Experience*, 2nd ed., edited by R. Michael Paige. Intercultural Press: 21-71.

Bennett, Milton. J. 2004. "Becoming Interculturally Competent." In *Toward Multiculturalism: A Reader in Multicultural Education*, edited by Jamie S. Wurzel. Intercultural Resource Corporation: 62-77.

Bennett, Milton J. 2017. *Development Model of Intercultural Sensitivity*. IDR Institute. https://www.idrinstitute.org/wp-content/uploads/2019/02/DMIS-IDRI.pdf

Betancourt, Joseph R. 2003. "Cross-cultural Medical Education: Conceptual Approaches and Frameworks for Evaluation." Academic Medicine, 78 (6): 560-569.

Blau, Peter M. 1964. *Exchange and Power in Social Life*. John Wiley.

Bryan College of Health Sciences. 2011. *Employee Requirement for Annual Completion of Diversity-Related Activities*. College Policies and Practices.

Bryman, Alan. 2008. *Social Research Methods*, 3rd ed. Oxford University Press.

Bureau of Health Workforce. 2024. "State of the U.S. Health Care Workforce Report 2024." Health Resources and Services Administration, November. https://bhw.hrsa.gov/sites/default/files/bureau-health-workforce/state-of-the-health-workforce-report-2024.pdf.

Cacioppo, John T., & Patrick, William. 2008. Loneliness: Human Nature and the Need for Social Connection. W.W. Norton & Company: 123.

Campinha-Bacote, Josepha. 2002. "The Process of Cultural Competence in the Delivery of Healthcare Services: A Model of Care." *Journal of Transcultural Nursing*, 13: 181-184.

Chekroud, Adam M., Everett, Jim A. C., Bridge, Holly, and Hewstone, Miles. 2014. "A Review of Neuroimaging Studies of Race-related Prejudice: Does Amygdala Response Reflect threat?" *Frontiers in Human Neuroscience*, 8:179. https://doi.org/10.3389/fnhum.2014.00179

Christopher, John C., and Hickinbottom, Sara. 2008. "Positive Psychology, Ethnocentrism, and the Disguised Ideology of Individualism." *Theory & Psychology*, 18 (5): 563-589.

Choi, Yoonsun, et al. 2013. "Bicultural Socialization, Ethnic Identity, and American Identity Development among Asian American Adolescents." *Journal of Youth and Adolescence*, 42 (2): 210–227.

Comer, Linda, Whichello, Ramona, and Neubrander, Judy. 2013. "An Innovative Master of Science Program for Development of Culturally Competent Nursing Leaders." Journal of Cultural Diversity, 20 (2): 89-93.

Connerly, Mary L., and Pederson, Paul B. 2005. *Leadership in a Diverse and Multicultural Environment*. Sage Publications: 2.

Coutu, Diane. 2002. "How Resilience Works." *Harvard Business Review*, 80: 46-50, 52, 55.

Creswell, John W. 2009. *Research design: Qualitative, Quantitative, and Mixed Methods Approaches*, 3rd ed. Sage Publications.

Creswell, John W. 2013. *Qualitative Inquiry and Research Design: Choosing Among Five Approaches*, 5th ed. Sage Publications.

Creswell, John W., and Plano Clark, Vicki L. 2011. *Designing and Conducting Mixed Methods Research*, 2nd ed. Sage Publications.

Cross, Terry L., Bazron, Barbara J., Dennis Karl W., and Isaacs, Mareasa R. 1989. *Towards a Culturally Competent System of Care*, Vol. I. Georgetown University Child Development Center, CASSP Technical Assistance Center.

Cunningham, William. A., Johnson, Marcia K., Raye, Carol L., Gatenby, J. Chris, Gore, John C., and Banaji, Mahzarin R. 2004. "Separable Neural Components in the Processing of Black and White Faces." *Psychological Science*, 15 (12): 806–813. https://doi.org/10.1111/j.0956-7976.2004.00760.x

de Leon Siantz, Mary Lou. 2008. "Leading Change in Diversity and Cultural Competence." *Journal of Professional Nursing*, 24 (3): 167-171.

de Leon Siantz, Mary Lou, & Meleis, Afaf. 2007. "Integrating Cultural Competence into Nursing Education and Practice: 21st Century Action Steps." *Journal of Transcultural Nursing*, 18(1suppl): 86S-90S.

Douglas, Marilyn K., Pierce, Joan U., Rosenkoetter, Marlene, Pacquiao, Dula, Callister, Lynn C., Hattar-Pollara, Marianne, Lauderdale, Joan, and Purnell, Larry. 2011. "Standards of Practice for Culturally Competent Nursing Care: 2011 update." *Journal of Transcultural Nursing*, 2: 317-333.

Dreachslin, Janice L. 2007. "The Role of Leadership in Creating a Diversity-sensitive Organization." *Journal of Healthcare Management*, 52: 151-155.

Emerson, R. M. 1976. "Social Exchange Theory." *Annual Review of Sociology*, 2: 335-362.

Erdogan, Berrin, and Liden, Rober C. 2002. "Social Exchanges in the Workplace: A Review of Recent Developments and Future Research Directions in Leader-member Exchange Theory." In *Leadership (Research in Management)*, edited by Linda. L. Neider and Chester A. Schriesheim Greenwich. Information Age Publishing: 65-114.

Exec. Order No. 13,166, 28 C.F.R. § 42.104(b)(2), reprinted at 65 FR 50121 (2000).

Fagan, Helen. "PsyCap and Impact on the Development of Intercultural Insensitivity Development in Healthcare Educators: A Mixed Methods Study." Unpublished manuscript, University of Nebraska-Lincoln. 2014.

Fagan, Helen A. S., Guenther, Samantha, and Wells, Brooke, 2022. "The Path to Inclusion: A Literature Review of Attributes and Impacts of Inclusive Leaders." *Journal of Leadership Education*, January. https://drive.google.com/file/d/1_r-NGnkKBhpu4cr BZP1M4w3uEJ51bff3/view

Fail, Helen, Jeff Thompson, and George Walker. 2004. "Belonging, Identity and Third Culture Kids: Life Histories of Former International School Students." *Journal of Research in International Education*, 3, no. (3): 319–338.

Fortier, Julia P., and Bishop, Dawn. 2003. "Setting the agenda for research on cultural competence in health care: Final report." US Department of Health and Human Services Office of Minority Health and Agency for Healthcare Research and Quality.

Gardenswartz, Lee, Cherbosque, Jorge, and Rowe, Anita. 2010. *Emotional Intelligence for*

Managing Results in a Diverse World: The Hard Truth About Soft Skills in the Workplace. Nicholas Brealey Publications: 2.

Giberson, Tomas R., Resick, Christian J., and Dickson, Marcus W. 2005. "Embedding Leader Characteristics: An Examination of Homogeneity of Personality and Values in Organizations." *Journal of Applied Psychology,* 90: 1002-1010

Giger, Joyce N, & Davidhizar, Ruth. 2002. "The Giger and Davidhizar Transcultural Assessment Model." *Journal of Transcultural Nursing,* 13(3): 185-188.

Giger, Joyce N., Davidhizar, Ruth., Purnell, Larry. Harden, J. Taylor, Phillips, Janice, & Strickland, Ora. (2007). "American Academy of Nursing Expert Panel Report: Developing Cultural Competence to Eliminate Health Disparities in Ethnic Minorities and Other Vulnerable Populations." *Journal of Transcultural Nursing,* 18 (2): 95-102.

Guenther, Samantha, and Wells, Brooke. 2020. "The Development and History of the Rural Future Institute Fellows Program." Department of Agricultural Leadership, Education and Communication: Dissertations, Theses, and Student Scholarship. https://digitalcommons.unl.edu/cgi/viewcontent.cgi?article=1116&context=aglecdiss

Haggis, Paul, dir. *Crash*: Lionsgate Films, 2004.

Hall, Edward T. 1973. *The Silent Language.* Doubleday.

Hammer, Mitchell. R. 2009. "The Intercultural Development Inventory." In *Contemporary Leadership and Intercultural Competence,* edited by Michael A. Moodian Thousand Oaks, CA: Sage Publications: 203-217.

Hammer, Mitchell R. 2011. "Additional Cross-cultural Validity Testing of the Intercultural Development Inventory." *International Journal of Intercultural Relations,* 35: 474-487.

Hammer, Mitchell R. 2012. "The Intercultural Development Inventory: A New Frontier in Assessment and Development of Intercultural Competence." In *Student Learning Abroad,* edited by Kris H. Lou, R. Michael Paige, and Michael Vande Berg Student Learning Abroad. Stylus Publishing: 115–136.

Hammer, Mitchell R. 2020. The Intercultural Development Inventory® (IDI v5). IDI, LLC.

Hancock, Dawson R., and Algozzine, Bob. 2011. *Doing Case Study Research: A Practical Guide for Beginning Researchers.* Teachers College Press.

Harms, Peter D., and Luthans, Fred. 2012. "Measuring Implicit Psychological Constructs in Organizational Behavior: An example Using Psychological Capital." *Journal of Organizational Behavior,* 33 (4): 589-594.

Harms, Peter D. and Luthans, Fred. 2012. "Telling stories: Validating an Implicit Measure of Psychological Capital." Presentation at Society for Industrial and Organizational Psychology, April.

Hart, A. J., Whalen, P. J., Shin, L. M., McInerney, S. C., Fischer, H., and Rauch, S. L. 2000. "Differential Response in the Human Amygdala to Racial Outgroup vs Ingroup Face Stimuli." *Neuroreport,* 11(11): 2351–2355. https://doi.org/10.1097/00001756-200008030-00004

Heifetz, Ronald A., Linsky, Marty, and Grashow, Alexander. 2009. *The Practice of Adap-*

tive Leadership: Tools and Tactics for Changing your Organization and the World. Harvard Business Press.

Herbert, Christopher E., Haurin, Donald R., Rosenthal, Stuart S., and Duda, Mark. 2005. *Homeownership Gaps Among Low-Income and Minority Borrowers and Neighborhoods.* Abt Associates Inc. https://www.huduser.gov/Publications/pdf/HomeownershipGapsAmongLow- IncomeAndMinority.pdf

Hoopes, D. S. 1979. "Intercultural Communication Concepts and the Psychology of Intercultural Experience." In *Multicultural Education: A cross-cultural Training Approach,* edited by Margaret D. Pusch. Intercultural Press: 9-38.

Huckabee, Michael J., and Matkin, Gina S. 2012. "Examining Intercultural Sensitivity and Competency of Physician Assistant Students." *Journal of Allied Health Online,* 41: e55-e61.

Institute of Medicine. 2003. *Unequal treatment: Confronting Racial and Ethnic Disparities in Health Care.* National Academies Press. https://doi.org/10.17226/12875

Janik, Rachel. 2015. "Time of Change: U.S. Census Projections on Race and Aging." *Time,* March 3. https://time.com/3730385/census-projections-diversity/.

Kahneman, Daniel. 2013. *Thinking, Fast and Slow.* Farrar, Straus and Giroux,

Kardong-Edgren, Suzan, and Campinha-Bacote, Josepha. 2008. "Cultural Competency of Graduating US Bachelor of Science Nursing Students." *Contemporary Nurse,* 29 (1-2): 37-44.

Katz, Ralph V., Russell, Stafanie, Kegeles, S.Steven, et. al. 2006. "The Tuskegee Legacy Project: Willingness of Minorities to Participate in Biomedical Research." *Journal of Health Care for the Poor and Underserved,* 17 (4). https://muse.jhu.edu/article/206217

Keppel, Geoffrey, & Wickens, Thomas. D. 2004. *Design and Analysis: A Researcher's Handbook,* 4th ed. Pearson Education, Inc.

Klein, Gary, Moon, Brian, and Hoffman, Robert. 2006. "Making Sense of Sensemaking: Alternative Perspectives." *Intelligent Systems,* 21 (4): 70-73.

Kline, Paul. 2000. *The Handbook of Psychological Testing,* 2nd ed. Routledge.

Landis, Daniel, Bennett, Janet M., and Bennett, Milton J. 2004. Handbook of Intercultural Training, 3rd ed. Sage Publications. 147-165.

Leininger, Madeleine. 1991. *Culture Care Diversity and Universality: A Theory of Nursing.* Jones & Bartlett Learning.

Leininger, Madeleine. 2002. "Culture Care Theory: A Major Contribution to Advance Transcultural Nursing Knowledge and Practices." *Journal of Transcultural Nursing,* 13 (3): 189-192.

Leininger, Madeleine, & MacFarland, Marilyn. 2002. *Transcultural Nursing: Concepts, Theories, Research and Practice,* 3rd ed. McGraw-Hill.

Lieberman, Matthew, MD. (2013). *Social: Why our Brains are Wired to Connect.* Crown, 2013: 45.

Li, Z. "Making Sense of 'Care' in an Intercultural Context: Intercultural Competence Development Barriers and Solutions Found in Canada" (paper presented at Second National Transcultural Health Conference, Calgary, Alberta, Canada. 2010.)

Lincoln, Yvonne S., and Guba, Egon. 1985. *Naturalistic Inquiry.* Sage Publications.

Locke, Lawrence F., Spirduso, Waneen W., and Silverman, Stephen. 2000. *Proposals That Work: A Guide for Planning Dissertations and Grant Proposals*, 4th ed. Sage Publications.

Long, Tracey B. 2012. "Overview of Teaching Strategies for Cultural Competence in Nursing Students." *Journal of Cultural Diversity*, 19 (3):102-108.

Lundgren, C. A. "Culturally Sensitive Teaching: Exploring the Developmental Process." Unpublished doctoral dissertation. University of Minnesota. 2007.

Luthans, Fred., Avey, James, Avolio, Bruce, Norman, Steven M., and Combs, Gwendolyn. 2006. "Psychological Capital Development: Toward a Micro-intervention." *Journal of Organizational Behavior*, 27: 387-393.

Luthans, Fred, Avey, James, Avolio, Bruce, and Peterson, Suzanne. 2010. "The Development and Resulting Performance Impact of Positive Psychological Capital." *Human Resource Development Quarterly*, 21: 41-67.

Luthans, Fred, and Avolio, Bruce. 2003. "Authentic Leadership Development." In *Positive Organizational Scholarship: Foundations of a New Discipline*, edited by Kim S. Cameron, James E. Dutton, and Robert E. Quinn. Berrett-Koehler: 241-258.

Luthans, Fred, Avolio, Bruce J., Avey, James B., and Norman, Steven M. 2007. "Positive Psychological Capital: Measurement and Relationship with Performance and Satisfaction." *Personnel Psychology*, 60: 541-572.

Luthans, Fred, Norman, Steven M., Avolio, Bruce, and Avey, James B. 2008. "The Mediating Role of Psychological Capital in the Supportive Organizational Climate: Employee Performance Relationship." *Journal of Organizational Behavior*, 29: 219-238.

Luthans, F., Youssef, Carolyn M., and Avolio, Bruce J. 2007. *Psychological Capital*. Oxford University Press.

Manyika James, Bughin, Jacques, Lund, Susan, et al. 2014. "Global Flows in a Digital Age." McKinsey & Company. https://www.mckinsey.com/business-functions/strategy-and-corporate-finance/our- insights/global-flows-in-a-digital-age#0

Matkin, Gina S., and Barbuto, John E. Jr. 2012. "Demographic Similarity/Difference, Intercultural Sensitivity, and Leader-member Exchange: A Multilevel Analysis." *Journal of Leadership and Organizational Studies*, 19 (3): 294-302.

Mattan, Bradley D., Wei, Kevin Y, Cloutier, Jasmin, and Kubota, Jennifer T. 2018. "The Social Neuroscience of Race-Based and Status-Based Prejudice." *Current Opinion in Psychology*, 24: 27–34. https://doi.org/10.1016/j.copsyc.2018.04.010

Merriam, Sharan. 2009. Qualitative *Research: A Guide to Design and Implementation*. Jossey-Bass

Merriam, Sharan, & Clark, M. Carolyn. 1993. "Learning from Life Experience: What Makes It Significant? *International Journal of Lifelong Education*, 12 (2): 129-138.

Montenery, Susan M., Jones, Angela D., Perry, Nancy, Ross, Debra, and Zoucha, Rick. 2013. "Cultural Competence in Nursing Faculty: A Journey, Not a Destination." *Journal of Professional Nursing*, 29 (6): e5-57.

Moodian, Michael A. 2009. *Contemporary Leadership and Intercultural Competence: Exploring the Cross-cultural Dynamics Within Organizations*. Sage Publications.

Nordstrom, Todd. 2024 "Outsourcing Emotional Intelligence: The Tools We've Built Aren't the Tools We Need." *Forbes*, June 14. https://www.forbes.com/sites/toddnord

strom/2025/07/05/outsourcing-emotional-intelligence-the-tools-weve-built-arent-the-tools-we-need/

Nguyen, Thuy, Whaley, Christopher, Simon, Kosali, I., and Cantor, Jonathan. 2022. "U.S. Health Care Workforce Changes During the First and Second Years of the COVID-19 Pandemic." *JAMA Health Forum*, 3. e215217. https://jamanetwork.com/journals/jama-health-forum/fullarticle/2789521.

Office of Minority Health. 2013. "What is cultural competency?" https://www.infanthearing.org/coordinator_toolkit/section10/36_cultural_competency.pdf

Onwuegbuzie, A. J., and Teddlie, C. 2003. "A Framework for Analyzing Data in Mixed Methods Research." In *Handbook of Mixed Methods in Social and Behavioral Research* by Abbas Tashakkori and Charles B. Teddlie. Sage Publications: 351-383

Paige, R. Michael, Jacobs-Cassuto, Melody, Yershova, Yelena, and DeJaeghere, Joan. 2003. "Assessing Intercultural Sensitivity: An Empirical Analysis of the Hammer and Bennett Intercultural Development Inventory." *International Journal of Intercultural Relations*, 27: 467-486.

Pajares, F. "Self-efficacy in Academic Settings" (paper presented at the Annual Meeting of the American Educational Research Association, San Francisco, California, April 1995).

Papadopoulos, Irena. 2003. "The Papadopoulos, Tilki, and Taylor Model for the Development of Cultural Competence in Nursing." *Journal of Health, Social and Environmental Issues*, 4: 5-7.

Parks, Sharon D. 2005. *Leadership Can be Taught: A Bold approach for a Complex World*. Harvard Business School Press.

Peus, Claudia, Wesche, Jenny S., Streicher, Bernhard, Braun, Susanne, and Frey, Dieter. 2012. "Authentic Leadership: An Empirical Test of its Antecedents, Consequences, and Mediating Mechanisms." *Journal of Business Ethics*, 107: 331-348.

Phelps, E. A., O'Connor, K. J., Cunningham, W. A., et al. 2000. "Performance on indirect measures of race evaluation predicts amygdala activation." *Journal of Cognitive Neuroscience*, 12(5): 729–738. https://doi.org/10.1162/089892900562552

Phinney, Jean S., and Ong, Anthony D. 2007. "Conceptualization and Measurement of Ethnic Identity: Current Status and Future Directions." *Journal of Counseling Psychology*, 54 (3): 271–281.

Picoult, Jodi. 2016. *Small Great Things*. Ballantine Books.

Pollock, David C., and Ruth E. Van Reken. 2009. *Third Culture Kids: Growing Up Among Worlds*, 3rd ed., Nicholas Brealey Publishing.

Purnell, Larry. 2002. "The Purnell Model for Cultural Competence." *Journal of Transcultural Nursing*, 13 (3): 193-196.

Quinn, Robert E. (1996). *Deep Change: Discovering the Leader Within*. Jossey-Bass.

Radley, David C., Collins, Sara R. and Zephyrin, Laurie C. 2024. "Advancing Racial Equity in U.S. Health Care: The Commonwealth Fund 2024 State Health Disparities Report." The Commonwealth Fund. https://www.commonwealthfund.org/publications/fund-reports/2024/apr/advancing-racial-equity-us-health-care

Rego, Arménio, Sousa, Filipa., Marques, Carla, and Pina e Cunha, Miguel. 2012.

"Authentic Leadership: Promoting Employees' Psychological Capital and Creativity." *Journal of Business Research*, 65: 429-437.

Reichard, Rebecca J., and Avolio, Bruce J. 2005. "Where are We? The Status of Leadership Intervention Research: A Meta-analytic Summary." In *Authentic Leadership Theory and Practice: Origins, Effects and Development*, edited by William. L. Gardner, Bruce J. Avolio, and Fred O. Walumbwa . Elsevier Press: 203-226.

Richard, Orlando C. 2000. "Racial Diversity, Business Strategy, and Firm Performance: A Resource-based View." *The Academy of Management Journal*, 43: 164-177.

Roberts, Brent W., Harms, Peter, Smith, Jennifer L., Wood, Dustin, and Webb, Michelle. 2006. "Using Multiple Methods in Personality Psychology." In *Handbook of Multimethod Measurement in Psychology*, edited by Michael Eid and Ed Diener. American Psychological Association: 321-335.

Sealey, Lorinda J., Burnett, Michael Burnett, and Johnson, Geraldine. 2006. "Cultural Competence of Baccalaureate Nursing Faculty: Are We Up to the Task?" *Journal of Cultural Diversity*, 13 (3): 131-140.

Seligman, Martin E. P. 2002. *Authentic Happiness: Using the New Positive Psychology to Realize Your Potential for Lasting Fulfillment*. Simon & Schuster: 91.

Sesma, A., Jr., Mannes, M., and Scales, P. C. 2005. "Positive Adaptation, Resilience, and the Developmental Asset Framework." In a *Handbook of Resilience in Children* edited by Sam Goldstein and Robert E. Brooks. Kluwer Academic/Plenum Publishers: 281-296.

Seong, Jeongmin, White, Olivia, Woetzel, Lola, et al. 2022. "Global Flows: The Ties that Bind in an Interconnected World." McKinsey Global Institute. https://www.mckinsey.com/capabilities/strategy-and-corporate-finance/our-insights/global-flows-the-ties-that-bind-in-an-interconnected-world

Shen, Karen, Eddelbuettel, Julia C. P., and Eisenberg, Matthew, D. 2024. "Job Flows Into and Out of Health Care Before and After the COVID-19 Pandemic." *JAMA Health Forum*, 5 (1): e234964. https://jamanetwork.com/journals/jama-health-forum/fullarticle/2814360.

Shore, Lynn M., Randel, Amy E., Singh, Gangaram, et al. 2010. "Inclusion and Diversity Work in Groups: A review and Model for Future Research." *Journal of Management*, 37 (4).

Skiba, Russell J., et al. 2016 "The Disparate Discipline of Students with Disabilities: A Multi-Level Exploration of Variation across School Contexts." *Exceptional Children*, 82, (2), 2016: 193–208. https://doi.org/10.1177/0014402915588789

Stake, Robert E. 1995. *The Art of Case Study Research*. Sage Publications.

Starr, Sharon, Shattell, Mona M., and Gonzales, Clifford. 2011. "Do Nurse Educators Feel Competent to Teach Cultural Competency Concepts?" *Teaching and Learning in Nursing*. 6: 84-88.

Suárez-Orozco, Carola, and Marcelo M. Suárez-Orozco. 2001. *Children of Immigration*. Harvard University Press.

Tavakol, Mohsen, and Dennick, Reg. 2011. "Making Sense of Cronbach's Alpha." *International Journal of Medical Education*, 2: 53-55.

Telzer, Eva H., Humphreys, Kathryn L., Shapiro, Mor, and Tottenham, Nim. 2013.

"Amygdala Sensitivity to Race is Not Present in Childhood but Emerges Over Adolescence." *Journal of Cognitive Neuroscience*, 25 (2): 234–244. https://doi.org/10.1162/jocn_a_00311

Tummala-Narra, Pratyusha. 2019. "Psychological Experiences of Immigrant Families: Fostering Resilience, Healing, and Well-being." *Transcultural Psychiatry*, 56 (4): 674–694.

Teddlie, C., and Tashakkori, A. (2009). *Foundations of Mixed Methods Research: Integrating Quantitative and Qualitative Approaches in the Social and Behavioral Sciences*. Sage Publications.

Useem, Ruth Hill, and John Useem. 1999. "The Third Culture Kid Experience: Adult TCKs Report on Their Cross-Cultural Childhood." The Interchange Institute.

US Census Bureau. 2012. "US Census Bureau Projections Show a Slower Growing Older, More Diverse Nation a Half Century from Now." http://www.census.gov/newsroom/releases/archives/population/cb12-243.html

US Department of Education. 2016. "2016 Civil Rights Data Collection: A First Look." Office for Civil Rights, https://www2.ed.gov/about/offices/list/ocr/docs/2013-14-first-look.pdf

US Department of Health and Human Services. 2000. Center of Cultural and Linguistic Competence in Health Care. Retrieved from http://minorityhealth.hhs.gov/templates/browse.aspx?lvl=1&lvlID=3

US Public Health Service Syphilis at Tuskegee. 2015. "The Tuskegee Timeline." https://www.cdc.gov/tuskegee/timeline.htm

Wahls, Zach. 2012. *My Two Moms: Lessons of Love, Strength, and What Makes a Family*. Gotham.

Walumbwa, Fred O., Luthans, Fred, Avey, James B., and Oke, Adegoke. 2011. "Authentically leading groups: The Mediating Role of Collective Psychological Capital and Trust." *Journal of Organizational Behavior*, 32: 4-24.

Wang, Hui, Sui, Yang, Luthans, Fred., Wang, Danni, and Wu, Yanhong. 2014. "Impact of Authentic Leadership on Performance: Role of Followers' Positive Psychological Capital and Relational Processes." *Journal of Organizational Behavior*, 35: 5-21.

Wikipedia. (n.d.). "Henrietta Lacks." Last modified June 9, 2025. Wikipedia. https://en.wikipedia.org/wiki/Henrietta_Lacks

Wilson, Astrid H., Sanner, Susan, and McAllister, Lydia E. 2010. "A Longitudinal Study of Cultural Competence Among Health Science Faculty." *Journal of Cultural Diversity*, 17 (2): 68-72.

Wilson-Stronks, Amy, and Mutha, Sunita. 2010. "From the Perspective of CEOs: What Motivates Hospitals to Embrace Cultural Competence?" *Journal of Healthcare Management*, 55(5): 339-351.

Witherell, Sharon. 2015. "Open Doors 2015 Report. The Power of International Education." November 16. https://www.iie.org/news/2015-11-16-open-doors-data/

Wolcott, Henry F. 1990. *Writing Up Qualitative Research (Qualitative Research Methods)*. Sage Publications.

Wood, K. C., Smith, H., and Grossniklaus, D. 2001. "Piaget's Stages of Cognitive Development." In *Emerging Perspectives on Learning, Teaching, and Technology*, by Michael

Orey. CreateSpace Independent Publishing Program. http://projects.coe.uga.edu/epltt/

Woodward, Kyla F., Dill, Jeanette, Trotter, LaTony, and Frogner, Bianca. 2025. "Beyond the Pandemic: The Relationship Between Macroeconomic Conditions and Healthcare Worker Shortages in the United States." BMC Health Services Research, 25. https://doi.org/10.1186/s12913-025-12780-z.

World Health Organization. 2024. "Nursing and Midwifery Fact Sheet." World Health Organization, 2024, https://www.who.int/news-room/fact-sheets/detail/nursing-and-midwifery.

World Health Organization. 2011. "World Health Statistics 2011." http://www.who.int/whosis/whostat/2011/en/index.html

World Health Organization. 2013. "Global Health Workforce Shortage to Reach 12.9 Million in Coming Decades." http://www.who.int/ mediacentre/news/releases/2013/health-workforce-shortage/en/

World Health Organization. 2014. "The Human Resources for Health Crisis." Global World Health Alliance. Retrieved from http://www.who.int/workforcealliance/about/hrh_crisis/en/index.html

Yin, Robert K. (2009). *Case Study Research: Design and Methods (Applied Social Research Methods)*, 4th ed. Sage Publications.

Youssef, Carolyn M., and Luthans, Fred. 2007. "Positive Organizational Behavior in the Workplace: The Impact of Hope, Optimism, and Resiliency." *Journal of Management*, 33: 774-800.

Acknowledgments

I am grateful to so many who have helped bring this book to fruition. From students to colleagues, to clients, to family, and friends, each person has given me the gift of themselves. What greater gift is there?

Cindy, you have been more than a colleague and editor; you've been a true friend. Your friendship and support have held me during so many of life's ups and downs since the day we met. Your commitment to the work at Helen Fagan & Associates has elevated the experience of our clients in ways that would leave a big void if you were not part of our team. Your editorial talents, patience, and wisdom have been a lifeline on the days I could write no more and on the days when my words made no sense. I'm deeply grateful for you.

Gina, Marilyn, Rich, Dana, Mary, and Tori, thank you for your willingness to read through the pages and provide guidance on the first edition. Samantha, Brooke, Amber, Jenny, and Jan, thank you for reading this new version and providing your insights as leaders, educators, coaches, and parents. Each of you represented the readers who will read these pages and hopefully find application to their own personal and professional lives.

Thank you to my sister, Helena, for your diligence in helping me find the perfect Persian quotes for each chapter. I loved having you as part of the creative aspect of this book.

To our sons, Jonathan and Alan, thank you for putting up with a student for a mom *most of your lives*. I always dreamt that my passion for learning would become your passion, too, and be passed on to your children. Nothing else in my life has taught me more about human differences and the gracious development of leaders than raising you. You've challenged me and inspired me to lead like people matter. To our bonus sons, Zane and Chanse, it's been fun to have you as part of our family since the day we met your parents in the early 1990s. I cherish the memories we have made with all four of you young men, and look forward to making new ones with you, your lovely brides (Liz, Kacy, Tori, and Holly) and your incredible children.

Beckett, Kash, and Wyatt, you are the future of the Fagan family. Berkley, Calhen, Atley, Dexter, Lennox, Drew, and Paxton, you are the future of the Strode family. I want to encourage each of you with the words that my dad used to encourage me: "Make sure you live your life in such a way that you represent your country and your family well." I am hopeful that, like your parents, you will grow into leaders who have a positive impact on the world around you.

Our future: The Fagan and Strode grandkids, 2025.

Most of all, I thank my favorite human (aka partner), Scott, for living every word of this book with me. This book would never have needed to be written the first time and rewritten this time had you not stepped up and said, "I will marry you and you don't have to pay me." Your sacrifices and commitment to the promise you made to my dad, to make sure I pursue my educational dreams, are the reasons we have come this far. I look forward to our years to come. Like the words of the song by Gladys Knight and the Pips, "You're the best thing that's ever happened to me."

-Helen

About the Author

Helen Abdali Soosan Fagan, PhD

As a leadership scholar, executive coach, and global strategist, Helen Fagan equips leaders to master the one thing that sets enduring organizations apart: the ability to unlock human potential while advancing meaningful results.

As the founder of Helen Fagan & Associates, she has worked across industries and continents, helping high-impact leaders move beyond checklists and competencies into true self-mastery. Her research and leadership development philosophy weave together Emotional Intelligence, Intercultural Mindset, Psychological Capital, and the Neuroscience of Transformation to create lasting change in people, culture, and legacy.

Dr. Fagan designs learning that challenges conventional leadership development models and raises the bar on what it means to lead with depth, discernment, and discipline. Her work is informed by lived experience, academic rigor, and a global lens. She has lived in three countries and spoken to audiences on four continents.

With a PhD in Human Sciences (Leadership) and decades of experience designing executive-level programs, she is also a trained executive coach and a Qualified Administrator of the Intercultural Development Inventory (IDI).

Dr. Fagan has been honored with the 2020 Inspire Leadership Excellence in Education Award and the 2021 University of Nebraska-Lincoln Fulfilling the Dream Award, but she measures success differently.

"People matter. And because people matter, leadership demands Olympic-level commitment to personal growth."

Dr. Fagan lives in Nebraska with her husband, Scott, and enjoys spending time with her children and grandchildren.

HelenFagan.com

Visit Helen on LinkedIn

Helen Fagan & Associates exists to change the world one leader at a time. Built on firsthand knowledge and resources developed by Dr. Helen Fagan through her thirty-plus years as a practitioner and researcher, we are here to guide individuals, teams, and organizations through a variety of leadership development experiences. Our services combine the power of emotional intelligence, the neuroscience of transformation, leadership theory, and intercultural mindset.

We believe that leadership mindset development is a journey, not a destination. Contact us to start your journey today.

HelenFagan.com

www.ingramcontent.com/pod-product-compliance
Lightning Source LLC
Chambersburg PA
CBHW060454030426
42337CB00015B/1582